FRENCH ENTRÉE 8

The Loire

The P&O European Ferries Guide

FRENCH ENTRÉE 8
The Loire
The P&O European Ferries Guide

Patricia Fenn

Quiller Press
London

Le Château des Réaux

First published 1989 by Quiller Press Ltd
46 Lillie Road, London SW6 1TN
Updated edition 1990

Line drawings: Ken Howard
Area maps: Paul Emra
Design and production in association with
Book Production Consultants, Cambridge

ISBN 0 907621 93 7

Printed in Great Britain by
Richard Clay Ltd, Bungay, Suffolk

Also published by Quiller Press:
The Legal Beagle Goes to France (£3.95)
Bill Thomas's brilliant guide to French law – and
what to do if things go wrong.

Contents

Notes on using the book

1 The area maps are to help the reader to find the place he wishes to visit on his own map. Each place is given a reference on the relevant area map, but they are not designed to replace a good touring map.
2 o.o.s. stands for 'out of season'. Other abbreviations such as f for francs, are standard.
3 H, R and C in the margin stand for 'hotel', 'restaurant' and 'chambre d'hôte'.
4 L, M or S in the margin, in combination with 3 above, indicate the standard of the hotel or restaurant: L = Luxury, S = Simple and M is used for those in between (e.g. (H)S, (R)L, etc.).
5 The ➤ symbol means the establishment fulfils exceptionally well at least one of the author's criteria of comfort, welcome and cuisine – see also pages 21–2.
6 Credit cards: 'A' = Access, 'AE' = American Express, 'V' = Visa, 'DC' = Diners Club, 'EC' = Eurocard and 'CB' = Carte Bleue.

7 ¶⑪| means Hotel of the Year.

8 ⓜ means market days.

9 The figures above the addresses, e.g. 62000, are the postal codes, which should be used in all correspondence.

Author's appeal

In order to keep *French Entrée* up to date I need all the latest information I can get on establishments listed in the guide. If you have any comments on these or any other details that might supplement my own researching I should be most grateful if you would pass them on.

Please include the name and address of establishment, date and duration of visit. Also please state if you will allow your name to be used.

Patricia Fenn,
c/o P&O European Ferries P.R. Dept.,
Channel House,
Channel View Road,
Dover, Kent.

Author's Foreword to Second Edition

In more ways than one it is good to be able to print an early second edition. Not only is it encouraging to see the success of FE8 in sales figures, but it gives me a chance to update promptly, to cover the considerable time that has elapsed since the manuscript first reached the printers. This edition is, I am confident, a better, wiser book than the first could ever be, thanks to the accumulated experience passed on to me by the multitudes of reader-spies who have praised, disapproved of and re-assessed the entries since I last visited them.

Their judgment is indicated with the thumbs-up or thumbs-down symbols in the margin. Unfortunately, for commercial reasons, it is not possible to up-date the prices, and the reader must add on at least inflation rates to those quoted. Even then they still represent bargains compared with UK rates, and not a single customer says he wouldn't go back for more.

The biggest disappointment has been at Dissay-sous-Courcillon, where my Hotel of the Year abruptly closed after an unexpected sale. I can only apologise to the many readers who read my enthusiastic account and arranged their holidays around a stay at the Château, and tell them that I feel as let down as do they. Eight of the 64 arrows have gone, either because standards have declined, because the management has changed, or, as in the sad case of the long-revered Auberge du XII Siècle at Saché, a death has meant closure. The *chambres d'hôte* continue to generate many triumphant letters, as readers discover for themselves the joys of this kind of holiday. The general tendency seems to be to save on bed and spend on food; perhaps the Loire attracts Foodies, since there have been more glowing restaurant confirmations than usual. Au Plaisir Gourmand at Chinon inspired the largest number of retrospective appreciative dribbles.

Please keep reporting – I need your ideas for the third edition.

Patricia Fenn.

Entrée to the Entrées

Categories

Old Entrée readers will know that hotels and restaurants are graded into three categories: 'L' for Luxury, 'M' for Medium, and 'S' for Simple. Value for money, with a smile, is the criterion in judging them.

This is a prosperous area, with easy access to Paris, and has a notably higher proportion of 'L' establishments than previous *French Entrées*. Their prices, at around 400–1,000f for a double room, and 250–350f for the menus, are high, but not so high as their British equivalent. However, I noticed with distress that there is a certain amount of complacency in this bracket and would therefore claim that an honest appraisal of their luxury offerings earns its keep. I get particularly twitchy and unsympathetic if standards are not very high indeed at this price level.

Two of my favourites, the Hôtel d'Espagne at Valençay (p. 168) and the Lion d'Or at Romorantin (p. 130), are evidence that luxury hotels can still have a heart, and if you're feeling like a treat or are just plain rich, you won't find better value.

Most of these sophisticated hotels run their own 'L' restaurants, often with a Michelin star. In fact the area is lavishly sprinkled with stars – no less than six two-star restaurants, at Tours, Montbazon, Romorantin, Bracieux, Les Bézards, Orléans. Every one produced outstanding cooking for me, and although prices seem to rocket with the award of the second star, I guarantee satisfaction.

There are also 15 one-star Michelin restaurants described here, edging into the 'L' bracket, but with some bargains. If you can catch the cheapest menu (usually not weekends, sometimes lunch only) of a young aspiring chef – Christian Gaillard at Le Rivage in Gien (p. 90) has one at an incredible 75f – you will be doing yourself a good turn.

Into the 'M' range come many of the most popular hotels. I would cite La Duchesse Anne at Saumur, Le Bon Laboureur at Chenonçeaux, (p. 69) and, especially, Le Castel de Bray-et-Monts at Bréhémont, as being outstanding examples. Most of them run their own good restaurants – they have to in order to keep going – but typical eat-out treats would include Au Plaisir Gourmand at Chinon (p. 73) and l'Automate Gourmand at Azay-le-Rideau. Think in terms of 150–300f for a room, 70–120f for a meal.

This is not an area where 'S' hotels are easy to locate. However, where they do exist, they offer outstanding value, with few lino-on-the-floor, pinned-up-curtains exemplars.

The Grand Hôtel St Aignan and the Hostellerie de la Gabelle at St-Florent are both reliable and cheap. Who says you can't get a double room in France nowadays for under £10?

'S' restaurants tend to be bistros and bars in the big towns, where you can eat for under a fiver, but there are still some simple country inns, like Le Petit Pêcheur at Varades (p. 169), where the same price buys four courses.

Rarely do I list chain hotels, however practicable they may be, since I believe that they are easily located without my help and descriptions are unnecessary – once you've seen one, you've seen 'em all.

The Loire is especially strong on *chambre d'hôte* accommodation, so popular with *FE* readers. So strong, that there has been no way, alas, that I could personally visit all those recommended to me. As I believe that it is more important than ever to vet this form of accommodation, since so much depends on the hostess, I decided merely to make a list of those un-visited (see p. 177), and hope that readers will soon fill in the gaps with intrinsic details. Those I have personally experienced and which I describe in detail have, without exception, been outstandingly successful, and most of them are arrowed.

The private-château-receiving-guests is yet another category strong in the Loire, and probably my favourite. To stay in such glorious surroundings and meet their (uniformly) charming and interesting owners has been the greatest pleasure. I do accept, though, that not everyone will agree that this intensely individual lodging is preferable to the safe anonymity of the predictable hotel. It is a pity too that some of their prices are beginning to emulate those of the 'L' hotels, who can better justify them in terms of professionalism and running costs. I cannot pick out particular examples of excellence, since I enjoyed every one in this category. I anticipate many enthusiastic letters from readers who sample this form of hospitality for the first time.

Arrows These are the paragons, the hotels and restaurants around which it is safe to arrange a holiday. They are outstanding, in their category, for at least one (normally several) of the desiderata of comfort, welcome, good food, pleasant site. See p. 21 for a list.

A Word on Wine Sore subject. The sting in the tail to all this bargain food is the far-from-bargain wine. It comes as a nasty shock to be expected to pay more for French wine in France than in Britain. Price blocking has been blamed but I'm afraid it's probably more a case of pure commercial greed.

House wines are getting rarer by the day. When they do

appear, at around 40f a bottle, they sometimes have an 80% mark-up on the bottle of plonk you might take home from the hypermarket. In more expensive restaurants the bill can easily double when appropriate wine is added. I cannot help – only warn what to expect.

Wine by the glass would be an innovation that I would much appreciate, especially at lunchtime with afternoon driving envisaged. Wine bars – *bistros à vin* – are incredibly slow to catch on in France, and it is only in the big towns, like Tours, that they will be found in this area. The alternative is a small glass of the cheapest, no-choice, gut-rot in a seedy bar. French chauvinist drinking habits die hard.

A Campaign It grieves me inexpressibly to note the disappearance of fresh veg. from French menus. With the neighbouring market stalls groaning with covetable fresh produce, the restaurants have the cheek to dish up khaki tinned beans and frites. It's an insidious process, paralysing imaginative vegetable cooking. Where are the well-chosen, lovingly prepared individual vegetable accessories that used to complement each dish? The best one can hope for nowadays, even in expensive restaurants, is a portion-controlled standardised side dish of the same selection for everybody.

If every *French Entrée* reader, and especially those who write to me about this very phenomenon, were to ask specifically for fresh veg. and make offensive grumbling noises if he didn't get them, it might be one small step for posterity.

Other titles *Areas covered by previous French Entrées, currently in print:*
FE3 – Normandy
FE5 – Brittany
FE6 – Boulogne, Pays d'Opal, Picardy
FE7 – Calais, Champagne, Ardennes, Bruges

Tips for beginners

Maps and Guides

Good maps are essential and I must stress that those in the front of this book are intended only as an indication of where to find the entries. They should be used in conjunction with the appropriate Michelin maps: 238 covers the Centre, Val de Loire; and 232 the Pays de Loire. The green Michelin guide *Châteaux of the Loire* is essential for more detail on individual sightseeing.

The red Michelin, apart from all its other virtues, has useful town maps. It's a bit slow to spot a newcomer though, unlike its rival Gault-Millau This gives more specific detail but has less comprehensive coverage and is strongly biassed in favour of *la nouvelle cuisine* (its authors did invent the label in the first place); it is useless for the really basic hotels and restaurants.

Logis de France do a good guide to their hotels, obtainable at the French Government Tourist Bureau at 178 Piccadilly. This is the place to go for general advice, free maps and brochures and details of the admirable gîtes system, which provides simple self-catering accommodation in farmhouses and cottages. We have stayed in gîtes all over France and found them invariably reliable and cheap, and often more comfortable and interesting than hotels, but you have to be quick off the mark to book the best in peak season.

Booking

Sunday lunch is the Meal of the Week, when several generations settle down together to enjoy an orgy of eating, drinking, conversation and baby-worship that can well last till teatime. You should certainly book then and on fête days. Make tactical plans and lie low, or it could be a crêpe and a bed in the car. French public holidays are as follows:

New Year's Day	France's National Day, 14 July
Easter Sunday and Monday	The Assumption, 15 August
Labour Day, 1 May	All Saints' Day, 1 November
VE Day, 8 May	Armistice Day, 11 November
Ascension Day	Christmas Day.
Whit Sunday and Monday	

If you wish to book ahead and do not speak French, try and find someone who does to make a preliminary telephone call. If necessary, write in English and let them sort it out, but make sure when you get the confirmatory letter that you understand what you've booked. Many hotels nowadays will ask for a deposit. My method is to send them an English cheque; they then either subtract the equivalent from the bill or return the cheque.

Make good use of the local tourist bureaux, clearly indicated in the centre of every town, where you will find English spoken. Let them do the booking for you if you have problems. This is the place to pick up maps and brochures.

Closing Times The markets, like the rest of the town, snap shut abruptly for lunch. I regularly get caught out by not shopping early enough; if it's going to be a picnic lunch, the decision has to be made in good time. From 12 p.m. to 2.30, and sometimes 3, not a cat stirs. At the other end of the day it's a joy to find shops open until 7 p.m. Mondays tend to be almost as dead as Sundays and it's likely to prove a grave disappointment to allocate that as a shopping day.

It does not pay to be casual about the weekly closure (*fermeture hebdomadaire*) of the restaurants. It is an excellent idea to ensure that not every restaurant in the same town is closed at the same time, but do check before you venture. Thwarted tastebuds are guaranteed if you make a special journey only to find the smug little notice on the door. 'Sun. p.m. and Mon.' are the most common and often it will take a good deal of perseverance to find a possibility open then.

Changing Money Everyone has their pet method, from going round all the banks to get a few centimes advantage, to playing it the easy and very expensive way of getting the hotel to do it. It depends on how much is involved and how keen a dealer you are as to how much trouble is worth it. I change mine on the boat, where I have always found the rate to be very fair. If you get caught outside banking hours, the *bureaux de change* stay open late.

Telephoning Most of the public telephones in France actually work. You put your 1f piece in the slot and watch it roll down for starters, then as many more pieces as you estimate you will need. If it's too much, out it all comes at the conclusion of the conversation.

To dial UK from France: 19, wait for tone, 44, then STD code minus 0, then number.

Inter-departmental:

Province to Province: Dial just 8 figures (e.g. 21.33.92.92.)
Province to Paris: Dial 16, then 1, then 4 followed by 7 figures (e.g. 16.1.4X.XX.XX.XX)

Paris to Province: Dial 16, then the 8 figures
Please note that all numbers you refer to should be 8
figures only (e.g. 21.86.80.48 not (21) 86.80.48).
To dial France from UK: 010, pause, 33, 8-figure code.
Emergencies: Fire 18; Police 17; Operator 13; Directory
Enquiries 12.

Markets　　We Brits go to France to sleep cheaply, eat well and to shop.
The markets are more than just a utility – they are part and
parcel of the French scene, and everyone loves them. Take
your time strolling round the colour and hubbub, and
experience the pleasure of buying from someone who knows
and cares about his wares. The man selling you a kitchen
knife will be an expert on knives and will want to know what
you need it for; the cheesemonger will choose for you a
cheese ready for eating today or in a couple of days' time,
back home. Trust them. Choose for yourself the ripest peach,
the perfect tomato, and buy as little as you need and no
more, so that you can buy fresh again tomorrow. Stock up on
herbs and spices, pulses and dried fruits, soap scented with
natural oils, honey from local bees, slices of farmers' wives'
terrines – every village a veritable Fortnums on market day.
The day of the market in the nearest town is listed in most
entries – (M).

Take with You　Soap (only the grander hotels supply it) and a decent towel if
you're heading for the S group and can't stand the
handkerchief-sized baldies. If self-catering, take tea, orange
juice, breakfast cereals, biscuits, Marmite, marmalade – all
either expensive, or difficult to locate, or horrible.

Bring Home　Beer is a Best Buy and the allowance is so liberal that you can
let it reach the parts of the car that other purchases fail to
reach, i.e.: load up. Coffee is much cheaper; cheeses are an
obvious choice if the pong is socially acceptable. If, like me,
you have a weakness for *crème fraîche* and resent paying
double at home, you can rely on it staying fresh for a week, so
long as it's not confined to a hot car. I buy early expensive
vegetables like asparagus, artichokes, mange-touts and the
wonderful fat flavoursome tomatoes. Electric goods are often
cheaper, as are Le Creuset pans, glassware. John Doxat's
notes on p.179 will help choose the best bargain of all – the
wine.

Breakfasts　A sore point. The best will serve buttery croissants, hot fresh
bread, home-made preserves, a slab of slightly salted butter,
lots of strong coffee and fresh hot milk, with fresh orange
juice if you're lucky. The worst – and at a price of between 15

and 40f this is an outrage – will be stale bread, a foil-wrapped butter pat, plastic jam, a cup of weak coffee and cold sterilised milk. Synthetic orange juice can add another 10f to the bill. If you land in an hotel like this, get out of bed and go to the café next door.

Tipping

Lots of readers, used to the outstretched British hand, worry about this. Needlessly – 's.t.c.' should mean what it says – all service and taxes included. The only exception perhaps is to leave the small change in the saucer at a bar.

Garages and Parking

Considerably older and wiser since I started travelling so often, I now have sympathy with readers who insist on a garage. I have to tell you that my locked car has been twice broken into and once stolen altogether (recovered three weeks later with £2,000 worth of damage). The latter disaster was from a well-lit street outside a very grand hotel, so my experience is altogether different from that of a reader who advises street parking after having all his belongings pinched from a car in an underground car-park. I can only advise removing any valued belongings, however tiresome that may be, and taking out adequate insurance.

Waterways

A lovely way to see the countryside is to take a holiday on one of the tributaries of the Loire. A week or two on a well-equipped, comfortable boat, gliding through the Sarthe, Mayenne, Odon . . . and stopping to eat at one of the riverside inns is a most agreeable experience – one that could be linked perhaps with a week's châteaux-bashing car tour. These rivers are never crowded, always peaceful even in school holidays. A company that specialises in boat trips in this area is Slipaway Holidays of 90 Newlands Rd, Worthing, Sussex; (0903) 821000. Highly recommended.

What Next?

FE9 will be a completely new book on Normandy. A good deal of changes have taken place since the best-selling '3' was written and readers have been diligent in keeping me abreast. Any new ideas welcome.

Thanks

To all my new friends in the regional tourist offices along the Loire, especially to Jean-Pierre Jacquin and Peter Gerhäuser in Nantes, Hélène Pouleau in Angers, Loïc Rousseau in La Flèche, Jeanne Prévost in Saumur, Marie-Odile Barthélémy in Orléans and Marie-Helen Lopez in Tours, for unstinting help and guidance; to Pauline Hallam of the French Tourist Office in London for all the introductions; and to Philippe Lazarus of Château Accueil and John Olhagaray of Grandes Étapes for all their assistance.

The Loire

How to define 'The Loire'? Unlike Normandy, Brittany, Burgundy, Alsace, it is not a finite area, with borders arranged by history, geography, politics. It belongs to many *départements*, and governs the lives of wildly diverse Frenchmen, influencing their character and customs, affecting the economy of their regions.

Confusion is compounded by the administrative designation of the area. The western Loire is termed 'Pays de Loire' by the tourist boards and map-makers, the eastern stretches become 'Centre, Val de Loire'. This means that if you visit the tourist office in Saumur, for example, you will find plenty of documentation for a journey westwards, as far into Brittany as the border of the Loire-Atlantique *département*, but nothing about Chinon next door in the rival 'Centre' district.

This inclusion of part of Brittany in the Loire administration area is even more bizarre. The battle rages. Should the Loire-Atlantique beyond Nantes, historically and demographically Breton, change its allegiance to suit the neat parcelling-out of Paris-ordinated regions? I think not, and as the area has already been covered in *French Entrée 5 – Brittany*, you will not find it mentioned here.

Moreover, the Pays de Loire territory covers other *départements* which, interesting though they may be, are not generally associated with a tour along the river. The Vendée and Mayenne I much admire, but believe would be interlopers in this book.

So the first decision in writing *FE8* was where to start and (even more difficult) where to stop. Follow the river by all means, but how far to deviate either side of its banks?

The eastern limit was easy, since the river before Orléans obligingly flows south–north, and its eastern banks become Burgundy (regretfully omitted). But how far south to follow? The green Michelin guide *Châteaux of the Loire*, my constant companion, made the choice for me. It fades away at Sancerre, and that seemed an excellent place to begin the year's research.

The western limit was easy too, with Nantes just out of bounds, but how far north to start and what about the bulge south of Orléans that encompasses the green and lovely Sologne, familiar to many readers from their earliest introduction to French literature via *Le Grand Meaulnes*. That must be recorded as far as possible. Reins had to be sharply drawn though. Before I knew it, I was wandering down into the Berry country, and indeed could have continued to do so very happily . . . but that's another story.

The northern approaches to the Loire Valley were even more tempting, since it is through them that most readers will travel, and lodgings here might well prove valuable. Time and space made the decision for me by simply running out. The Chartres, Le Mans country, and most of the Sarthe will have to wait for the next version of *FE8*, which could easily be twice as fat.

Fascinating and diverse though the territory may be, following not only the course of the parent river but those of its many (sometimes even more) delightful tributaries, the Mayenne, Sarthe, Indre, Indrois, Loir, Vienne, Thouet, Maine, Sauldre, Beuvron, Cosson, Cisse (see pp. 14 and 34 for holidays thereon), is not usually the principal *raison d'être* for a tour in the Loire area. To visit the region and overlook the châteaux would be unthinkable.

There are dozens of them, strategically sited to defend, enhance and profit by the mighty river that used to be the main highway through the land. The temptation is to gobble them up in one gulp and suffer violent indigestion subsequently. Rather they should be taken singly, before or after meals, and swallowed slowly, relished the while, and long after.

There are some, such as mammoth Chambord, stunning Chenonçeau, verdant Villandry, which no first-timer can afford to miss. Others, such as Le Lude, Loches, Valençay, are perhaps for second-time-around delectation. These are the diamonds, fabulous, famous; the pearls, such as Serrant, Montrésor, Le Plessis-Bourré, may not glitter so obviously but, for the connoisseur, are just as desirable.

I have listed the 31 châteaux that I visited and re-visited in 1988 on p. 175–6 with a Fenn rating system designed to help readers make their own choice. But don't forget that this is an essentially subjective list, based on personal taste as well as incidentals such as the company, the guide, the weather, the time of day.

A BRIEF RUN ALONG THE RIVER, FROM EAST TO WEST

There are generally good roads on either bank; I recommend
zig-zagging, according to time and mood.

Sancerre–Orléans (131 km)

The area starts at what I consider to be the most attractive
scenery of the whole route. **Sancerre** is completely different
from anything else, with its considerable hills and valleys and
a mediaeval village keeping guard over the vine-dotted
slopes. The Loire, far below, is fast-running, island-dotted,
with (rare) opportunities for swimming and sailing.

Between here and Gien lies a disappointing stretch, with
nothing much to see from either bank. I recommend the
minor road on the left bank, the D 951.

The first château appears at **Gien**, then comes the next
bridge at **Sully**, with another important fortress-castle. The
river banks are sandy, the countryside flat. The right-bank
road, the D 60, will reveal two important ecclesiastical
monuments, at **St-Bênoit** and **Germigny des Prés**.

Châteauneuf is a pleasant, underestimated town and the
river here is impressively wide. Further north the Forest of
Orléans, dotted with lakes, is unspoilt and worth a detour.

Orléans–Blois (59 km)

Orléans is the administrative capital of the Centre – Val-de-
Loire region, mostly new, but with fine cathedral and strong
sense of history, well laid-out, good shops.

South of Orléans begins redoubtable **Sologne**, wooded
hunting country, peppered with lakes, good for picnics and
hot summer weather, a little sad out of season.

Along the river the châteaux begin to assemble. This is the
most-trafficked stretch, with the northern-bank route
nationale in parallel with the new autoroute. I prefer the
south bank, from which a diversion can be made to
Chambord and **Cheverny**, but **Meung** and **Beaugency** are
both interesting.

Blois–Tours (63 km)

Blois is the first big château-town and correspondingly
congested. Then begins another very busy stretch of road,
but this time with more visual attractions on both banks. I
prefer the southern route, but if time doesn't press, there is a
pleasant minor road, the D 58, that runs parallel and slightly
inland from the northern nationale. **Amboise** is most
attractive out of season. Its site, castle and town are all
delightful, but spoiled by too many tourists in summer. Both

banks from here to Tours are surprisingly rural – I would pick the northern one.

A diversion from Tours to St-Aignan follows the river Cher, with **Chenonçeau** the jewel in the crown. **Montrichard** is a narrow strip of a town; **St-Aignan** is more attractive altogether.

Tours–Saumur (66 km)

Tours is a lively university city, with some appealing new restoration work. The north bank from there on is extremely busy, and badly signposted, since new ring-roads are planned. Better by far to take the southern route and visit **Villandry** and **Azay-le-Rideau** on the way. But then I would back-track to **Bréhémont**, a little-known, quiet, fishing village, and take the minor D 16 to fairy-tale **Ussé**.
Chinon, on the **Vienne**, is delightful, with probably the most historically interesting château of them all. The abbey of **Fontevraud** is one of the area's greatest treasures; its Plantagenet tombs should be of particular interest to the Brits.

Saumur–Angers (45km)

This would be my first choice for a base area, with lots to see and do in both directions, and fewer crowds than further north. **Saumur** is a lively town, with plenty to entertain in and out of season. The south-bank road from here is peaceful and uncrowded and passes through pretty villages such as **Chênehutte**, past the Romanesque abbeys of **Cunault** and **Trêves** to **Gennes** and **Les Rosiers**, well served with good accommodation and eating places.

Angers–Nantes (89 km)

The south bank is one of the most attractive stretches along the whole Loire, passing through the **Corniche Angevine**, with good views down to the river and vineyards. Many islands now, with **Béhuard** the biggest and most interesting. **St-Florent** is a delightful village and from here the D 751 corkscrews up to the viewing point of **Champtoceaux**. Unspoilt fishing villages continue right up to the outskirts of the Nantes agglomeration.

But both the autoroute and the nationale on the north bank are painless, fast and relatively uncrowded means of covering this distance very quickly.

Nantes is one of my favourite French cities, with lots of good shops, open spaces, water, restaurants, a château and a strong cultural involvement. Read more about it in *FE5*!

FOOD AND DRINK

This is the Garden of France, rich, fertile, moist, warm. Fruit is particularly renowned and many varieties have been named after Loire celebrities – La Reine Claude, wife of François I, gave her name to a greengage, Bon-Chrétien pears were first planted by St Francis of Paola in an orchard near Tours; Beurre-Hardy pears grow here too, and the Williams, from which the scented Poire William liqueur is made.

Saumur's strawberries are famous and around Angers grow all manner of soft fruits and the bitter cherries that make the aperitif Guignolet. Open fruit-tarts glow in every *pâtisserie*. Dessert apples, such as la Reinette, are used for Tarte Tatin. This reversed apple tart appears regularly on Norman menus, but it was in Lamotte-Beuvron that the blessed Demoiselles Tatin first accidentally caramelised the apples.

Early vegetables beat those from the Paris region by about a fortnight; asparagus is grown around Vineuil, and mushrooms from the Saumur tufa caves account for three-quarters of the national consumption.

As any market day will witness, cheeses from cow's, sheep's and goat's milk are produced throughout the area, with the Crottin de Chavignol, from the village of the same name, near Sancerre, probably the best known. A particularly distinctive goat's cheese is the cylindrical St-Maure, with a straw running through it. *Crêmets* are soft cream-cheeses, eaten with sugar and sometimes fruit.

Freshwater fish from the Loire, its many tributaries and the *étangs* of the Sologne, appear on every menu. In sophisticated restaurants the perch, pike, zander, tench, carp and salmon will appear in many guises, with sauces made from red Chinon wine, or with the beurre blanc that derives from Nantes; in the simple hostelries along the river banks the more modest varieties come crisply fried in *fritures*, along with garlicky eels, which everyone must try at least once. A *matelote* is an eel stew, with mushrooms and onions, simmered in white wine, sometimes with other fish added.

This hunting country – one of the reasons for the existence of the royal residences in the first place – and several *musées de la chasse* (Gien, Montpoupon) boast formidable specimens, stuffed, painted, of indigenous beasts. Particularly in the Sologne, the formal hunt is very much part of the scene; elsewhere it's a matter of shooting anything that runs, creeps or flies, and game features strongly on autumn menus.

The appearance of the first wild mushroom is the signal for a frenzy of fungi-hunting. The locals have their secret caches (they can't understand why we don't bother), and strolls round the market stalls in autumn are even more fascinating than usual, wondering at the range of wrinkled/smooth, vivid/grey varieties.

Rillettes are a Touraine speciality – an obvious ready-made bring-home present – along with a range of other *charcuterie* from pig and game – *boudins, rillons, terrines.*

The little town of Cormery is famous for its macaroons, made from the local almonds; abundant chestnut trees produce *marrons glacés*. Prunes are ubiquitous in Touraine cooking, in both savoury (rabbit stew, with pork and game) and sweet (macerated in Vouvray, in tarts, and in stuffed sweetmeats). Quinces are made into jellies and a very sweet hard *pâté* from Beaugency.

See also Wines and spirits by John Doxat, p. 179

SPECIAL RECOMMENDATIONS

The hotels and restaurants marked by an arrow ➤ have been selected for the following reasons:

Amboise. *Le Choiseul* (HR)L. Position, cooking.
Angers. *Hôtel du Mail* (H)S–M. Calm in city centre, good value.
Azay-le-Rideau. *Clos Philippa* (C)M–L. Comfort, welcome, position.
   Grand Monarque (HR)M. Sustained high standards.
   L'Automate Gourmand (R)S–M. Atmosphere, value.
Beaugency. *Sologne* (H)S–M. Value, welcome.
Les Bézards. *Auberge des Templiers* (HR)L. Sublime cooking.
Bléré. *Le Cheval Blanc* (H)S (R)M. Value, food.
Blois. *Le Relais Bleu du Château* (HR)M. Comfort, food, position.
Bourgueil. *Le Thouarsais* (H)S. Value, welcome.
Bracieux. *Le Relais de Bracieux* (R)L. Exceptional cooking.
Candé-sur-Beuvron. *La Caillère* (HR)M. Exceptional cooking.
Champigné. *Les Briottières* (C)L. Comfort, style, welcome.
Champtoceaux. *Auberge de la Forge* (RM)L. Exceptional cooking.
Château-du-Loir. *Dianne Legoff* (C)S. Value, welcome.
Chênehutte-les-Tuffeaux. *Le Prieuré* (HR)L. Comfort, setting.
Chenonçeaux. *Le Bon Laboureur* (HR)M. Sustained high standards.
Chinon. *Au Plaisir Gourmand* (R)M–L. Outstanding cooking.
Combreux. *L'Auberge* (HR)M. Atmosphere, welcome.
Cravant-les-Côteaux. *M. et Mme Chauveau* (C)L. Comfort, welcome, position.
La Flèche: *Le Vert Galant* (HR)S. Value.
Fondettes. *Manoir du Grand Martigny* (C)L. Comfort, welcome, situation.
Fontevraud-l'Abbaye. *La Licorne* (R)L. Outstanding cooking.
Genillé. *Auberge Agnès Sorel* (H)S (R)M. Value, atmosphere.
Gien. *Le Rivage* (HR)M. Value, comfort, cooking.
La Jaille-Yvon. *Château le Plessis* (C)L. Comfort, welcome, style.
Joué-lès-Tours. *Château de Beaulieu* (HR)M–L. Value, situation.
Montbazon. *Domaine de la Tortinière* (HR)L. Comfort, style, position, food.
Montrésor. *Hôtel de France* (HR)S. Atmosphere, situation.
Montsoreau. *Le Bussy* (H)M, and *Diane de Meridor* (R)M–S. Value, food, welcome, position.
Orléans. *La Crémaillère* (R)L. Outstanding cooking.
   Les Antiquaires (R)M. Cooking, value.
Port Boulet. *Château les Réaux* (C)L. Comfort, welcome, style.
Richelieu. *Hôtel le Puits Doré* (HR)S. Value.
Romorantin-Lanthenay. *Grand Hôtel Lion d'Or* (HR)L. Comfort, good food.
Les Rosiers. *Auberge Jeanne de Laval* and *Résidence Ducs d'Anjou* (H)M (R)L. Comfort, welcome, superb food, position.
Saché. *La Sablonnière* (C)M. Comfort, good breakfasts.
St-Dyé-sur-Loire. *Manoir Bel Air* (HR)M. Efficiency, welcome, situation.

St-Florent-le-Vieil. *Hostellerie de la Gabelle* (HR)S. Good value, pleasant position.
St-Hilaire-St-Mesmin. *L'Escale du Port Arthur* (HR)M–S. Good value, pleasant position near Orléans.
St-Patrice. *Château de Rochecotte* (HR)M–L. Efficiency, style, friendliness, location.
Sancerre. *Joseph Mellot* (R)S. Simplicity, value.
Saumur. *Central Hôtel* (H)S. Welcome, efficiency.
  Anne d'Anjou (H)M. Value, situation.
  Les Ménéstrals (R)M. Cooking, setting.
Souvigny-en-Sologne. *La Croix Blanche* (HR)M. Food.
Tours. *Hôtel Akilène* (HR)M. Value, situation.
  Hôtel Mirabeau (H)M. Value, welcome.
  Jean Bardet (HR)L. Outstanding cooking.
  La Roche le Roy (R)M–L. Outstanding cooking.
Valençay. *Espagne* (HR)L. Comfort, cooking, welcome.
Varades. *Le Petit Pêcheur* (HR)S. Value, situation.
Vernou-sur-Brenne. *Hostellerie des Perce-Neige* (HR)M. Value, comfort.

Here is a list of readers' discoveries, for which I accept no responsibility! Please keep reporting.

Bléré. Le Boeuf Couronné (R)S. Miss S.V. McDonnell.
La Chartre-sur-le-Loir. Hotel France (HR)M. Pl. de la Republique.
Château du Loir. Manoir du Riablay (HR)L. Rte St Jean. 43.79.45.86.
Château-sur-Sarthe. Les Ondines (HR)M. F.A.M. Tait.
Chinon. La Ste Maxime (R)M. 31 Pl. du Ge. de Gaulle. 47.93.05.04.
Onzaine. Aub. du Beau Rivage (HR)S. G.A. Lloyd.
Parçay-sur Vienne. Les Granges (HR)M. Barbara Chaumeau.
Richelieu. Château de St. Bonnet (Ch. d'hôte). 49.86.01.55.
St Martin-de-la-Place. M. Dusser (Ch. d'hôte). 18 rue des Turcres. 41.38.43.05. Dr. P.W. Jeffreys.
St Michel-sur-la-Loire. Auberge de la Bonde (HR)M. 47.96.83.13. L.T. Evans.
Saulges. L'Ermitage (HR)S. F.A.M. Tait.
Saumur. La Croix de la Voulte (Ch. d'hôte). St Lambert des Levées, Rte de Boumois. 41.38.46.66.
Savonnières. Le Prieuré. Mme Caré (Ch. d'hôte). 10 rue Chaude. 47.50.03.26. Dr. A. Abrahams.

The Maps

The maps which follow are to be used in conjunction with a
good touring map – for instance Michelin 238 and 232.

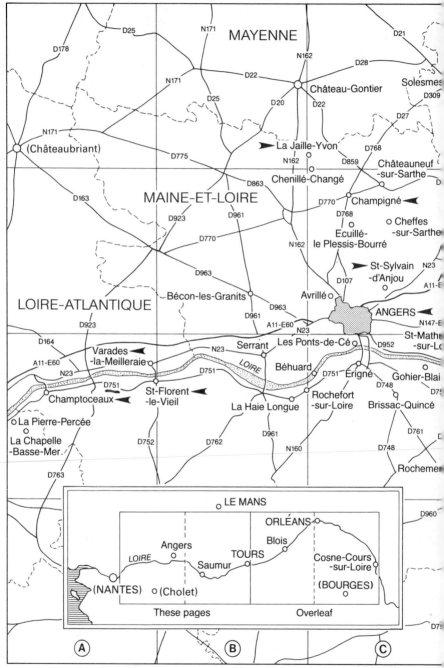

MAYENNE

D178
D25
N171
D21
N171
D22
N162
D28
Solesmes
D309
N171
D25
D20
D22
Château-Gontier
D27
(Châteaubriant)
D775
La Jaille-Yvon
D768
Châteauneuf
N162
-sur-Sarthe
D859
D163
Chenillé-Changé
D770
Champigné
MAINE-ET-LOIRE
D863
D923
D961
D768
Cheffes
-sur-Sarthe
D770
Ecuillé-
le Plessis-Bourré
N162
D963
St-Sylvain
N23
-d'Anjou
LOIRE-ATLANTIQUE
Bécon-les-Granits
D107
A11-E
Avrillé
D923
D963
D961
ANGERS
N147-E
D164
A11-E60
N23
St-Math
-sur-Lo
Varades
Serrant
Les Ponts-de-Cé
D952
-la-Meilleraie
N23
LOIRE
Béhuard
A11-E60
N23
D751
D751
Erigné
Gohier-Blai
Champtoceaux
St-Florent
D751
Rochefort
D748
D75
-le-Vieil
La Haie Longue
-sur-Loire
Brissac-Quincé
La Pierre-Percée
La Chapelle
D752
D762
D961
D748
D761
-Basse-Mer
N160
Rochemen
D763

LE MANS
D960
ORLÉANS
Blois
Angers
LOIRE
TOURS
Cosne-Cours
Saumur
-sur-Loire
(NANTES)
(Cholet)
(BOURGES)

These pages | Overleaf

Ⓐ | Ⓑ | Ⓒ

24

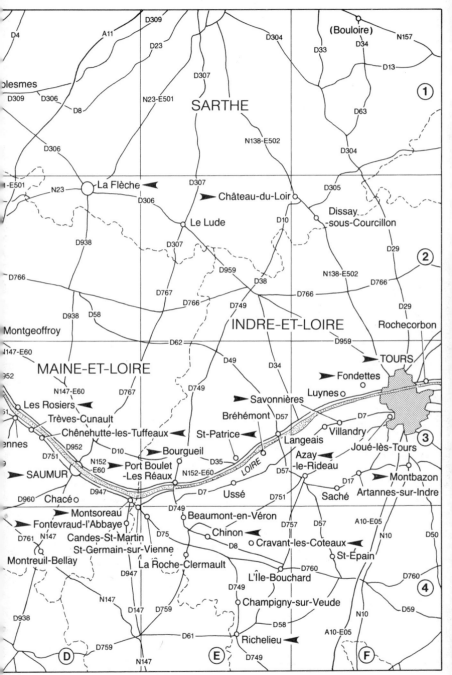

D4

A11

D309

D23

(Bouloire)

N157

D304

D33

D34

D13

lesmes

D309 D306

D8

N23-E501

SARTHE

D307

D304

①

D63

D306

N138-E502

D304

D305

-E501

N23

La Flèche

D307

Château-du-Loir

D306

Le Lude

D10

Dissay -sous-Courcillon

D938

D307

D29

②

D766

D959

N138-E502

D766

D767

D38

D766

D29

D938 D58

D766

D749

INDRE-ET-LOIRE

Rochecorbon

Montgeoffroy

D62

J47-E60

D49

D959

TOURS

J147-E60

MAINE-ET-LOIRE

D34

Fondettes

352

N147-E60

D767

D749

Savonnières

Luynes

Les Rosiers

Bréhémont

D57

D7

Trèves-Cunault

St-Patrice

Villandry

Chênehutte-les-Tuffeaux

Langeais

Joué-lès-Tours

ennes

D952

D10

Bourgueil

Azay -le-Rideau

D751

N152 -E60

Port Boulet -Les Réaux

D35

LOIRE

D17

Montbazon

SAUMUR

N152-E60

D57

Artannes-sur-Indre

D960

Chacé

D947

D7

Ussé

D751

Saché

Montsoreau

D749

Beaumont-en-Véron

D757

D57

A10-E05

Fontevraud-l'Abbaye

D75

Chinon

N10

D50

D761 N147

Candes-St-Martin

D8

Cravant-les-Coteaux

St-Germain-sur-Vienne

St-Épain

Montreuil-Bellay

La Roche-Clermault

D760

D760

D947

L'Île-Bouchard

④

D749

N147

D147

D759

Champigny-sur-Veude

D59

D938

D58

N10

D61

Richelieu

A10-E05

Ⓓ

D759

N147

Ⓔ

D749

Ⓕ

25

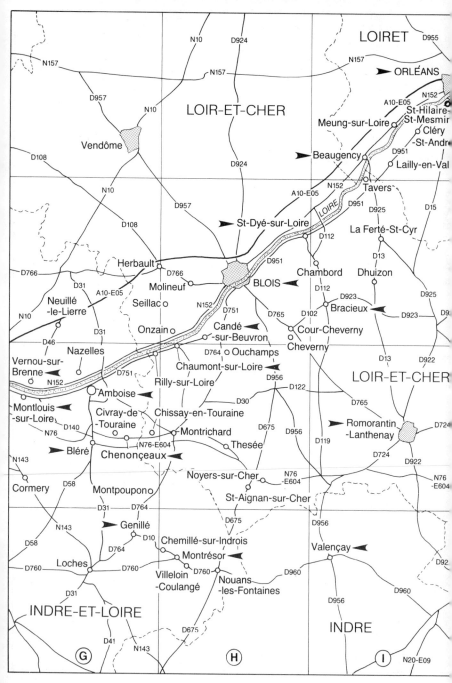

LOIRET

ORLÉANS

LOIR-ET-CHER

Vendôme

St-Hilaire-St-Mesmir
Meung-sur-Loire
Cléry-St-André
Beaugency
Lailly-en-Val
Tavers
St-Dyé-sur-Loire
LOIRE
La Ferté-St-Cyr
Chambord
Dhuizon
Herbault
Molineuf
BLOIS
Seillac
Neuillé-le-Lierre
Bracieux
Onzain
Candé-sur-Beuvron
Cour-Cheverny
Cheverny
Ouchamps
Chaumont-sur-Loire
Nazelles
Vernou-sur-Brenne
Rilly-sur-Loire
Amboise
Montlouis-sur-Loire
Civray-de-Touraine
Chissay-en-Touraine
Montrichard
Romorantin-Lanthenay
Bléré
Chenonceaux
Thesée
Cormery
Montpoupon
Noyers-sur-Cher
St-Aignan-sur-Cher
Valençay
Genillé
Chemillé-sur-Indrois
Loches
Montrésor
Villeloin-Coulangé
Nouans-les-Fontaines

INDRE-ET-LOIRE

INDRE

LOIR-ET-CHER

Roads: N157, D924, N10, D955, N157, N152, A10-E05, D957, D951, D108, D924, D108, D766, D31, A10-E05, N10, N152, D112, D925, D15, D112, D923, D925, D9, D765, D102, D751, D46, D31, D764, D13, D922, D956, D122, D765, D751, N152, D30, N76, D140, D675, D956, D119, D724, N143, D58, D31, N76-E604, N76-E604, N143, D58, D764, D10, D760, D31, D760, D724, D922, D675, D956, D960, D92, D960, D41, N143, D675, N20-E09

G   H   I

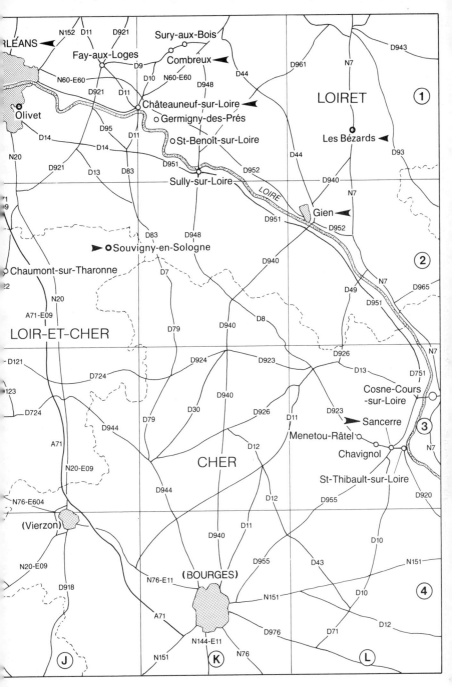

ORLÉANS
N152 D11 D921
Sury-aux-Bois
Fay-aux-Loges
Combreux
D9
Sury-aux-Bois
D943
N60-E60
D10 N60-E60
D948
D44
D961
N7
LOIRET
Olivet
D921 D11
Châteauneuf-sur-Loire
Germigny-des-Prés
D95 D11
St-Benoît-sur-Loire
Les Bézards
D14
D14
D44
N20
D921 D13 D83
D951 D952
D93
Sully-sur-Loire
D940
LOIRE
N7
D83 D948
Souvigny-en-Sologne
D951
Gien
D952
Chaumont-sur-Tharonne
D940
N20
D7
D49
N7
D965
A71-E09
D951
LOIR-ET-CHER
D79
D940
D8
D121
D724
D924
D923
D926
N7
123
D13
D751
D724
D79
D30
D926
Cosne-Cours
-sur-Loire
A71
D944
D923
Sancerre
N20-E09
CHER
D12
Menetou-Râtel
Chavignol
N7
N76-E604
D944
D12
St-Thibault-sur-Loire
(Vierzon)
D955
D920
N20-E09
D940
D11
D918
D10
N76-E11
(BOURGES)
D955
D43
N151
A71
N151
D10
N144-E11
D976
D71
D12
N151
K
N76
L
J

27

The regions

AMBOISE (I.-et-L.) 25 km NE of Tours; 35 km SW of Blois

37400
(m) *Fri.,*
Sun. a.m.

Try and approach Amboise from the north, so that the splendid site of its **château** can be best appreciated. Over the centuries it has been regularly enlarged and demolished and rebuilt, but its domination, high on a rocky spur in the very heart of the little town, remains total.

The late 15th and early 16th century was its apogee. Both Louis XI and Charles VII, married to the ubiquitous Duchesse Anne, were born here, and extended and embellished their home. On his return from Italy in 1495 Charles brought with him, to impress his wife, not only a wealth of Italian treasures but an army of craftsmen, to paint, sculpt, and lay out an ornamental garden along the river terrace.

For the first three years of his reign, François I lived at Amboise and he and his court organised flamboyant festivals, masques, tournaments in the glittering castle. He it was who was responsible for bringing Leonardo da Vinci to Amboise, to spend the last years of his life (and to be buried) here. He invited him to stay at the 15th-century house of **Clos Lucé** on the outskirts of the town, where he eventually died. Just picture the drama of his arrival, having trekked over the Alps carrying on his mule two of what are now the most famous pictures in the world, the Mona Lisa and the Virgin of the Rocks!

Sketches and models of Leonardo's machines are on show at Clos Lucé – a mind-blowing example of his scientific prescience hundreds of years ahead of his time. There is a very pleasant Renaissance garden, with a photogenic view of the château. It can be visited 9 a.m.–7 p.m. 1/6–31/9; 9 a.m.–12 noon and 2–7 p.m. for the rest of the year (except Jan.).

The most gruesome event in the castle's history, described with some relish by the guides, was the Tumult of Amboise, in 1560. The Guises, protectors of François II and his girl-queen, Mary Stuart, on hearing of a Protestant plot to seize the king, moved their court from Blois to the stronghold of Amboise. From there the attackers were routed and annihilated, their corpses strung around the town on makeshift gibbets and from iron hooks on the front of the castle, from trees on the terrace and from the balcony of the King's Lodging, still known as the Balcon des Conjurés. When the stench became insupportable the court, hastily and understandably, withdrew.

In 1631, during one of the many rebellions against Louis XIII's brother, the duc d'Orléans, who had taken over the castle, the Royalist troops razed the outer fortifications to the ground, and from then on its fortunes declined – used as it was as a prison, allowed to decline still further by Napoleon, and then damaged by 1940 bombing. Via Louis Philippe, the citizen king, whose portrait hangs in his room in the castle, it passed to the Pretender to the French throne, the comte de Paris, and is now part of a foundation set up to preserve national heritages.

The approach to the castle is up a long ramp, lined with souvenir shops and tourists, and the entrance is between the 16th-century Hôtel de Ville and the Church of St Florentin. The terrace, with its bust of Leonardo, has splendid views over the Loire and the old walls and roof-tops of the town. Look out for the lovely flamboyant 14th-century Church of St Hubert (said to contain Leonardo's bones), the King's Apartments, Gothic and Renaissance wings and the Tour des Minimes or Tour des Cavaliers, with a ramp up which horsemen could ride to deliver provisions to the castle.

Visits: 9 a.m.–12 noon and 2–6.30 p.m. 1/4–30/6; 9 a.m.–6.30 p.m. 1/7–31/8; 9 a.m.–12 noon and 2–5 p.m. during the rest of the year. *Son et lumière* in summer.

The ancient centre of the town, beneath the castle, is highly picturesque and interesting, but concentrated in a very small area, so crowds and parking problems are endemic. Keep well away from the traffic confusion on the quays if you can and leave the car perhaps in the place Richelieu, which leads to a pleasant short walk through quiet streets beneath the château. The pedestrianised area, under the ancient colourful archway, is delightful, lined with a variety of simple very French shops, particularly *chocolateries* and *pâtisseries*.

➤ **Le Choiseul**
(HR)L
*36 quai Ch.
Guinot
47.30.45.45
Closed 5/1–15/3
CB, EC
Parking*

Recently face-lifted and a highly impressive member of the classy Grandes Étapes chain, Le Choiseul is now a delight. It's a dignified 18th-century white mansion built by the duc de Choiseul, facing onto the river, with a nice rear garden terrace and swimming pool. The 23 rooms have been decorated with great style and cost from 380f, up to 980f for an apartment.

The restaurant has the best view of any in the town, with wide windows overlooking the river on one side and the gardens on the other. It is light and airy thanks to the white tufa walls, enlivened with vivid curtains, and made even more agreeable by the friendly welcoming staff. The food was among the best we sampled along the whole Loire. The new chef comes without the usual requirement for smart restaurants – an impressive track record in other smart restaurants – but whoever hired him knew what they were doing, and I wouldn't mind betting that starry Michelin recognition will come his way in due course.

Here we ate the best salmon ever, as the second course of a 200f menu. Cooked to the magic moment when the flesh has just lost its transparency but is not beginning to fall apart, it was the ultimate in tender juiciness. 'Loire salmon are rare', said the nice *maître d'hôtel*. But worth waiting for.

Before that came a velouté of the first green asparagus of the season, in which swam ravioli stuffed with foie gras, then pink noisettes of lamb with caramelised turnips, a perfect cheeseboard served by a well-informed waiter and then a coffee mousse with a jasmine tea cream. A memorable meal.

Arrowed on all counts, in the luxury bracket. If you can afford it you could hardly do better than to stay in great comfort in such a central position, with lovely food served on site.

Le Lion d'Or
(HR)M–S
17 quai Ch.
Guinot
47.57.00.23
Closed 30/11–1/
4
EC, V
Garage

A little white hotel at the foot of the château, overlooking the river, with some recently renovated rooms. The range is 127–248f. Breakfasts are said to be particularly good, with home-made bread and croissants. Restaurant prices struck me as disproportionately high, from 117f to 196f.

La Belle-Vue
(H)M–S
12 quai Ch.
Guinot
47.57.02.26
Closed 30/11–
15/3
EC, V

Modern rooms, in a hotel a few doors along from the Lion d'Or, with some good views of river and château, at 170–296f, including breakfast.

Château de Pray
(HR)M–L
2 km E by the D
751
47.57.23.67
Closed 1/1–10/2
AE, DC, EC

An attractive Louis XIII château, set peacefully in the countryside. Readers' experiences have been mixed. There has been some praise for the rooms, at 250–402f, but not for the restaurant, and as *demi-pension* is obligatory in season, at 445–465f, this poses a problem.

'We have one important criticism. The menu never changed over the five days we stayed there. After the third night we could try nothing new and therefore had to retrace our steps.' A pity, because the site and building have great potential. I have the feeling that changes are in the offing here, so reports particularly welcome.

Le Mail St Thomas
(R)L–M
Pl. Richelieu
47.57.22.52
Closed 3/11–17/
11; 15/1–1/3
AE, DC
Parking

A Renaissance house in a lovely garden. Owner François Le Coz moved here two years ago from the Auberge du Mail, and brought with him a tradition of classic cooking, which earns him a Michelin rosette.

Lots of atmosphere in the impressive dining-room, with sculpted fireplace and painted ceiling. Menus 170–220f. Superb Touraine wines.

La Clôserie
(R)S
2 r. Paul Louis
Courier
47.23.10.76

Follow the Loire towards Tours and turn left to find this simple little bistro, well liked by locals on a budget. At lunchtime they do a good-value three-course 56f menu; in the evenings it costs a little more, for a little more choice.

Le Paradoxe
(R)S
3 bis r.
Mirabeau
47.57.50.07

A tiny bistro, with small garden at the rear, where you can draw breath after the château crowds and partake of an ice-cream (home-made). Inside, most of the food is cooked on open grills, with menus at 55f. All very pretty and agreeable.

Le Fournil,
'Chez Bigot'
(R)S
Pl. du Château
47.57.04.46
Closed Tue.
o.o.s. Open 8
a.m–10 p.m

Penetrate through the *salon de thé* of this old-established pastry shop opposite the château for the ideal light lunch. Profit from the *pâtissier's* expertise by eating a quiche, feuilleté or croissant, flavoured with onion, cheese, ham or herbs, or a salad (mine was Roquefort, hazelnuts), or an omelette *au choix*.

Follow up with one of the wonderful pastries of the house, wash it down with freshly squeezed fruit juice or a choice of teas or cafetière coffee (N.B. no alcohol) and you will have done exceedingly well. You could go back at teatime.

In Vino Veritas
(R)S
14 r. Nationale
47.30.53.60
Lunch only
Closed Sun.

In the attractive old pedestrianised area near the château a young couple, Gilles and Florence Martinetti-Monge, have recently opened up a *bar à vins*, a species surprisingly rare in France. They say that the locals are deeply suspicious of anything as un-trad. as a bar that sells wine by the glass not by the bottle, and that their trade perforce relies heavily on the more sophisticated Parisiens (even they have no more than a handful of wine bars to their credit), and on the tourists. In October, when the latter were thin on the ground, their light and bright little bar was empty at lunchtime; the French were all tucking their napkins under their chin(s) and settling down to two hours on a typical 60f menu elsewhere.

Such a pity because I ate so well – a salad, rillettes, some cheese – and drank a glass each of the wines recommended by the knowledgeable Gilles – a not-too-dry Vouvray and a richly rewarding Bourgeuil, resulting in a bill of under a fiver.

They deserve all possible support.

Map 2C   **ANGERS** (M.-et-L.) 45 km NW of Saumur; 109 km E of Tours

49000
(M) *Mon.,*
Wed., Fri.

The former capital of Anjou stands 8 kilometres north of the Loire, on the banks of the Maine – a very short river indeed, formed by the confluence of the Sarthe and Mayenne. The splendid view from the château ramparts reveals how all this wateriness sorts itself out around the town.

It is not generally considered a tourist town. Mistakenly I feel, for there is much to see, and the liveliness that comes with a busy industrial and farming centre, independent of seasonal visitors, is agreeable and unusual in the area. The cafés in the main square, the place du Ralliement, are always full of students and shoppers, and the department stores and boutiques are of high quality. Bad weather – and the Loire seemed to get more than its fair share of rain on my visits throughout the year – is not much fun anywhere, but I'd rather be wet in Angers than in any empty rain-sad village.

It prides itself on being the centre of the arts for the *département* and during the second fortnight in June and first week in July the locals flock in to see the festivals of music, drama and art it hosts.

The fine feudal **château** is a must, dominating the centre of the city with its 17 chunky red and white towers, strung out for over a kilometre. They look down far below to the moat, now laid out in pleasant gardens, with a herd of deer in occupation.

It dates from the early 13th century, on the site of an earlier castle, built by one Foulques Nerra (987–1040), whose name will undoubtedly crop up repeatedly whenever the history of Anjou and Touraine is discussed. His passion for building fortresses – 20 of them in the area – was only equalled by his bouts of religious fervour, when he sought to cancel out the effects of his appallingly ruthless and avaricious nature by showering gifts and endowments on monasteries and churches. During his reign, the power of the House of Anjou rivalled that of the ruling house of France – the Capets. He was the founder of the dynamic dynasty of Foulques, culminating in Geoffrey, who married William the Conqueror's granddaughter Matilda, and who bequeathed the name of Plantagenets (*plante à genêt*) to his descendants (Henry Plantagenet was his son) by wearing a sprig of broom (*genêt*) in his cap.

Good King René is another name likely to be encountered frequently by the traveller here. He was the last and one of the most civilised dukes of Anjou, eventually seceding the dukedom to his nephew Louis XI.

Ruminating on all these colourful previous residents of the castle, it is time to proceed inside to see a unique treasure, the **Tapestry of the Apocalypse**, preserved in a specially designed room, where its great length – 350 feet of the original 460 feet – can be seen to advantage. It's an awe-inspiring sight as well as a stunningly beautiful one; the tapestry was made in Paris six hundred years ago and its colours, if not as brilliant as when they were so painstakingly stitched, are still amazingly vivid. The sequence of seven sections, each 16½-feet high, tells the story of the Apocalypse, as related by St John. Its purpose was to put heart into persecuted Christians by portraying the ultimate triumph of the Church, but even without the message, the beauty and purity of the design would make this work of art quite outstanding. Do go.

There is more tapestry on view on the upper floor of the castle, reached by King René's staircase. This is the Passion Tapestry, four late-15th-century Flemish works, again marvellously rich in colour. And if that's not enough, cross the river to the **Lurçat Museum**, housed in the former St Jean Hospital – a mediaeval hospital (1175) founded by Henry II as part of his penance for the murder of Thomas à Becket. It's a beautiful building and it was a clever idea to make it the home for the brilliant colour and swirling pattern of the Chante du Monde, made at Gobelins in 1966 to the design of Jean Lurçat, who had been inspired by the Tapestry of the Apocalypse to produce this personal attestation of faith.

Another clever utilisation of an existing building is the restoration of the 13th-century former abbey church of Toussaint into a light and airy gallery, to house the work of the sculptor **David of Angers**. (Jean-Pierre David is not to be confused with his contemporary Jacques-Louis David the painter.) An example of his work can be seen at the foot of the castle – the powerful statue of Duke René, around which nowadays too much traffic surges to make considered viewing feasible.

The **Fine Arts Museum**'s home is a beautiful Renaissance mansion, the Logis Barrault. A feast of goodies here: primitive treasures, Renaissance furniture, many fine 18th-century works – by Fragonard, Watteau, Boucher, Greuze – and 19th-century representations by the other David, Ingres, Géricault, Delacroix, Corot, Jongkind; but alas, currently nothing is displayed to its best advantage. A rearrangement is planned and then here will be a treasure-house indeed.

The **Cathedral of St Maurice** stands imposingly at the head of a gentle flight of wide steps leading down to the river, often scattered with students, chattering, picnicking. The splendid carvings around the porch can be taken in gradually during the upward climb. The 12th-century building is unusual in having a single nave, and that roofed with one of the earliest examples of Gothic vaulting. The magnificent stained-glass windows were miraculously preserved during the 1944 bombing, when the RAF attacked the castle, used by the Germans as an arsenal.

Angers is also a good base from which to cruise the rivers Maine, Mayenne, Sarthe and Oudon. A variety of trips are on offer through these lovely green peaceful waterways. Information from the Compagnie Féerives, 19 rue Valdemaine, 41.88.88.78. See also p. 14.

Although there is plenty to see in Angers, I'm not sure I would choose to stay in the town itself. It does lack green spaces and pleasant walks and the quays have not been exploited except as busy thoroughfares. In kind weather better by far to stay somewhere quieter outside and drive into the town. The exception, however, might be in winter, and so I have tracked down one or two possible lodgings, with that idea in mind.

Hôtel d'Anjou
(H)M
and its
restaurant
Restaurant Salamandre
(R)M
1 bvd Mar.-
Foch
41.88.24.82
Rest. closed
Sun; hotel open
all year round
All credit cards
Garage

A smartly restored old hotel on the main boulevard, at a busy crossroads; the rooms would be decidedly noisy were it not for the efficient triple-glazing and soundproofing. Most of the 50 rooms have been redecorated very attractively and are now comfortable, spacious and well equipped. At 260–360f they represent very good value in this central position.

The restaurant seems very English, with its panelling, latticed windows, stained glass, chandeliers, white starched napery. Definitely for serious eating. In spite of all this solid dignity, the prices come as a pleasant surprise, especially for the quality of cooking on offer. The 88f menu, e.g. terrine of hare, fillet steak with mustard sauce, dessert, is excellent value, as is the 120f, e.g. six Breton oysters, escalope of salmon, beurre blanc, cheese and pud. The food, though classical in concept, is not as heavy as the décor might suggest (though forgo the desserts – a trifle leaden). Fish, vegetables and home-made bread are particularly commendable.

➤ **Hôtel du Mail**
(H)S–M
8 r. des Ursules
41.88.56.22
Open all year
EC, V
Parking

This would be my first choice, if only by virtue of its calm. Angers is a noisy, busy city and its other hotels tend to be noisy and busy too. The Hotel du Mail is the only one qualifying to belong to 'La Chaine de Silence'.

It's an old, grey, very French-looking house, set behind a courtyard, in a quiet street just behind the Mairie. Nearby is the colourful Jardin du Mail, a pleasant spot in which to sit and watch the fountains play, so near the town and yet so far away from the bustle.

The nice patron is very proud of his wife, a florist. There are photographs of her impressive, stiff arrangements for Versailles all up the staircase (the French do not admire the softer, more natural English approach to flower arranging). Here is one hotel where the flowers are never plastic.

The bedrooms have all recently been renovated and are now fitted with *tout confort*, but are still simple and good value at 135–270f.

With private parking, lots of character, and this privileged site, the Hôtel du Mail qualifies for an arrow.

St Julien
(H)S–M
9 pl. du
Ralliement
41.88.41.62
Open every day
CB

Angers is not well served for cheap hotels, so I was particularly pleased to find the St Julien, in the same building as the best restaurant in town (see below), bang in the centre of all the activity but with efficient soundproofing. The rooms are good sized and well equipped, and remarkable value at 130–220f. No restaurant, but a special service-on-trays in the bedrooms, and a bar.

For those who like to economise on their bed and go Banco on their food, I would recommend staying here and eating at Le Quéré.

Le Quéré
(R)M
9 pl. du
Ralliement
41.87.64.94
Closed Fri.
p.m.; Sat.; 1
week school
hols in Feb.; 1/
7–20/7
AE, CB, DC

MOVED
TO NEW
ADDRESS

The best in town, perhaps in the whole of Anjou, but, oh dear, what a let-down setting, on the first floor of a dreary building overlooking the square. On the other hand, when the new premises, now being sought, are finally located, the prices might rise in proportion to the prestige of a smarter address. Currently the 149f menu, for cooking of this class (Paul Le Quéré trained at Robuchon) is a gift. And the 220f version too for that matter.

Martine Le Quéré is a phenomenon – a youthful female *sommelier*. And, moreover, one who knows her stuff, passionately interested in everything to do with wine, but an encyclopaedia on those of the Loire.

She will counsel a glass of the wonderfully subtle and relatively unknown delicately sweet Layon to go with her husband's sublime terrine of duck livers, served with asparagus in season. You could follow this, perhaps, with local carp, its juices preserved in a casing of cabbage leaves, sprinkled with bacon, or a fricassée of zander and crayfish daringly combined with a purée of Brussels sprouts, and finish with a rich fondant of bitter chocolate, freshened with a sorbet of chocolate and mint.

Who cares about the site when the cooking's this good?

Le Logis
(R)M
17 r. St Laud
41.87.44.15
Closed Sat.
p.m.; 1/6–15/6;
Sun., 11/7–4/8
AE, CB

The place for fish, both river and sea, with some original variations. Small, rustic, in the centre of town.

Try house fish pâté, goujonettes of turbot with saffron and bitter cherries, and forget puddings. Menus from 110f. Carte 230f.

Le Grand Cercle
(R)S–M
18 bvd Foch
41.87.37.20
All credit cards
Open every day

A pleasant surprise was the restaurant attached to the modern chain hotel La Concorde. At lunchtime, particularly, it's a vibrant, agreeable place to partake of anything from a meal (menus from 70f) down to an ice-cream and coffee. Outside on the pavement is a shellfish bar from which to order perhaps a half-dozen oysters (from 25–31f), which, with a glass of fruity Loire wine, could make the perfect light lunch. In summer the stall goes and is replaced by white tables from which to watch the Angevin world go by.

No eyebrows were raised when I ordered just an entrée – a seafood salad – and a mere half-carafe of rosé wine. My 'salade marine' was full of fishy delicacies, including a sprinkling of red 'caviare', with fresh beans and designer lettuce, all for 35f.

With swift and efficient service, this could be a useful all-year-round address. Certainly the locals think so – it's always packed.

These restaurants are the pick of the bunch for serious eating at serious prices, but *bistros*, *crêperies*, and *brasseries* abound in this university city. Here is a selection recommended to me, on which readers' reports would be particularly welcome:
Le Campagnard, 69 r. du Mail, 41.88.50.40. Closed Sun. and Mon. Menus from 49f. Rustic, simple.
La Croque au Sel, 8 r. Botanique, 41.86.86.30. Closed Sun. Menus from 56f. Old-fashioned cooking.

Le Jardin, 31 r. Boreau, 41.43.24.16. Closed Wed. and Sat. Salads, carte only, say 50f.
Crêperies: Boisnet, r. Boisnet; Clementine, r. Delage.
Good meat, grills: La Côte du Boeuf, r. Madeleine; La Cour Foch, 13 bis bvd Foch.
Fish: Le Départ, 28 bvd Arnault; L'Écume, r. des Deux Haies; La Marée, Les Halles.
Brasseries: Brasserie de la Gare (good wines too); Le Pub St Aubin (fun décor).
Bars and cafés: Le Bar Belge, bvd Arnault (students, wide choice of beers); La Civette, pl. Romain (in fashion, artists, terrace); Le Glacier, Jardin du Mail (pleasant setting).

SHOPPING

G. Benoit, 1 r. des Lices, *chocolaterie,* wonderful Cointreau truffles; Galloyer, 7 r. Lenepveu, *pâtisserie;* Au Petit Lord, r. St Aubin, *pâtisserie;* Le Cave du Roy, r. Monthault, wines; Le Sang au Terroir, wines; Vinothèque, r. de la Roë, wines; Carterie Toussaint, 19 r. Toussaint, presents, postcards, posters.

Map 3F | **ARTANNES-SUR-INDRE** (I.-et-L.) 12 km E of Azay; 10 km W of Montbazon

---

37260
Monts
(M) *Sun. am.*

An unremarkable village on the D 17.

Mme Odette Pointreau
(C)S
123 av. de la Vallée du Lys
47.26.80.85

Set well back from the road, approached through an avenue of young limes, the house looks spic from the first impressions onwards. And that's not common in France! Inside the place positively gleams, from polished floor to polished furniture and any other surface remotely shineable. Dust or grime wouldn't have a chance here. It's like an advert for good housekeeping.
    The four bedrooms have flowery name-plaques neatly nailed to their new paint. I like 'Myosotis' best, with its own bathroom a step across the landing, at 160f. The others are all fine, good sized, at 135f. They share a loo and shower but I bet Mme Pointreau nips in between showerers to make sure the next occupant finds it perfectly ship-shape. A good inexpensive reliable stop.

Auberge de la Vallée du Lys
(R)S–M
47.26.80.02
Closed Sun. p.m.; Mon.

In the village centre on the hill leading down to the river. A bright and cheerful little restaurant with locally approved food. Interesting menus from 75f.

Map 2C	**AVRILLÉ** (M.-et-L.) 8 km NW of Angers

49240

Le Cavier
(HR)S–M
41.42.30.45
Rest. closed
Sun.; 1/8–15/8;
24/12–8/1
AE, DC, EC, V

On the N 162.

A motel, recommended as a convenience stop, perhaps for those who do not want to get embroiled in Angers, with a quiet night guaranteed, in spite of its proximity to the route nationale. 29 rooms from 170f to 240f with bath; menus from 55f, and good carafe wine.

Map 3F	**AZAY-LE-RIDEAU** (I.-et-L.) 21 km NE of Chinon; 28 km SW of Tours

---

37190
(M) *Wed.*

Along with Chenonçeau, everyone's favourite château. The two have much in common, both being inspired by women – in this case, Phillipe Lesbahy, wife of Gilles Berthelet, the financier, who had the château built in the early 16th century. Perhaps the female touch accounts for the gracefulness of both châteaux, lacking aggressiveness, with only token fortification, and the surrounding waters mellow and soften the general effect.

Azay was certainly Balzac's favourite; he called it a diamond cut in facets. It's true that the deep moats, and the river Indre which partly surrounds it, throw back some of their sparkle onto this photogenic, turretted, minaretted gem of a castle, whose architecture combines the best of the Gothic heritage with the Renaissance lightness and brightness.

Inside, the four-storey Great Staircase, illuminated with double windows, is the most striking Italianate feature. It is a delight to be able to wander through the furnished rooms at one's own pace, accompanied by helpful documentation in a choice of languages, rather than by a possibly uncongenial guide (but guided tours are also available every half hour).

Château open: between 9.30 a.m. and 12 noon and 2 p.m. and 6.30 p.m. from Easter to 30 September; closes at 5 p.m. from 1 October to 15 November; closes at 4.45 p.m. 16 November to Easter. A particularly good *son et lumière* performance starts in late May and continues through to September. Info: 47.61.61.23, ext. 2160.

The little town of Azay revolves round the château and tends to get hopelessly traffic-entangled. Parking in peak periods is a nightmare, with irritable gendarmes blowing their whistles at the hapless motorist looking for a slot. Best leave the car in the château park on the Chinon road. In any case, this is a very pleasant spot to picnic, peacefully by the river in off-peak days; alternatively there is a café and snack-bar by the park.

Lucky those with parking facilities on the spot, as at:

➤ Clos Philippa
(C)M–L
10 r. Pineau
47.45.26.46

If you've ever wondered what goes on behind those forbidding, blank, begrimed walls of many a French town house, you'll get an answer here, having driven through the iron gates adjoining Clos Philippa, bang on the Saché road, near the town centre.

Inside is an altogether different story from the outward appearance. It's a nice, faded, 18th-century house, with two arms enclosing a courtyard, looking down to a substantial garden, burgeoning with Easter daffodils when we were there, and leading on to the grounds of the château.

Mme Bernadette Wilmann is the most helpful of hostesses, anxious to please even to the extent of making a cup of 'English' tea. 'I'm not very good at it – is this all right?' It was, served on a nice tray, as we collapsed after a long drive, in our pretty, spacious bedroom, looking over the garden, with a fine view of the château whetting our appetites for a post-revival visit.

Mme Wilmann proudly shows you round her home – the wide salon and dining-room furnished mostly with antiques.

As we came down for breakfast, a little note was propped up on our table: 'Excuse me – just popped out for some fresh croissants.' (Do the French know how lucky they are?) Fresh bread, too, home-

Clos Philippa, Azay-le-Rideau

made jam and unlimited coffee made it a good start to the day. Cost: 350f for our bedroom, which was the nicest, 200f for one of the other three. All have private bath/shower and loo.

A unique position for château-bashing, nice Mme Wilmann, and comfortable accommodation add up to an arrow.

➤ **Grand**
Monarque 🏨
(HR)M
Pl. République
47.45.40.08
Rest. closed 15/
11–15/3
AE, EC, V

For three generations the Jacquet family ran this delightful old, very French, hotel in the town centre, and it seemed nothing much changed during that time. Now the fourth generation claims to have taken a *chemin différent* and there is a fresh sense of direction under Mme Forest. All the old *équipe*, including the chef and the *maître d'hôtel*, have rallied round her, and the hotel is enjoying a new lease of life, with all the old successes.

Some of the bedrooms have already been done up, and very nice they are too. Those on the front could be noisy but there is another quieter block across an unexpected green courtyard, where I would ask to be. A double with bath costs 305f, while one of the older rooms is 145f.

The food is as good and as traditional as ever, featuring home-made foie gras, Loire fish and good desserts. No need to spend more than 80f for a menu but the next one up at 120f is good too. Splendid wines.

An arrow for sustained high standards in a popular tourist town.

Hôtel de
Biencourt
(H)M–S
7 r. Balzac
47.45.20.75
Closed 15/11–
15/2
V

A nice little Logis, tucked away in a quiet street near the château. The rooms are fresh and bright and good value at 175–250f, and there is a charming breakfast area, freshly papered in a wistaria-covered lattice, looking out on to a little garden.

No hardship, in this little town with several choices within walking distance, to have no restaurant.

Hôtel Val de
Loire,
Restaurant Le
Commerce
(HR)M–S
50 rte Nationale
47.45.23.67 and
47.45.40.22
Closed 15/11–
15/3
EC, V

A cheerful, newly decorated modern hotel, hung about with geraniums, with friendly helpful owners. The bedrooms are all bright and clean, furnished in country style, and range from 160 to 205f. Ask for one overlooking the garden.

Le Commerce next door, under the same management, also has rooms. They are unrecommendable, but the food is fine. Menus at 84f, 110f and 175f.

'We visited the Hôtel Le Commerce and met the hyperactive and very friendly M. Dovale, who assured us that the rooms were not good but the restaurant was! He recommended we stay at the Val de Loire and we did. We were very pleased with our choice. If you have dinner at the Commerce then you receive a complimentary aperitif.

'We consider the food to be very good value and enjoyed all the meals, but would particularly recommend the "pièce de boeuf flambée aux herbes fraîches" on the 110f menu. This is prepared at the table by M. Dovale's brother, who is an expert. Madame Dovale attends to the Val de Loire when Monsieur is at Le Commerce.'

L'Aigle d'Or
(R)M
10 r. Adelaide-Richer
47.45.24.50
Closed Sun.
p.m. o.o.s.;
Wed. 15/
1–15/2; 13/12–
21/12
CB

A former *maître d'* from the high and mighty Château d'Artigny recently bought and transformed this little town house. Mercifully he is not applying château prices or château standards, but his menu is quite ambitious, with a salad of langoustines and foie gras, zander with wild mushrooms, roast pigeon. Menus from 72f weekdays only. The 98f is better. Nice garden for fine weather eating.

Local opinion is divided as to which is better – this or L'Automate (see below). What is agreed is that they are both very good indeed. Catch it while it's new.

➤ **L'Automate Gourmand**
(R)M–S
11 r. du Parc,
Chapelle-St-Blaise
47.45.39.07
Closed Sun.
p.m.; Wed; 20/
12–20/1
CB

Everyone loves L'Automate Gourmand for a lively evening and fun atmosphere, generated by the astonishing décor of old toys, displayed in cabinets on the walls of the little bistro.

The food is excellent, simple but imaginative, from a humble terrine of *tripier* (brains, tongue, head) on a bed of cabbage, to a lobster cooked in its own juices. Extraordinary value on the 66f menu, and the 109f is a winner too.

Arrowed for unusual atmosphere, and good value.

Map 1I **BEAUGENCY** (Loiret) 25 km SW of Orléans, 31 km NE of Blois

45190
Ⓜ *Wed. a.m.,*
Sat.

The best approach to this once walled and fortified town on the banks of the Loire is from the south. This way leads across the 23 arches of the 14th-century bridge, crossing the river, wide and swiftly flowing here, with a fine view all the way of the steeply sloping old town, dominated by the Tour St-Firmin and its keep. Parking is easy either side of the bridge along the river bank.

Unfortunately for its townspeople, Beaugency's bridge used to be the only one between Blois and Orléans and so the town was the obvious target for enemy attack. During the Hundred Years' War it was taken by the English four times, until eventually delivered by Joan of Arc in 1429. Legend has it that it was built by the Devil, no less, in exchange for the first soul to cross it. When he saw that it was a cat who made the first transition, Old Nick thought it so good a joke that he let out a mighty guffaw that blew the top off the keep. Those who doubt the story have only to look at the tower – its top is certainly missing.

The Devil must have been very attached to Beaugency, since he decided to live there in another smaller tower, the Tour du Diable, near the old abbey, and some say he is still there. Perhaps he would approve of all those litter-leaving, beer-swilling tourists in the bar beneath his former home.

To find the most attractive part of the town walk up the rue du Pont and turn left under an old stone archway to the precincts of the 12th-century abbey church of Notre Dame. Unfortunately the fine Romanesque vaulting was destroyed by fire and the Gothic wooden replacement has been painted, in an unfortunate attempt at *trompe l'œil*, to look like stone.

And that's about it; apart from the immediate picturesque impact, I found the rest of the town somewhat disappointing. Its proximity to Orléans and the more popular châteaux leads to overcrowding and traffic-fret and the stalls up the rue du Pont are pretty tatty. However, the main market up in the place du Martroi is genuine enough and worth a puff up the cobbled streets.

Hôtel de l'Abbaye
(HR)L
Quai Abbaye
38.44.67.35
AE, DC, EC, V
Parking

A bit intimidating perhaps, this vast grey pile, previously the abbey, rebuilt in the 18th century to replace the 12th-century original, and I found the atmosphere somewhat impersonal and very conscious of l'Abbaye's station as *the* hotel of the town. But it does have a truly impressive interior, with grand reception rooms, great beamed galleries and a restaurant with a prime view overlooking the river. Even a drink on the terrace would be a treat.

I though the price of the set menu – 98f – comparatively modest for an establishment of this standing, but locals say that the cooking varies wildly. Catch the young chef, Patrick Cartier, on a good day and he is very very good . . . Other menus with more choice are 138f and 175f.

Some of the bedrooms are conjured up from erstwhile cells and are accordingly small and darkish. At 400f they cannot be said to be good value. The apartments, for another 100f, are probably a better bet. Their decor varies considerably. One, obviously geared to transatlantic tastes, gave me the giggles with its tartan coverings and scarlet carpet but next door was delightful – all calm greys and slate blues.

Écu de Bretagne
(HR)M
Pl. du Martroi
38.44.67.60
Closed 25/1–1/3
AE, DC, EC, V

A nice old-fashioned hotel facing on to a square, with tables outside on the terrace, from which to observe the market-day bustle. Rooms are 80–230f, menus from 80f to 180f.

➤ **Hôtel Sologne**
(H)S–M
Pl. St-Firmin
38.44.50.27
Closed Sun.
p.m. o.o.s.; 15/
12–1/2
V

A find. A really pretty little grey stone hotel, laden with geraniums, in a steep square, central but away from the through traffic. It has a green and cool interior, courtyard, very modestly priced comfortable bedrooms, at 90–230f, and best of all, a charming and helpful Breton patronne, the unfortunately named Mme Rogue.

Arrowed for convenience, *accueil* and good value.

Le Petit Bâteau
'Chez Yvette'
(R)S
54 r. du Pont
38.44.56.38

Mme Rogue assesses her clients' needs and incomes and sends them to a range of local eateries, but there is one that brings them back rubbing their stomachs in appreciation. Top choice is 'Chez Yvette', a little restaurant in the main street, shaped, they claim (though it would never have struck me), like a boat. Menus at 46f, 65f, 90f and 120f.

Map 4E

BEAUMONT-EN-VÉRON (I.-et-L.) 5 km N of Chinon

37420
Avoine

Signposted off the D 749.

La Giraudière
(H)M
Rte de
Bourgueil et de
Savigny
47.58.40.36
Open every day
AE, CB, DC, EC

Maybe it was overkill that spoiled La Giraudière for me. After reading its praises in every known guide to the area, I put it top of my list as a base. Certainly it met the bill in terms of position – deep peaceful countryside but still near the man-made attractions – and certainly the owners are kind and helpful, but the disappointment was that it was not something special. The lack of a restaurant means no heart to the place – I hate being asked what time I want breakfast in my room next day as soon as I arrive, as though the management has now done all that is required; and when breakfast came it was depressingly plastic. As my husband gloomily opined 'Just a B and B really, without the personal touch.'

Our room, up two freezing and drably carpeted flights of stairs, was fine, with functional bathroom, for 300f. I'm told the others vary in size and character, as in price (from 140f to 365f).

Oh dear, I wonder if I'm not being fair, as I didn't discover this one myself. Here is a reader's letter, to adjust the balance:
'It is good old-fashioned rural France – clean with no pretensions to style although there are signs that some sort of refurbishing is in progress. It has no restaurant and breakfast is basic; the garden is an unkempt orchard and apart from some garden furniture in the courtyard there is nowhere to sit. We found it to be a good base from which to go out to the neighbouring rivers with a picnic, but for anyone wanting anything more from their hotel than that it would be a disaster. The guests were very cosmopolitan and it was always full with people sent out from the tourist office in Chinon.' – Betty S. Carr.

Château de
Goulaine
M. Jacques de
Bonnaventure
(C)M–S
47.93.01.27

The château is clearly visible from the Chinon–Bourgueil road, and from here I decided to give it a miss. It looked one of those typical decaying châteaux, where the guests have to excuse all manner of aberrations for the privilege of staying in so aristrocratic a building. However, a local recommendation made me think again and I encountered nice Mme Bonnaventure going out to the stables. She told me that all her rooms were taken and very honourably regretted I could not therefore inspect (I admire that – so embarrassing to be shown other people's dirty socks). A nice young couple sitting sunning on the terrace, however, offered their room as an example and it was fine – spacious, furnished with antiques, shower and loo attached, all for 165f. Good value, especially for families – 3 people – 200f; singles 80f.

| Map 2B | **BÉCON-LES GRANITS** (M.-et-L.) 10 km NW of Angers |

49370
Lelouroux
Béconnais

On the D 963.

Des Trois Marchands
HR(S)
Pl. de l'Église
41.77.90.21
Closed Fri. p.m.
and Sun. p.m.;
15/12–31/12

Only six rooms in this simple Logis de France, usefully situated on the approach road to Angers. Readers have praised the cooking of M. Lechêne (from 55f) and been happy to return another time to the comfortable bedrooms (from 120f to 140f).

| Map 2C | **BÉHUARD** (M.-et-L.) 13 km S of Angers; 5 km N of Rochefort-sur-Loire |

49170
St-Georges-sur-
Loire

Cross the river Louet from Rochefort and the island of Béhuard will be marked from the bridge over the Loire, or take the pleasant river road, the D 111 from Angers.

The most interesting and attractive of the Loire's many islands, Béhuard is some two miles long, with the ancient village, dating from pre-Christian times, in the middle of its green pastures. Take time, do, to walk around the peaceful, time-warped lanes, down an avenue lined with soaring poplars to the river for a fine watery view; find the deserted beach on the south side for a picnic and a paddle, and be sure to visit the church, built into the rock face, for Louis XI, who used to lodge in the chaplain's house alongside it. The war memorial gives pause for thought. So many souls lost from one tiny island.

In and near the square are several simple restaurants, ideal for an excursion lunch. **Notre Dame** specialises in fritures of eels and river fish (46f), **Les Tourelles** (75f) has a nice terrace, and **Au Rocher** (65f) is the best-known and gets the thumbs-up from the lorry drivers – always a good sign.

Actually on the bridge, and with a good view of the river is:

Le Grand Pont
(R)S
41.72.21.64
Open every day

A popular destination on fine days for the consumption of eels, pike and other river fish, served on the terrace. In winter make for the rustic restaurant inside. Menus 75f.

Map 1L   **LES BÉZARDS** (Loiret) 16 km NE of Gien

45290
Nogent-sur-
Vernisson

On the N 7.

►**Auberge des
Templiers**
(HR)L
38.31.80.01
Closed mid-
Jan. to mid-
Feb.
AE, DC, EC, V
Parking

I knew quite a lot about the Auberge des Templiers before I got there.
From other guides and foodie articles I learned that it was one of the
best-known and valued gastro-shrines in the whole area, backed up
by a highly luxurious hotel complex, all run by the same family for
many years. Superlative followed superlative, Michelin gives it two
stars, Gault-Millau 19 out of 20. Heady stuff. From all this verbiage I
had drawn a mixed bag of impressions, some accurate, some way off
the mark.

First the name: the Auberge des Templiers I had pictured as a
rustic ancient hostelry, as picturesque as other 'Knights Templar'
lodgings dotted about France; its address, with Nogent-sur-
Vernisson the nearest village, sounded deeply rural. So to find that
this auberge stands near a crossroads on a very busy route
nationale, near no village, was the first shock. If the original building
were indeed ancient, the antique irregularities of its walls have now
been heavily plastered over to produce the smart, well-groomed
effect the French admire.

The next disappointment was the room. Ours was the most
expensive throughout a year's research in the area. At 880f (breakfast
another 80f), it was in the middle of the hotel's price range.
Cheerfully decorated in sunny yellow admittedly, it was of modest
size, with tiny windows letting in minimum light via its north aspect.
Bathroom OK but hardly the hedonist asses'-milk variety I had been
looking forward to with that price in mind. We were lucky in drawing
a room in the block furthest away from the highway, but, even so, the
traffic noise was considerable (OK, we shouldn't have been so Brit as
to sleep with our windows open). It looked out on to a swimming
pool, in which I had been looking forward all day to washing away
the cares of a long journey. No luck again. 'Swimming pool closed at
5.30', said the bossy notice. Rebelliously, thinking of all that entrance
fee, I stepped over the gate and dipped a toe in the water, but had to
admit defeat. On a September evening the water was too chill for
even the most stalwart.

So far, so bad, and if it were only accommodation that the Auberge
had to offer, it wouldn't figure here. To strike a balance, it must be
emphasised that its *raison d'être* is the food, and that the rooms
came later, as an accessory. And the food we ate that night at dinner
more than merited the journey, the two stars and all the lavished
praise.

There have been disturbing changes in the kitchen, with chefs
coming and going, disasters prophesied but triumphantly overcome.
The policy of the percipient patron, Philippe Depée, has always been
to retain the best of the retiring chef's repertoire, while gently
introducing the new man's successes, so that Les Templiers' regular
clients are not rudely deprived of their favourite dishes (and in fact
are barely aware of the back-stage dramas). Which does seem to
make refreshing sense in this age of mega-star chefs. Here it is

Philippe and his ex-model wife Françoise who are the stars. Before he stepped into centre-stage he served a thorough apprenticeship under his parents, who ran the Templiers before him; the threads of continuity extend to many of the staff – the *sommelier* and the gentle and gentlemanly porter Jean to name but two.

Since the cheapest menu was 295f (240f at lunch), we decided that as rape was going to be inevitable, we should not resist some of the house specialities, and ate à la carte. Each course was quite sublime. Mousse of chicken livers studded with fresh grapes, Loire zander with Sologne girolles and an unforgettable dessert *dégustation* of all the house favourites, a raspberry mousse, a mango ice-cream, a strawberry tart, and the famed vanilla mille-feuille.

So we went to bed very happy and faced the enormous bill next day (nearly £200) with guilty resignation.

Advice here would be to make the most of Les Templiers' undeniable culinary genius and sleep in a tent if needs be. The arrow for wonderful extravagant food. Thumbs-down for the hotel.

Map 3G	**BLÉRÉ** (I.-et-L.) 25 km E of Tours

37150
(M) *Tues.,*
Fri.

On the south bank of the Cher.

Not a very exciting little town on a not very exciting stretch of river, but forgive all this in view of:

Le Cheval Blanc
(H)S (R)M
Pl. de l'Église
47.30.30.14
Closed Sun.
p.m. and Mon.
except Jul. and
Aug.

A very model of what a modest little French hotel should be. The Association de Logis de France thought so too, when in 1985 they awarded it the 'Fleur d'Or d'Accueil' award.

All black and white and hard to miss, it's set on the little church square, and once upon a 17th-century time formed part of the monastery. Nowadays it is run, with lots of success, by a young couple, Michel and Micheline Blériot. He willingly took time in the late afternoon, a chef's low, when he is resting his aching feet after one onslaught and gathering strength for the next, to show me the bedrooms. There are 13: 8 with double beds, 5 with twins, all with bathrooms, pristine and bright, at 190–210f. I would ask for one at the rear.

He cooks straightforwardly and very well, using local fresh ingredients, including veg. and herbs from his garden. In fine weather you can eat in the flowery little courtyard, with its 18th-century fountain refreshingly splashing. Good menus start at 95f.

A winner on all counts.

Hôtel Cher
(HR)S
R. du Pont
47.57.95.15
V

I was so pleased with the Cheval Blanc, I looked no further in Bléré, but here's someone who knows better:

'This must be one of the better Michelin red 'R' restaurants, with menus from 47.50f, super value and with carafe wine available.' –Geoff Woollen.

But, for reasons I know not, the red R has gone. The menu is now 58f – I should like to know if it is still as good.

BLOIS (L.-et-Ch.) 60 km NE of Tours; 56 km SW of Orléans

41000
(M) *Every day*

A city built around its château, one of the Loire's most-visited. It has always struck me as being an integral part of the city, not standing aloof, as it does at Saumur and Angers for example. The best view is from the south, where the old roofs tumbling down to the river set off the imposing castle most appropriately. Once across the elegant 18th-century bridge, it is the traffic that dominates and I am afraid spoils the place for me. Parking is diabolical. Sometimes there is room up in the comparative calm of the place du Château, along with coaches galore; otherwise it's a matter of cruising and meter-spotting. My advice is to abandon the car at the very first opportunity and hoof the rest.

This involves a fair amount of climbing, some of it mercifully pedestrianised, through steep and narrow mediaeval streets, now being restored after the 1940 destruction. Take a walk round old Blois, east of the château, where there are many half-timbered houses and mansions, mediaeval turrets, and tempting glimpses of enclosed courtyards. Look out for the rues de la Fontaine-des-Élus, du Puits-Châtel, des Papegaults, des Juifs, Pierre de Blois, Honoré, Chemonton, Lion Ferré, for the most interesting walks.

In the main shopping street, the rue Denis Papin, there are some good food shops, especially *chocolatiers*, which seem particularly to thrive here.

The list of associations with the château is too long, complicated and interesting to try and compress into a couple of paragraphs. Buy a guide book!

The building is a history book in itself – they call if four châteaux in one – with its fascinating hotchpotch of periods and styles, most of them heavily restored, a cross-section of French architecture from the 13th to the 17th centuries. Once a mediaeval fortress belonging to the counts of Blois, it became a royal residence in 1498 under Louis XII. He added a graceful brick and stone wing, and his successor, François I, contributed the Renaissance wing, with its famous openwork staircase and Italian façade. Then Gaston of Orléans, brother of Louis XIII, directed Mansart to build the majestic classical wing. The most striking feature of course is the staircase, built originally as a kind of grandstand for watching the goings-on in the courtyard.

With the exception of the apartments of Catherine de Médicis, much of the interior is a disappointment, with so many blank rooms, failing to evoke any atmosphere.

Blois is strangely short of good hotels, but it is not in any case a place I would choose to stay in this area – there are many other possibilities only a short distance away in altogether less traffic-polluted areas. However, more by luck than judgement, I did come across one hotel, opened only two weeks, which I believe would well serve most requirements of those who need a central Blois base.

→ **Le Relais Bleu du Château** (HR)M
22 r. Porte Côté
54.78.20.24
Open every day

This is an old French-style hotel, which used to be the Hôtel du Château, recently acquired and restored by a small and select chain called les Relais Bleus. If the others are as good as this example, here is one chain I will not despise.

The position is ideal – at the foot of the château, with no need to use the car for sightseeing within the city. The rooms have all been attractively refurbished and are now light and bright, cheerful and mod-conned; excellent value in this central position for 250f.

The restaurant is a real find, both for hotel residents and for passers-by, since I found central Blois oddly deficient too in any kind of restaurant. It was in desperation that I called in here at 2 p.m., wanting a light lunch and not expecting too much.

I found a delightfully furnished bar/salon which would be ideal for tea/coffee/drinks, and, further through the hotel, the restaurant in an interior courtyard full of flowers, lots of light, exposed stonework and a delightful rustic feel in the heart of town.

So far so very good, but even better was the food, which was the cheapest and most interesting in many a long day. Menus are 65f and 85f, with some really first-class fish and meat dishes.

Because I wasn't hungry, I chose two starters, a gâteau of chicken livers, studded with grapes and served with a coulis of fresh tomato (20f) and a feuilleté of asparagus with a chive and chervil sauce (30f). All the sorbets and ices are home made every day, with titillating unusual flavours, but I chose a mousse of white chocolate with a fresh fruit sauce. Wine equally good value.

Go soon before word gets round that the young chef, Yves Raffault, should be lionised.

Arrowed for central position in tourist town, good cooking.

Hôtel Viennois (HR)M–S
5 quai A
Contant
54.74.12.80
Closed Sun.
p.m. and Mon.
lunch o.o.s.

On the south bank of the Loire, near the bridge, a small hotel (26 rooms) long popular with English visitors (booking strongly advisable). Rooms are 51–100f – excellent value – and menus start at 55f.

'This provides an excellent base. A room for four people, including a bath and loo, was 160f. Dinner was excellent – four courses included.' – David G. Thomas.

La Péniche
(R)M
Promenade du
Mail, quai St-
Jean
54.74.37.23
Open every day
AE, CB, DC, EC

Well, at least it's something different. *Péniche* means barge, and this one, tied up between the two bridges on the right bank, is a restaurant of quality, not just a tourist trap. The bearded patron, Germain Bosque, serves classic food, particularly fish, in comfortable surroundings, on a 135f menu. Carte 250f.

La Bocca d'Or
(R)M
15 r. Haute
54.78.04.74
Closed Sun.;
Mon. lunch; 31/
1–7/3
AE, CB

Blois is no gastronomic paradise and to say this is the best restaurant in town might seem faint praise, but Patrice Galland's cooking would win applause anywhere. His restaurant is not Italian, as its name indicates, but based on his inventive French modern cooking and served in a magnificently vaulted 19th-century cellar.

He comes from Picardy, where the natives like their food in quantity, *à l'ancienne*, so although his ideas – galettes stuffed with langoustines, chaud-froid of oysters and asparagus, breast of pigeon with a feuilleté of the bird's liver, might sound *nouvelle*, you will not leave hungry. The 100f menu is the one to go for.

His wife Francine comes from California, so there should be no language barrier.

Le Médicis
(R)M
2 allée François
Ier
54.43.94.04
Closed Fri.
p.m.; Sun.
p.m.; 24/12–1/
2; 22/8–30/8

An agreeable, comfortable restaurant near the station, with a covered-in terrace. M. Garanger cooks good ingredients imaginatively – zander with a cream of carrot sauce, feuilleté of sweetbreads on spinach – and his 70f menu is a bargain. Others at 110f, 140f and 210f. Carte 230f.

Au Rendez-
Vous des
Pêcheurs
(R)M
27 r. de Foix
54.74.67.48
Open every day
CB

A charming little bistro, contrived from an erstwhile grocer's shop, no distance at all from the Loire, whence cometh many of M. Jegonday's ingredients. Simple fresh cooking – fillets of carp, skate with cabbage, goats' cheese tart. All the requirements for an enjoyable meal. Menu 120f.

Aux Trois
Marchands
(R)S–M
21 r. des Trois
Marchands
54.74.30.31
Closed Sun;
Mon. lunch;
Feb. school
hols
AE, CB, DC

Particularly hard to locate in Blois are inexpensive but interesting restaurants. Plenty of fast-fooders, bars, pizzerias, but those who like to eat real food at realistic prices don't have many choices here. The little Aux Trois Marchands fits the bill admirably – in an ancient house, all dovecotes and exposed beams, with seafood a house speciality. That doesn't come cheap but there is a good 50f menu. Another at 81f. Carte around 150f.

Map 1F	**BOULOIRE** (Sarthe) 22 km E of Le Mans

72440
(M) *Tues.*

On the N 157.
An interesting little town with a castle dominating its market square, on the main route towards the châteaux country from Le Mans.

Auberge du Château
(R)M–S
Pl. de l'Église
43.35.64.54

When I spotted the Auberge in the autumn of '87, and on closer acquaintance decided that it was a real find and worthy addition to the rather thin ground of this area, M. Michel Ducrot, patron/chef, had just heard from Michelin that he would be included in the next year's guide. Probably the best news any chef can imagine. He had been cooking in Bouloire for two years – just about the statutory time before Michelin is satisfied that the entry is merited.

I am very pleased for him, because his food, on menus from 55f to 150f, deserves recognition. It is interesting, fresh and well presented. I just hope that prices won't rise with his new standing. Reports particularly welcome.

Map 3E	**BOURGUEIL** (I.-et-L.) 17 km N of Chinon; 45 km SW of Tours

37140
(M) *Tues.*

5 km north of the Loire, by the D 749.
A charming, friendly little town at whose eastern end (park here) stands an imposing collection of monastic buildings on the site of a 10th-century Benedictine abbey.

It is famous for its full-bodied red wines, produced by the 'Breton' grape, probably brought from Nantes by river in mediaeval times. Buy some of the high quality, relatively low priced wines to take home and lay down – far cheaper than claret. It is generally said to taste of raspberries, and, sure enough, if you hear this claim often enough, you can believe it readily.

An annual wine exhibition is held in the elegant stone-arcaded market-place at Easter. Tuesday is market-day throughout the year and the whole town becomes a pleasing jumble of stalls selling everything from local cheeses to pink cotton brassières of redoubtable magnitude.

➤ Le Thouarsais
(H)S
Place Hublin
47.97.72.05
Closed Sun.
o.o.s. and 15
days in Feb.

A delightful little hotel facing on to a pleasant square in the town centre. It has a small garden and is proud of its *'confort, repos et calme'*, which claim I think is perfectly justified. What is more, Mme Caillaut is a friendly and welcoming hostess, and I think a stay in her bargain hotel would be an extremely agreeable one. Rooms range from 65f to 190f for one with bath. Arrowed for value in a real French town, very near the fleshpots.

Germain
(R)M–S
R. A.-Chartier
47.99.72.22
Closed Sun.
p.m. and Mon.
except fêtes;
26/9–24/10

Everyone I asked, from guests at aristocratic dinner parties to the local chemist, was unanimous – 'Eat at Germain' they said.

They were right. The little restaurant in the centre of town is bright, cheerful, stylish, next door to the *pâtisserie* of the same name (which is hardly surprising since *restaurateur* and *pâtissier* are one and the same).

You will eat simply and well here on the 85f menu.

Map 2I	**BRACIEUX** (L.-et-Ch.) 8 km S of Chambord

41250
(M) *Thurs.*

Take the D 112 from Chambord, through the park.

▶ **Le Relais de Bracieux**
(R)L
54.46.41.22
Closed Tues.
p.m.; Wed.; 20/
12–25/1
V

A very well-known restaurant indeed, qualifying for two stars in Michelin and attracting American tourists and well-heeled locals alike. It is extremely pretty, set in a pleasant garden, with elegant decor and elegant patronne at the reception desk. All this means that patron Bernard Robin has to turn away many aspiring clients, and so he has plans to open another hotel/restaurant not far away, on which I hope to be able to report soon.

His cooking is in the modern idiom – light, inventive, beautifully presented. His 'Menu Potager' at 200f would certainly appeal to me, with clever interpretation of mostly vegetable dishes, but the 120f version is excellent value for cuisine of this standard, as indeed is the next one up at 175f. Arrowed for outstanding cooking.

Map 3E	**BRÉHÉMONT** (I.-et-L.) 6 km SW of Langeais; 25 km SW of Tours

37130
Langeais
(M) *2nd Fri.
of each month*

On the south bank of the Loire.

The southern stretch of the Loire on the D16 is infinitely preferable to its northern counterpart. The contrast between the lorry-ridden N 152 as it struggles through Langeais, and the green and peaceful little road across the bridge is one of the charms of the Loire, where the clever driver, armed with a map and a bit of common sense, can usually find a choice of fast/busy or meandering/stress-free roads, to suit his mood. Even the inhabitants are races apart. Here on the flat sandy soil – the *varennes* – live a breed of hardworking smallholders, rough and ready to till their living from the land, very different from the gregarious *vignerons* across the river and further south.

Bréhémont is a pretty, tranquil village, once a port, with stone *levées* running down to the river, where the fishermen make their base. Just one street back from the river is a real find:

Le Castel de Bray-et-Monts
(HR)M
47.96.70.47 and
47.96.63.98
Closed Wed.
o.o.s.; 2/1–30/1
🚩

The delightful 18th-century manor house was transformed into a comfortable hotel and restaurant by M. and Mme Maxime Rochereau on their return from a sojourn in the US four years ago. M. Rochereau was once a chef at the Ritz, and now offers cookery classes – three hours every morning, with the afternoon given over to sightseeing arranged by the charming and helpful Éliane Rochereau (apply direct for details).

His cooking is inventive and makes good use of local ingredients. On menus from 75f to 165f he suggests dishes like salmon stuffed with crayfish, eel with beurre blanc and sorrel, roast quail with garlic and at least ten varieties of local cheese. On Saturday night dinner is candlelit, with a small orchestra for dancing; in summer you can dine underneath the magnolias on the terrace.

Mme Rochereau has furnished the rooms in the most individual style imaginable. Each one is different, enlivened with patchwork quilts, antique furniture, brass light-fittings, light and bright curtains

Le Castel de Bray et Monts

and wallpapers, lots of basket chairs and wickerwork. Because there are only seven rooms, the hotel cannot qualify for three stars (how ridiculous) and so the prices are very reasonable – 180–360f, all with bathroom, all quite charming.

Outside, at the end of a pretty garden, is an apartment built into a pavilion, which was once a chapel for the de Valois family. With two rooms downstairs and one up, here is another bargain for 360f. There is also a duplex with its own terrace, whose two double rooms cost 640f.

Everything about the proposition seems unbeatable – even the breakfasts are superb, with home-made jams. Arrowed for comfort, good food, perfect position and friendly welcome.

Map 3C	**BRISSAC-QUINCÉ** (M.-et-L.) 18 km SE of Angers

49320
Ⓜ *Tues. a.m.*

Turn off the D 748 and follow signs to the château.

An unremarkable village, with just one disappointing hotel (changes rumoured, so any accounts of recent experience welcomed). However there is a good reason for a visit here:

Château de Brissac
(C)L
41.91.23.43 and 41.91.22.21
Open by appointment for B & B and dinner.

Not one of the best-known châteaux, but certainly one of the more interesting, not least because of the family that lives, as its ancestors have done for five centuries, in the castle.

The future Henri II said 'Were I not the Dauphin, I would wish to be Brissac'. It is certainly one of the oldest warrior families in France.

In 1502 Charles II de Cossé, 1st Duke of Brissac, bought the forbidding fortress, and added the 'new' part. The present Duke has written an admirable guide book to his castle and its history, which is packed with far too much fascinating detail for me to go into here. It is on sale at the entrance lodge, with a better selection of souvenirs than in most châteaux. The Duke and Marquise are excellent proponents for their admirable property and make ingenious use of its many facilities, like the amazing 200-seat theatre built by the Duke's great-grandmother, which still possesses the original scenery and *belle époque* décor. In the magnificent dining-room, galleries and guardrooms are held receptions, concerts and candlelit dinners, where 700 people can be entertained in great style.

The most immediately striking feature of the vast building with its 150 rooms is the immense height – seven storeys in the central Renaissance part, which is flanked with the two old fortress towers, all that remains of the earlier building. It stands in a pleasant park, running down to the little river Aubance. Good for strolling, picnicking, photographing.

Inside, the furnishings are mind-boggling, so rich and rare are the painted lounges, golden ceilings, crystal chandeliers, Gobelin tapestries.

Brissac

To stay here is obviously an unforgettable experience, but only for the mega-rich. There are suites and the Queen's Room, where Marie de Médicis slept in 1620 after her reconciliation with her son, who occupied what is now called the Louis XIII suite, hung with Aubusson tapestries. The Royal Hunt Suite is named after the 16th-century Flemish hunting-scene tapestries which line the walls; the Chambres des Dames and des Demoiselles are so called because their portraits are all of ladies; their windows open on to a magnificent view of rolling parkland. The Metamorphoses Suite has an intriguing ceiling, representing butterflies being turned into women. Not sleep-inducing I would have thought.

The Duke and Marquise are very much in evidence to look after their guests and are kind and interesting hosts. Suites (of two rooms each) cost 2,760f; candlelit dinner, breakfast, all drinks included.

Chateau visits from 1/4–30/6: 9.30 a.m.–5.15 p.m.; 1/7–31/8: 9.30 a.m.–5.45 p.m.; 1/9–15/10: 9.30 a.m.–5.15 p.m.; 16/10–1/9: 9.30 a.m.–4.30 p.m. Closed Tues. 1/4–30/6 and 15/9–1/11.

Map 2H   **CANDÉ-SUR-BEUVRON** (L.-et-Ch.) 6.5 km N of Chaumont; 14 km S of Blois

41120
Les Montils

On the south bank of the Loire.

The road following the south bank west from Blois, the D 751, swings well inland and then rejoins the river bank near Candé; it is an altogether more peaceful, less trafficked road than the northern route, which undeniably has the better views, Candé is a hamlet built where the little river Beuvron joins the Loire; its valley makes a pleasant exploration for those with time to spare from the busyness of ticking-off châteaux. There are several windmills along its course, and at Seur it even becomes wide enough to accommodate a diving board over a fair-sized pool.

Proceed through the Forêt de Russy to the unique **Château de Beauregard**, one of the most interesting smaller châteaux in the area. It was built in the early 16th century as a hunting lodge for François I. In the following century the showpiece of the house, the long gallery, was added. Around three of its walls are 363 portraits of 15 sovereigns of France and other famous historical personalities. Each row is devoted to the reign of one particular king, so that those, like me, who have a lot of catching up to do on French history can put in some worthwhile homework. In fact I would give Beauregard an early date in planning a châteaux tour, so that the fascinating emblems of the various sovereigns can be noted and spotted later on in all manner of situations in other royal residences.

The floor, too, of this long gallery is remarkable – it has retained the old Delft tiles depicting an army of cavalry, artillery and infantry in period costume.

Le Lion d'Or
(HR)S
54.44.04.66
Closed Tues; 1/
2-11/2
EC, V

It's not easy to find cheap accommodation in this popular area, and the rooms at this little Logis may not be very exciting, but might well prove a welcome find at 130f, or 180f with bath. Menus from 56f. You could always spend what you save on your room on a slap-up meal at:

► **La Caillère**
(HR)M
R. Montils
54.44.03.08
Closed 15/1–1/
3; rest. closed
Sun. p.m. o.o.s.
and Wed.
AE, CB, DC, EC

A few kilometres west on the road towards Chaumont is another strong reason for visiting the area. La Caillère is a picture-book creeper-covered cottagey old house, set in a lovely old-fashioned garden, where Jacky Guindon cooks some of the best food around. Imaginative use is made of local ingredients – carp and pike from the river, wild mushrooms and wood pigeons all feature on his menus – 98f weekdays, or 128f, 178f, 235f.

He does have six rooms, with bath, which sound very good value at 190–210f, but I have not been able to see them or garner any specific idea of what they involve. So any personal accounts would be most welcome. Meanwhile the arrow goes to the restaurant for outstanding cooking.

Map 4D

CANDES-ST-MARTIN (M.-et-L.) 2 km E of Montsoreau

37500

On the south bank of the Vienne.

Drive along the quay eastwards from Montsoreau and enter another world.

The mediaeval village of Candes rises in tiers, from green river bank (ideal for picnicking) through rose-covered stone houses, up cobbled alleys, past the wonderful 11th-century church, now being restored from crumbling annihilation, thank God, up more steep, polished cobbles, past time-warped cottages, whose owners emerge to gaze at any car, let alone a GB numberplate, on and up to the 'Panorama', a well-marked wide view back again over the village and river sweeping far below. I had not dared to hope to find something remotely like this in the valley of the Loire – in Burgundy perhaps, but between Saumur and Chinon, hardly.

Mme de Bony
(C)M
47.95.92.60

Mme de Bony's house, too, is built on steep terraces (and therefore unsuitable for the elderly or very young). Once through her front door, slap on the main road, opposite the church, the ground drops sharply and so practically every room is on a different level, all with little terraces attached for private sun-worshipping.

She has two spacious rooms, each with its own kitchen and bathroom, furnished sparely but with a great deal of character. No nylon carpet on the walls – they are whitewashed stone – nor on the floors for that matter – they are tiled – but the beds are comfortable and all is clean and spic.

There is also a suite of two rooms, kitchen, bathroom and private terrace to let by the week – 600f for four people, except July and August, when the cost doubles.

Breakfast is usually prepared by the guests themselves (a considerable saving to be able to do this, and picnic lunches too) but nice Mme de Bony will supply a simple *café complet* if required. She charges 160f for two people.

Le Confluent
(R)S
Place de l'Église

Recommended by Mme de Bony for those clients who want a good simple meal, and seconded by me. Newly opened in an old building by the church, it is light and bright and cheerful and run by a friendly young patron who is trying hard to please. I wanted some change in order to buy a vast wicker basket being sold by some itinerant gypsies and he cheerfully changed my large note without any hint of so-what's-in-it-for-me. (So of course I went back and tried his galettes (around 10f), which are A1 and his salads, ditto, around 20f.) Just the thing for a light lunch, and he's open every day of the year.

Map 3D

CHACÉ (M.-et-L.) 3 km S of Saumur

49400
Saumur

Take the D 93 from Saumur.

Auberge du Thouet
(HR)S
46 pl. de la Mairie
41.52.97.02
Closed school hols, and weekends from 1/10–1/3; Mon. o.o.s.

Several readers have commended this little Logis, strategically situated just outside the Saumur straggle. They praise M. Perrot's cooking on menus from 65f, and the cleanliness of the 14 rooms from 85f to 195f.

    'Excellent food, including many regional dishes. Our bedroom was particularly pleasant and spacious.' – Sue Biggart.

Map 2I

CHAMBORD (L.-et-Ch.) 18 km E of Blois; 45 km SW of Orléans

41250
Bracieux

A village, cut out of the great forest, almost totally devoted to the cult of its château.

Le Château de Chambord is larger than life. It has to be high on everyone's list, simply because of its scale. It was never intended as a home, but merely as a monumental show-off by François I, to impress his fellow reigning monarchs, such as Henry VIII and the Holy Roman Emperor, at a time when one-upmanship contests like the Field of Cloth of Gold were all the rage. François preferred the Loire to Paris, and although he had other bijou residences like Blois down the road, he fancied a hunting lodge in the Sologne forests. So the show-piece of Chambord was vaguely conceived in 1519, never completed in François' lifetime, never built to a coherent plan, never benefited by a woman's touch (like graceful Chenonçeau and Azay).

    Pepperpots, towers, turrets, curlicues, steeples and 365 chimneys appear to have been added to its skyline at random, as if by the capricious hand of a child building with bricks. The view up here from the flat roof is spectacular and far-reaching, as it has always been – it was from here that the ladies of the court used to follow the hunt in the forests far below.

The staggering staircase is the château's core and *raison d'être* – with the building whimsically built around it. It spirals up and it spirals down again, so that there should be no need to meet undesirables on the way. Along with the terrace, this is the best part of the visit, since the interior is sparsley furnished – understandably with 440 rooms to fill.

Mock though one might at this *folie de grandeur*, this Disney-château, a tour of the Loire would not be complete without a boggle at Chambord and I guarantee that the very first glimpse down the avenue approach will bowl you over.

Open 1/4–30/9 from 9.30 a.m. to 12 noon and 2–6 p.m.; the rest of the year it closes at 5 p.m. *Son et lumière.*

Hôtel du Grand St-Michel (HR)M 54.30.31.31

Being the only hotel in Chambord, virtually in the grounds of the château, can bring problems. I heard that the management here were spoilt and difficult. Having listened to their side of the story, I am perhaps more sympathetic. Madame thought I was an American, and has no time for that race: 'They telephone, they write, but they do not arrive. Or if they arrive they look at the rooms and say "Guess we'll go on to Paris".'

I can't think why they should do that. The rooms here are mostly very pleasant and at 160–310f not expensive, with that eyeful of a view thrown in. They were good enough for Presidents Giscard d'Estang and Mitterand, who have been frequent visitors during the period of *la chasse*. They occupied the two best rooms, Nos. 5 and 7, which at 310f are bargains, with twin beds, lots of space, good bathrooms.

Unfortunately, being let down so often has led to an insistence on a deposit or arrival before 6 p.m., a sometimes unsmiling welcome, and obligatory eating on site. The food is O.K. but not outstanding, with menus at 85f; with several more interesting possibilities in the area, I consider the *demi-pension* requirement a big snag, but it would certainly fit the bill for a first night in the area, and in the season you get *son et lumière* thrown in.

Map 2C   **CHAMPIGNÉ** (M.-et-L.) 32 km N of Angers

49330

Take the N 162 and D 768 from Angers. In deeply rural countryside between the rivers Mayenne and Sarthe.

➤ Les Briottières (C)L 41.42.00.02 Closed 1/11–1/4

One could go on about the elegance of the 18th-century château, the peacefulness of the park surrounding it, the picturesqueness of the lake, the comfort of the bedrooms, all with justification, but what I shall go on about is the warmth of the welcome from the young owners, François and Hedwige de Valbray.

From the moment the car winds up the drive for the first glimpse of the truly lovely house, with the ever-alert, ever-hospitable François already leaping to meet and greet, you cannot fail to feel pampered, welcomed and privileged. You will also feel at ease, for the de Valbrays wear the grandeur of their home lightly. Not a hint of pomposity mars the relaxed ambience. The gravel in front of the tall shuttered windows was being raked – by Ingrid, the 2½-year-old daughter! No lackey, but François carries the cases up to the bedroom, points out the mod-conned bathroom and suggests you come down at leisure for *un petit verre* (champagne it proved to be, of which François always seems to have a ready supply on hand). Breakfast is carried in next morning by Hedwige. But their transparent enjoyment of their roles helps to cancel any embarrassment at being thus waited on and one is forced to the conclusion that they are both very fortunate to recognise their good fortune and relish it.

Château-hosting came to François in a fortuitous way, with the family deciding, upon his grandfather's death, that he could take on the pleasures and pains of ownership, if he so wished, when he was a bachelor of only 28. The alternative, which has been the fate of so many lovely French houses, would have been to allow Les Briottières to crumble away, since under the Code Napoléon the property is divided equally among the children, none of whom is likely to have the means to support the financial drain. François has applied himself enthusiastically to the formidable task of restoring the fading old building, getting the business going with several ancillary schemes – a farm, a wine shop, a dried-flower project. Soon the old walled vegetable garden will enclose a swimming pool and tennis court. So many things to do and, in his case, so much time to achieve them.

Chateau des Briottieres, Champigné

His main handicap is that Les Briottières is not bang on the Loire. Tourists to the area apparently can't see this particular wood for the trees of that royal and over-publicised route. In fact Champigné is in a particularly green and pleasant part of Anjou, unspoilt, squeezed in between the alternative and often preferable rivers Mayenne and Sarthe. Just 25 kilometres north of Angers, it also happens to be on the route from the Normandy ferries to the Loire valley, so would make an ideal first or last stop of a tour of the region.

The bedrooms, as one might expect in a home not a hotel, are all different in style, size and content. Mine was blue and white, flowery and spacious, furnished with modest antiques. Lovely. All have bathrooms, lights that work, views of the park and not a TV or minibar in sight. They cost from 400f to 500f.

Dinner is certainly not obligatory, but I imagine that most guests would wish to sample the experience of sitting at the de Valbray's hospitable table at least once. Hedwige somehow manages to cook three courses with the help of one au pair and still smile throughout the evening, which starts with champagne and introductions in the salon, and continues to coffee and digestifs, with much conversation and wine in between. The inclusive cost is 250f, with pot-luck fellow guests thrown in.

Arrowed for an unusually agreeable experience.

Map 4E	**CHAMPIGNY-SUR-VEUDE** (I.-et-L.) 6 km N of Richelieu

La Sainte
Chapelle

19 km south-east of Chinon on the D 749.

Do make the slight detour off the main road into the village of Champigny, which stretches out along the little river Veude, to visit La Sainte Chapelle, a private historic monument (open every day between 1/4 and 1/10 from 9 a.m. to 12 noon and 2–6 p.m.).

Cardinal Richelieu was not happy to have as his neighbour the magnificent castle, built by Louis I and II, that once stood here, lest it should lessen the impact of his own castle and estate so nearby. And when Cardinal Richelieu was not happy, the obstacle to his happiness usually had to go. As in this case, where he ordered total destruction. All that remains to hint at the castle's erstwhile grandeur, so sadly lost to us, are a few outhouses, but by the intervention of the Pope, the chapel was mercifully spared, and so now we have this impressive and utterly beautiful white Renaissance gem standing incongruously isolated in the centre of a rather grey village.

Best of all are its superb 16th-century stained-glass windows. Allow plenty of time to study the stories they so movingly and colourfully portray.

The owners are currently restoring the gardens but already a stroll there, along by the river, is a very pleasant diversion.

Map 3A	**CHAMPTOCEAUX** (M.-et-L.) 31 km NE of Nantes; 10 km SW of Ancenis

49270
St-Laurent-des-
Autels

On the south bank of the Loire.

Here is the last bridge over the river before the outskirts of Nantes, and the last river village of any size. The route west on this bank is infinitely preferable, scenically, to the nationale and autoroute on the north, but allow plenty of time for twists and turns and hairpin bends.

Champtoceaux stands on one of the highest spurs, with a spectacular view down over the river from the Promenade de Champalud, a balcony behind the church, with viewing table, whence the many arms and islands, creeks and inlets can be identified. The gardens here make a perfect place for a picnic, which is just as well, because it's a dull little town, apart from the unvisitable castle ruins that guard the headland.

➤ **L'Auberge de la Forge**
(R)M–L
1 bis pl. des Piliers
40.83.56.23
Closed Sun. p.m.; Tues.; Wed.; 30/6–8/7; Oct.
AE, CB, DC

Once a *buvette* outside the castle gates, the modest exterior leads on to a chic but still rustic restaurant, its beams and grey stone lightened by lots of windows leading on to a flowery terrace. At night the castle's illumination spills over and attractively floodlights the garden and its sparkling fountain.

Paul Pauvert has a Bocuse background and cooks sophisticated dishes, but with strong regional affiliations. He has an arrangement to have first pick of the catch from the local fishermen, and alose (shad), salmon, zander and lamprey feature regularly on his menus. Stick with the 115f version (weekdays only) or the 168f, and you have a bargain.

His specialities include a miraculous mousseline of shad with a purée of frogs' legs. Not a dish to try out back home! But there is generally nothing chi-chi about cooking or portions here, and you'll not eat a better version of simply cooked fish with beurre blanc.

Arrowed for outstanding cooking.

Map 3A	**LA CHAPELLE-BASSE-MER** (M.-et-L.) 11 km SW of Champtoceaux, 20 km NE of Nantes

44450

On the south bank of the Loire, by the D 751.

The road hugs the river and swiftly loses Nantes' agglomeration to become distinctly rural. There are willowed islands and peaceful inlets where fishermen persist.

La Pierre Percée
(H)S (R)M
40.06.33.09
Closed Sun. p.m. and Mon.

Rather than a hotel, this is definitely a restaurant with rooms. Mme Raballaud sometimes does not even wish them to be used, especially o.o.s., when heating costs count. But there are three, very simple, for 69f or 90f or 110f with shower, which might be useful after a good meal here, either in the small and rustic ground-floor restaurant or in the panoramic room on the first floor looking over the water, above the little boats tied up to the quay.

The discerning Nantais drive out on a fine day to lunch or dine here on the splendid adaptations of regional dishes cooked by chef–patron M. Raballaud. Eels and river fish feature strongly on menus from 70f to 166f.

Map 2F	**CHÂTEAU-DU-LOIR** (Sarthe) 41 km E of La Flèche; 42 km NW of Tours; 40 km S of Le Mans

72500
(M) *Sat. p.m.*
Fri. (fêtes)

There are some pleasant drives around this area, either north along the D 73B, following the little river Yre, or eastwards on the D 64 along the valley of the Loir, which follows the cliff face pierced with troglodyte homes.

The name of the lttle town is misleading, since it is sited on the Yre not the Loir and the château is but a ruined keep.

On the bustling market square I spotted a *chambre d'hôte* sign and was delighted to find:

▶ **Dianne Legoff**
(C)S
*24 pl. de l'Hôtel
de Ville*
43.44.03.38

'Bonjour Madame' I said. 'Hello', said Dianne. 'You're English, aren't you?'

Dianne hails from Plymouth and is now married to a Frenchman and into PGs. Her trim little house standing behind a garden would make a splendid, cheap, and comfortable base from which to explore the Loir valley and to pay an essential visit to Le Lude. She is a kind and welcoming hostess, and, of course, those shy of airing their French need have no problems here.

130f for a really comfortable double room, 160f for a family room, 20f for a good breakfast. A valuable find in this area so short of accommodation.

Map 1K	**CHÂTEAUNEUF-SUR-LOIRE** (Loiret) 25 km SE of Orléans

45110
(M) *Fri.,*
Sun.

A delightful little town, gravely underestimated by tourists on the better-known stretches of the river hell-bent on fitting in as many châteaux as possible before lunch. Even in July I parked easily outside the château and had the grounds to myself.

The 'new château' has the perfect setting – formal gardens lightened with roses and geraniums, gravel walks between square tubs of orange and lemon trees (yes, with fruit on them too); oleanders, palm trees and giant cacti give the feeling of Monte Carlo rather than New Castle.

Wind down the old lichened stone steps to the moat far below for the perfect picnic stop, with stone benches thoughtfully provided beneath the shade of ancient trees. It's all wonderfully soothing watching the ducks duck and the fish plop. I was sorely tempted to say to hell with the book and spend the day walking along one of the tempting routes laid out from the château grounds, through the trees, along the river. Instead I dutifully visited the **Musée de la Marine de Loire** in the château and was rewarded by finding a fascinating story of the life of the Loire and its locals. Anyone interested in matters marine should pass a profitable hour or so here, looking at engravings, clothes, models and tools used when the Loire was a commercial route.

La Capitainerie
(HR)M
Grande Rue
38.58.42.16
Closed Feb.;
rest. closed
Mon.
EC, V
Parking

Prime position, with terrace overlooking château grounds. A smart little hotel, with pleasant bedrooms at 240f and a good restaurant. The 80f menu looked dullish – crudités, chicken, pud or cheese – so it would probably be necessary to pay 135f for the next one up.

Le Nouvel Hôtel
du Loiret
(HR)S–M
Pl. A.-Briand
38.58.42.28
AE, DC, EC, V

By the main gates to the château, another Logis, more attractive in than out, though it too has a geraniumed terrace. The dining-room is particularly agreeable and spacious; menus at 69f, 125f and 145f. Bedrooms are newly redecorated with flowery papers and represent good value at 89f to 168f with bath.

Auberge du
Port
(HR)S
83 Grande Rue
du Port
38.58.43.07
Closed Wed.;
19/2–12/3; 17/
9–8/10
V

NEW OWNERS

A misleading address. The Grande Rue is not very *grande*, and the port takes some finding, but that is the only complaint I have to lay at the door of this charming, simple inn not many yards from the bridge across the river. The Loire, imposingly wide here, leaves deposits of sand in banks on either side, so that the term *plage* might just be justified. There are cool tree-lined walks along the bank nearby and it is altogether a delightful and interesting spot.

The Auberge, run by M. and Mme Patrick Berthier, is unpretentious, popular with the locals, and excellent value. The four rooms cost an amazing 65f; they are simple but perfectly comfortable. The menus are equally attractive – 37f buys four courses: soup, plat du jour, cheese and dessert; for 48f you get melon, liver, cheese and fruit. Arrowed for unusual value, an attractive site.

Auberge du Port.

Hôtel de la Sarthe

Auberge des Fontaines
(R)M–L
1 r. des Fontaines
38.58.44.10
Closed Sun. p.m.; Sept.

Even on the other side of the castle walls there are delightful walks past old stone cottages with gardens brimful of flowers. Here, in a cul-de-sac, is a pretty little restaurant with tiny garden. In the rustic, balconied dining-room the food is so good that it is essential to book. There is no set menu, and three courses à la carte are likely to cost 200f, but are worth every franc.

Map 2C

CHÂTEAUNEUF-SUR-SARTHE (M.-et-L.) 31 km N of Angers; 33 km W of La Flèche

49330
Ⓜ *Fri.*

There are lovely walks along the river bank from the little town of Châteauneuf, and the Sarthe flows attractively fast and clear through the arches of the stone bridge. You can take a pleasure boat on a voyage of exploration. A mere 32 kilometres away from the main tourist area ensures a totally different concept in hotels and restaurants, and prices will be way down in comparison.

Hôtel de la Sarthe
(HR)S
41.69.85.29
Closed Sun. p.m. and Mon. o.o.s.; 3 weeks in Feb.; Oct.

A prime situation, overlooking the river, has not spoiled this pleasing little Logis de France. The rooms are country-charming and good value at 90–180f.

In summer it is one of the most agreeable things imaginable to eat a grilled fish on the wide terrace, with all that splish-sploshing going on just below. Lots of local specialities in the pleasant restaurant too – beurre blanc and a lovely garlicky friture of Sarthe eels. Menus from 55f.

Map 3H   **CHAUMONT-SUR-LOIRE** (L.-et-C) 17 km SW of Blois; 17 km
               NE of Amboise

41150   A village of a single street strung along the south bank of the river,
Onzain   totally dominated by the château. The mall by the river is a very
               pleasant tranquil spot to sit and watch the fishermen, eat a picnic,
               and to abandon the car prior to a château visit.

               I do find the green Michelin star rating puzzling. Chaumont would
               probably be the centre of many a pilgrimage were it to be situated
               anywhere else, but in this area, where impressive châteaux are
               ten-a-penny, I can see little justification for its two-star rating against
               Le Lude's one (to be rectified, I am happy to say, this year). It's worth
               paying the lower admission rate, however, to take the stroll up the
               lengthy incline (infirm walkers beware), to the cliff-top site, and to
               walk around the castle and admire the view. Inside there is little of
               great interest and it has an unloved air, perhaps because of its sad
               history.

               The interlaced 'D's in the stonework are a reminder that the castle
               once belonged to Diane de Poitiers. Catherine de Médicis gave it to
               her as a poor exchange for Chenonçeau, from which she ousted
               Diane on the death of her husband (and Diane's lover) Henri II. Diane
               didn't think much of the substitution and soon deserted it. Mme de
               Staël rented it during her Revolution banishment but, pining for
               Paris, thought the view of the Loire not a patch on that of the gutter
               beneath her home in the capital.

               The only owner to fall in love with the place was a 16-year-old,
               Marie Say, who in 1875 persuaded her rich Daddy to buy it for her.
               When she married the Prince de Broglie they spent a fortune
               restoring the building and the stables (and most of the village too)
               but once again good luck went missing – her father's business
               collapsed, there was no more subsidy forthcoming, and the château
               was unwanted until the State bought it in 1938.

               Open 9–11.20 a.m. and 1.30–5.20 p.m. 1/4–30/9; and 9–11.20 a.m.
               and 1.30–3.30 p.m. 1/10–31/3.

Hostellerie du   Unfaultable really. All the rooms are different, individually furnished,
Château   all extremely comfortable, most overlooking the river and the
(HR)M   swimming pool. I liked the pink room best. They cost 300f, 380f and
2 r. du Mlle de   480f.
Lattre de
Tassigny   The dining room is delightful and the food is well cooked and
DC, EC, V   plentiful on menus from 65f. Best of all, the management is friendly
Parking   and helpful. An excellent base from which to explore the stretch of
                     the river from Blois to Amboise. Arrowed for all-round excellence.

La Chancelière   A nice old grey stone building facing the river, housing a small rustic
(R)M   dining-room, where M. Cabret cooks local specialities. Highly
1 r. de Bellevue   recommended locally but, alas, unsampled by me, since I chose a
Closed Wed.   Wednesday to visit. Menus from 65f. Reports needed.

Map 2J	**CHAUMONT-SUR-THARONNE** (L.-et-Ch.) 35 km S of Orléans

41600

On the D 922.

In the heart of the lake-spattered Sologne, five roads converge in the centre of this village, and in the centre, covered in creeper, is:

La Croix Blanche
(HR)L
54.88.55.12
5 pl. Mottu
Closed Thurs.
lunch; Wed; 5/
1–13/2; 29/6–
10/7
AE, DC, EC
Parking

The kind of contrived rusticity that the Parisiens love to find when they drive out at weekends. Countrified La Croix Blanche may be but unsophisticated it is not. The stags' and boars' heads look down on tapestried chairs and lace tablecloths, the flowers tend to be potted azaleas not daisies, and the *maître d'* is black-suited and suave.

His is an odd position, because La Croix Blanche has a unique claim – it is the only restaurant in France where, for over two hundred years the cooks have been ladies. The current patronne, Mme Giselle Crouzier, carries on the tradition. She is a native of Périgord, and the dishes of that region appear alongside those of the Sologne on her menus. Many ingredients come from her own farm: geese, duck, wild mushrooms, to meet in the kitchen the produce from the waters and woods of the neighbourhood: the pike, quail and game.

This will not be a cheap meal, especially as the wines, appropriately chosen mostly from the Loire and the South West, are of high quality, but there are two weekday menus at 100f and 160f; à la carte will cost around 300f for three courses.

Similarly the rooms are elegant and comfortable, but perhaps overpriced, at 320–360f, or 400–420f for an apartment. But the Parisiens don't mind.

Map 3L	**CHAVIGNOL** (Cher) 3 km N of Sancerre

18300
Sancerre

There are several ways to arrive at the village of Chavignol; follow the 'Circuit de Fromages' signs from Sancerre, either west (D 183) or east about, via the D 955 and D 7 or D 183, to gain a charming glimpse of the surrounding vineyards.

Chavignol is synonymous with goat's cheese, and crottins de Chavignol are offered in various forms at several little bars and bistros in the village centre – try La Bonne Auberge or Le Petit Chavignol – so a drive in this direction makes a very pleasant lunchtime excursion. For something slightly more upmarket:

La Treille
(R)M
Pl. de l'Orme
48.54.12.17
Closed Tues.
p.m. and Wed.
p.m.

A pretty little restaurant in a leafy triangle at the top of the main street. Jean–Luc Pinard plays variations on the crottin theme: hot mousse of crottin with chive sauce, crottin flan, hot oysters with crottin-flavoured butter, fillet steak with sauce crottin . . . All good stuff and something different. Allow 100f.

Map 2C	**CHEFFES-SUR-SARTHE** (M.-et-L.) 24 km N of Angers; 3.5 km W of Tiercé

49125 Tiercé	By the D 52 and D 74. In deepest lush-green water countryside, Cheffes is a pretty little village with good picknicking down by its *port* on the river Sarthe.

Just a few kilometres west, in Ecuillé is the stunning 15th-century **Château du Plessis-Bourré**, owned and lived in by a nice young couple and their children. The atmosphere, therefore, in spite of the grandeur, is still that of a seigneurial home. It was built in just five years, and the harmony of the building is immediately obvious. The white castle appears to float in the wide moat which surrounds it; corner towers, capped with grey witches' hats, are peacefully reflected in the still water.
   Once across the many-arched bridge into the vast courtyard, the feeling of a house rather than a fortress is even stronger, and inside the castle there is lovely furniture to admire, along with the Parliament chamber and a 15th-century coffered wooden ceiling to the guardroom, whose allegorical paintings are worth spending a bit of time deciphering.
   The publicity blurb says 'The castle has welcomed Louis XI, Charles VIII, Anne de Beaujeu, the Hungarian Ambassador [?], why not you.' Why not indeed – worth a visit this one.
   Open: 9 a.m.–12 noon and 2–7 p.m. Closed: 12/11–15/12 and Weds.

Château de Teildras (HR)L *41.42.61.08* *Closed Tues.* *lunch; 1/11–1/4* *AE, CB, DC*	A happy compromise between the impersonality of some of the most luxurious manager-run Relais et Châteaux members, and the sometimes erratic and eccentric service in the privately owned châteaux that receive paying guests. Teildras is very much a home still, with family furniture and the belongings of the aristocratic family who live there embellishing the décor, but it is efficiently run and managed.

It's a lovely old – 16th-century – manor house, very French, with white shutters, grey slate roof; in summer a lot of sitting and reposing goes on on the wide, wide terrace, generously planted with roses. Absolute peace and quiet prevails, much appreciated by care-worn Parisiens. But that's not to say it's one of those resolutely smart hotels that intimidate rather than soothe. The dining-rooms are warm and intimate and the 11 bedrooms, with every mod con, are all differently decorated. Their price of 555–895f (cheaper than at home remember) seems well justified.
   I haven't eaten there personally, but met several faithful regulars, who love the food as much as the atmosphere. Sophisticated menus – 200–280f. Good wine list.

Map 4H	**CHEMILLÉ-SUR-INDROIS** (I.-et-L.) 3 km W of Montrésor; 7.5 km E of Genillé

37460	A pretty village on the pleasantly green D 10.

Ferme Auberge du Grand Gouard
(R)S
47.92.77.09
Open by reservation only

Something definitely different, recommended by Rosemary Farley of the Château des Genêts (see p. 174). All the cooking is done in an ancient bread oven and all the ingredients – goose, duck, rabbit, veg., are home-grown. Very rustic, with the opportunity to hire *les poneys* for delightful rural rides.

Lunch 65f, including wine, sitting round an old oak table, is very good news.

Map 3D | **CHÊNEHUTTE-LES-TUFFEAUX** (M.-et-L.) 8 km NW of Saumur

---

49350
Gennes

The D 751 between Saumur and Gennes is a pretty, peaceful stretch of river road, passing through ancient villages and the tufa cliffs which give their name to Chênehutte-les-Tuffeaux (the Chênehutte bit no longer applies – not many oak huts left in the area nowadays).

➤ **Le Prieuré**
(HR)L
41.67.90.14
Closed 5/1–1/3
CB

I would rate Le Prieuré very high indeed in the pecking order of Loire Relais et Châteaux. It's another of the clever M. Traversac's projects (see Château d'Artigny, Montbazon), well-promoted through his Grandes Étapes chain, efficient but not impersonal, thanks to the friendly staff, and not as intimidatingly grand as d'Artigny.

The erstwhile priory stands high, high above the river, affording from its terrace a splendid panorama far, far below. The rooms are lovely, furnished in what used to be called cretonnes, spacious, mostly with the same spectacular river aspect.

I found the whole set-up very peaceful, with quiet gardens to stroll through and a swimming pool surrounded by trees – not the smart Greek-pillar marble variety – more a pool in a forest clearing. Not the place to go to be seen, more a luxurious retreat, with the evening aperitif on that wonderful terrace a treat to be looked forward to.

I was sorry on a balmy June evening not to be able to eat out of doors, but the picture windows of the dining-room made the most of the view. Cooking is modern, restrained. I greatly enjoyed my aspic of sole and langoustines in a cream sauce, duck roast with honey and lime, cheeses, and double chocolate mousse and mocha cream. Menus are 200f lunch weekdays, with wine included, or 265f, 335f, 380f.

I like Le Prieuré very much, but must add two caveats: it is not an ideal choice for the elderly or infirm. In order to get down to the reception/dining-room or up to the bedrooms it is necessary to negotiate numerous winding stone steps, and one friend of mine, on crutches after an accident, quite justifiably reproached me for not warning her of the hazards.

The second reservation concerns the *bungalows* which serve as fall-back accommodation when the hotel is full. I should have been pretty miffed to find myself bedded in one of these, which, although comfortable enough, are isolated from the attractions and views of the hotel and not things of beauty in themselves.

Notwithstanding, given a room in the hotel itself, with comfort, good food, friendly staff, in such a delightful setting, the arrow is merited.

| Map 2C | **CHENILLÉ-CHANGÉ** (Sarthe) 25 km N of Angers; 8 km NE of Le Lion d'Angers |

49220
Le Lion
d'Angers

The Mayenne is a delightful river, very different from the Loire. Here is a good opportunity to explore it, by the day or week, taking one of the boats from the Maine-Anjou-Rivières company from Chenillé-Changé; a lovely spot, this, orchestrated by the splashing of the wide weir. Information: 41.95.10.83.

The owner of the boats, René Bouin, has set up a splendid little restaurant to feed his customers and many more besides:

**La Table du
Meunier**
(R)S–M
*41.95.10.83,
41.95.10.98*

An old stone house, cleverly converted into a smart/rustic restaurant, full of character. It has tables outside in fine weather. Lots of local specialities, and menus from 65f.

| Map 3G | **CHENONÇEAUX** (I.-et-L.) 12 km S of Amboise; 35 km SE of Tours |

37150
Bléré

Incomparable Chenonçeau (the name of the town usually has an 'x' at the end, that of the castle has not). Number 1 on every tourist's list and rightly so. Somehow, no matter how many coaches in the car-park, how many cameras clicking, how many promenaders through the gardens, how many school children giggling, the staggering good looks of the site and building triumph. Perhaps it should be the last (but essential) château to visit, because after Chenonceau others pale.

They say it is so beautiful because its history has been controlled so often by women. This, alas, is not the time and place – a novel could do better justice to the story – to go into the fascinating history in any detail, but of the six ladies involved it is Diane de Poitiers and Catherine de Médicis, mistress and wife of Henri II, whose ghosts linger most forcibly.

Henri gave the château, built on a perfect site overlooking the river Cher by Catherine Briçonnet around 1513, to his mistress in 1547. It was Diane who planned the accessories to the château – the beautiful Italian pleasure gardens stretched along the bank, the graceful five-arched bridge over the river. She loved Chenonçeau dearly and was heartbroken when, after Henri's death, she was forced to yield it to his widow Catherine and retire to the despised Chaumont.

Catherine, the Magnificent, loved it too. She it was who improved on Diane's schemes by extending the gardens, adding the park, building on to the bridge the double-storey gallery that makes it so distinctive, and extending the ensemble with stables, orangeries and outbuildings. To show off her magnificent acquisition, she made Chenonçeau the site of the kind of festivities that an oil magnate or pop star could not even envisage today.

One *fête* was in honour of François I and Mary Stuart (Catherine's daughter-in-law), another for Charles IX, when the moats were full of singing mermaids and the woods alive with leaping nymphs and satyrs. Mock naval battles were fought, fireworks cost thousands of livres, banquets went on for days. *Son et lumière* displays, clever though they are, with every modern scientific miracle, can be only a shadow. What would the gutter press today make of the feast to celebrate Henri III's visit, which involved all the most virtuous, aristocratic and beautiful ladies of the court serving the guests while naked to the waist?

One more lady ought to be thanked for her contribution to Chenonçeau – the 19th-century Mme Pelouze, who rescued and restored the château, re-creating the interiors of the time it was built. It now belongs to the Meunier (chocolate) family.

The approach, through an avenue of magnificent planes, is as perfect an introduction now as it must have been for visiting royalty. Then cross a drawbridge to reach the terrace, surrounded, as so delightfully often at Chenonçeau, by water, the most striking feature of the château being that it stands on two piers resting on the bed of the Cher.

There are too many visual riches inside and out to describe here; suffice to say it is very agreeable to be able to wander freely through the rooms admiring the treasures at one's own pace and inclination. Guides are there, if you need to ask a question, but they never intrude. A model way to show off a château.

In the grounds – and at least half a day should be allowed to appreciate the castle, grounds, village, river and to absorb a little of the atmosphere – there is another model. The self-service restaurant in the orangery is not only attractive, clean, efficient and cheap – it serves very good food. There is a more expensive restaurant too; it was closed when I last visited but if it's run the same way as the rest of the establishment here, it must be excellent.

Open 16/3–15/9 from 9 a.m. to 7 p.m.; 16/9–30/9 from 9 a.m. to 6.30 p.m.; Oct. from 9 a.m. to 6 p.m.; 1/11–15/11 from 9 a.m. to 5 p.m.; 16/11–15/2 from 9 a.m. to 12 noon and 2–4.30 p.m.; 16/2–28/2 from 9 a.m. to 5.30 p.m.; 1/3–15/3 from 9 a.m. to 6 p.m.

July and August – electric tram from entrance gate to main courtyard. Sometimes boat trips on Cher. *Son et lumière.*

➤ **Le Bon Laboureur et Château**
(HR)M
6 r. du Dr Bretonneau
47.23.90.02
Closed 1/12–1/2
AE, CB, DC, EC

How admirable and consoling that for two hundred years an inn here has looked after Chenonçeau visitors. Even more admirable is that the present patron/chef M. Jeudi, the fourth of his family to run the well-known restaurant and hotel, never allows the traditional high standards to drop in accordance with the Bon Laboureur's popularity and easy trade. You have to be very quick off the mark to get a booking here – visitors from all over the world are queuing up to do so, but if you're successful, count yourself very fortunate. Perhaps sometimes the strain shows, but even in very busy times I have always found the welcome unfailing.

It's a nice old-fashioned building, dominated by a venerable maple, in whose shade many a glorious summer's meal has been taken. The food is classic but not dull, with lots of lovely vegetables. Terrine from four Loire fish, zander with a red wine sauce, and a nougat ice-cream with Vouvray jelly are examples. Menus 100f (lunch midweek), 160f, 210f and 260f.

The bedrooms look out on to an interior courtyard and are

peaceful, well equipped, and good value at 280f with bath and 270f with shower. 380f if you want a telly (*telly* – at Chenonçeau!). Arrowed for sustained high standards.

Hôtel du
Manoir
(HR)M
1 r. de la Roche
47.23.90.31
Opening times
not yet settled

I felt a bit sorry for Carlo Mazella; the Bon Laboureur next door were busy turning customers away while he had plenty of rooms going begging. He has only been patron of the Manoir for a couple of years – a long way short of the Laboureur's record – and has yet to establish a reputation. Certainly you could fare worse than giving his hotel a chance. It's an incongruous scene for an Italian – the Manoir is mock English Tudor, a bit gloomy perhaps downstairs with all that olde worlde oak, but the rooms are fine and not expensive: 250f for a double with bath. There is a nice garden – and Italian cooking.

NEW OWNERS

Hôtel Ottoni
(HR)M
47.23.90.09

Just opposite the Laboureur, on the corner. The reception is grim and the welcome less than warm, but the bedrooms are good, especially those with a terrace overlooking the garden. They cost from 240f to 350f. Nice dining-room; don't know anything about the cooking. Menus from 75f. Please tell me if my suspicion is wrong that this is a hotel that knows it's on to a good thing and won't put itself out unduly. However, when others are full, it might be a good reserve.

Hostel du Roy
(HR)M
47.23.90.17

An old white building dating from the 16th century on the main road, with a nice family atmosphere. M. Goupil features regional specialities on his 70f menus, served in the beamed dining-rooms. Rooms are rustic and pleasant – ask for one at the rear. From 220f.

La Renaudière
(HR)M
47.23.90.04
Closed Tues.;
15/11–1/2
EC, V

A big, red, faded mansion on the outskirts of the town – the kind with red Turkey patterned carpet runners and dried ferns in Moroccan pots inside. Nice garden with lots of loungers and new restaurant built on the back.
   Good value in this area – rooms 95–245f; menus from 65f.

Gâteau Breton
(R)S
47.23.90.14
Closed Tues.;
15/11–1/2
EC, V

One of those red-check-tableclothed, beamed, determinedly rustic little bistros that are easy to find in other less ritzy parts of France, and even more delightful to come across here in overpriced *nouvelle-cuisine* land. Menus start at 40f and continue to offer much for little. Simple French cooking in the old style – veal steaks, 'bifsteacks', egg mayonnaise. You can eat outside in the little rear garden in summer. And very nice too.

Map 4E   **CHINON** (I.-et-L.) 29 km SW of Saumur; 48 km SW of Tours

---

37500
Ⓜ *Thurs.*

Try, if you can, to approach Chinon from the south, across the old bridge over the Vienne. From here you get the best first impression of a delightful little town, strung out along the river, backed by jagged castle ruins. From the southerly approach you can appreciate a good view of the castle's dominance over the river and town, and pick out from left to right; the Fort du Coudray, the massive Château du Milieu, and then, after a stretch of wall, the clock tower, the Tour d'Horloge, which forms the entrance to the castle.

You could perhaps precede your arrival by a visit to **La Devinière**, 5 km south-west on the D 117, said to be the childhood home of Rabelais. Here, in the little museum dedicated to the writer, scholar, priest, physician, you can catch up on all you half-knew about Gargantua and Pantagruel, whose names will undoubtedly recur in any visit through the region.

They certainly do in Chinon, jostling for precedence with an extraordinary range of other famous names and connections – the quai Jeanne d'Arc, the rue Voltaire, the rue Descartes, the rue Jean-Jacques Rousseau, and the shops and cafés named after Rabelais characters.

The author gets a prominent statue in the **Jardin Anglais** along the quays, a good place for a stroll among the flowers and (not-so-English) palm trees that flourish in the mild climate.

Parking is not easy, especially in high summer. Try along the quays or drive up to the castle and abandon the car there, for a hassle-free, leisurely exploration of all the gems that the little town has to offer.

Although visually the **château** is no more than a skeleton, historically it is probably the most interesting of all the hundreds of châteaux from which to choose, and a must on anyone's tour. As you approach, from the route de Tours, across the moat, there are several souvenir shops from which to buy guide books for more detailed information about history and layout.

The basic points of interest are that it was mainly built by Henry Plantagenet, King of England, who died in Chinon in 1189. The castle passed from the hands of John Lackland, youngest son of Henry and Eleanor of Aquitaine, into French hands, in 1205. While Henry IV, King of England, was also King of Paris, the uncrowned Charles VII was only King of Bourges when he brought his court to Chinon in 1427. Two years later, the peasant girl Joan of Arc, 18 years old, travelled from Lorraine to Chinon to convince the vacillating Charles that he would be anointed and crowned in Reims and become King of France. After three weeks' cross-examination before a court in Poitiers to determine whether she was mad or inspired, she won the confidence of both courtiers and the Dauphin and was armed and equipped in Chinon, whence she set out for her incredible journey with Charles to Reims.

You enter by the restored clock tower into the middle castle, where, in the 15th century there was the royal residence. The southern curtain wall hugs the very edge of the escarpment; the gardens with their fine views are a favourite photo-opportunity. The northern wall encompasses five towers, including the Dogs' Tower, where the kennels used to be. A second bridge crosses to the Fort du Coudray, where Joan lodged on the first floor. On the ground floor are the evocative graffiti drawn by the Knights Templar, some of them very skilfully done, during their incarceration here in 1308. Did they know, as they scratched, that their next move would be to the pyre in Paris? All that is left of the great hall where Joan was first received and recognised her King is the giant fireplace.

The castle is open, except Wed., from 15/3 to 30/9, 9 a.m–12 noon and 2–6 p.m; it closes earlier in winter and amazingly stays open even in the sacred lunch hours in July and August. There is a café/bar on the terrace, run by very jolly owners, from which to get a splendid view over the ancient roofs of the mediaeval town, down to the snaking river and along its valley.

Hard by the castle car-park are the vineyards of the Clos de l'Écho, where you can taste and buy some choice Chinon wine. It is named after the echo of the north cliff of the castle, where a doubtful lover may ask: 'Les femmes de Chinon, sont-elles fidèles?'
Echo: 'Elles?'
'Oui, les femmes de Chinon.'
Echo: 'Non.'

Follow the cobbled twisting path down to the old town, whose narrow streets always retain their cool calmness,in contrast to the main road and quays, which can be noisy and fraught at busy times. Take a stroll along the rue Voltaire, lined with recently restored old houses, beamed, gabled, mullioned, carved, if you can cope with the exhausting cobbles that is – definitely not for the unsteady.

Along its length look for the spot where Joan is said to have watered her horse, visit the fascinating wine museum, call in at the **Caves Peintes**, where Rabelais used to drop in for a drink, ponder at the 15th-century **Maison des États Généraux**, where they claim (probably erroneously) that Richard Coeur de Lion died of his wounds, and look up at the charmingly half-timbered **Maison Rouge** on the corner of the Grand Carroi.

The main shopping area is around the place de l'Hôtel de Ville; there is a friendly wine shop, the **Vinothèque Charles VII**, on the quay, where you can taste the local wine, including the classy Clos de l'Écho, before you buy.

Hostellerie Gargantua
(HR)M–L
73 r. Voltaire
47.93.04.71
Closed Wed.
o.o.s.; 15/11–
15/3
AE, DC
Parking

A striking 15th-century palace in the centre of the mediaeval area, where Rabelais' lawyer father once practised. Its five-storey high pointed roof and witch-hatted turret is a landmark in the town. Perhaps because of its obvious attraction and too easy custom, it has in the past been a somewhat unworthy, run-down tourist trap, but four years ago a new owner, Jean Fossé, moved in with a programme, almost completed, of restoration and embellishment, and it is now a very agreeable place to eat and stay.

The dining-room, with its tented ceiling and cream stone walls, has the finest view over the river of any Chinon restaurant. There is one secluded little table in the tower, where a perforce somewhat self-conscious dinner à deux by candlelight might bring rewards other than gastronomic.

Menus are 120f and 150f, of the kind of cooking the French now call *classique allégée*. In other words, some traditional dishes lightened to suit modern palates. A seafood pot-au-feu, escalope of sweetbreads, pear gratin, are examples.

At present there is a wide choice of room style and price, depending on whether or not they have been restyled. Those that are still awaiting their turn cost 110f a double; those that have received the treatment are 450f. The latter are goodly accoutred, with mock four-posters, chintz-hung, lots of space, excellent bathrooms. If you chose to economise and stay in one of the cheaper rooms, you could always abandon it at breakfast time and make a good start to the day by eating on the most attractive terrace.

M. Fossé has an arrangement with the nearby Château de Danzay at Beaumont-en-Véron, whereby overflow guests, or those who prefer to sleep in the countryside, can stay at the 15th-century château, in great style. Rooms are slightly more expensive here, but probably worth it.

Chris' Hôtel
(H)M
12 pl. Jeanne
d'Arc
47.93.36.92
AE, DC, EC, V
Parking

A nice old house, white stone, grey slate roof, whose 30 bedrooms have recently been redecorated in pleasing Louis XV style. Some overlook the river, all have private bathrooms, and cost from 170f to 300f.
My first choice in Chinon, because of its friendly owner, quiet situation, near river and old town, and good value. Arrowed accordingly.

Hôtel Diderot
(H)M
4 r. Buffon
47.93.18.87
Closed 15/12–
15/1
EC, V
Parking

Another attractive 18th-century house, creeper-covered, white-shuttered, in a quiet street behind the place Jeanne d'Arc. Again the bedrooms, all with bathrooms, have been attractively furnished, with antique furniture; the breakfast-room has a good fire in the vast fireplace for chilly mornings, and in more clement weather there is a pleasant garden. 150–270f.

La Boule d'Or
(HR)M
66 quai Jeanne
d'Arc
47.93.03.13
Closed Mon.
o.o.s.; 15/12–1/
2

A Logis, right on the quay, so you have the choice of a room overlooking the river, possibly noisy, or a smaller quieter one looking out onto a rear courtyard. All cost 240f.
The food looked promising, on menus from 65f to 190f, so this would be a good choice for those who like to eat in.

**Au Plaisir
Gourmand**
(R)M–L
2 r. Parmentier
47.93.20.48
Closed Sun.
p.m.; Mon.; 11/
1–31/1; 14/11–
30/11
V

A charming old house tucked away in a maze of cul-de-sacs between the quay and the château. Jean-Claude Rigollet and his nice wife, Danielle, arrived here in 1984 from the prestigious Auberge des Templiers at Les Bézards, followed by a spell teaching at a catering college in Orléans, and have established a reputation as the best restaurant not only in the town but for miles around. Tourists must book ahead in order to wrest one of the few tables (not more than 30 covers) from local gourmets from Saumur, Loudon and the nearby atomic centre. Worth an advance phone call, though, to sample on modestly priced menus Jean-Claude's unfussy skilful cooking of prime ingredients.

All three menus are recommendable. They are no-choice, so you have to be lucky to find that the cheapest, 'La Cuisine du Terroir', four courses for 146f, offers what you fancy. The next one up, 'La Cuisine Tourangelle' at 185f, slides in another course, or there's the admirable 250f 'Dégustation', 7 mini-courses for the whole table. On the first of these a terrine of baby hare, chunks of tender meat encircled in natural jelly, served with a cream of foie gras, then a fillet of carp in a *red* wine sauce, an admirable selection of cheeses, especially local varieties, and a superb chocolate marquise with a coffee sauce did us very nicely indeed thank you, especially as the feast was accompanied by a marvellously fruity young Clos de l'Écho wine from Jean-Claude's own vineyard.

With a pretty little secluded garden in which to sip a summer aperitif and the cosy candlelit dining-room, here is an essential detour at any time of the year.

L'Orangerie
(R)M
79 bis r. Voltaire
47.98.42.00
Closed Mon.

A newly restored old house in the centre of the old town, now extremely pretty, all light and airiness, with interesting menus at 65f and 95f.

'The Orangerie is built into the town wall, is very simple inside with washed bare stone walls, green "tennis court" flooring and white garden furniture. The general atmosphere was cool and quiet. The food was simple, good and inexpensive.' – Betty S. Cairns.

L'Océanic
(R)M
13 r. Rabelais
47.93.44.55
Closed Sun.
p.m.; Mon.

A real find. The rue Rabelais is not so tourist-orientated as the rue Voltaire on the other side of the square, but is nonetheless old and interesting, with real shops and real Chinonois using them.

They also use this little fish-dedicated restaurant with enthusiasm, so you must be quick off the mark to get a table. Menus from 80f include a variety of perfectly fresh fish from sea and river.

Fish restaurants in the area are few and this one is recommended for good unpretentious value.

Map 3G   **CHISSAY-EN-TOURAINE** (L.-et-Ch.) 3 km W of Montrichard

---

41400
Montrichard

Take the D 115 out of Montrichard.

Château de Chissay
(HR)L
54.32.22.01
Closed 1/1–15/3
All credit cards
Parking

Once a Royal palace, then passed down from noble hand to noble hand until 1952, and still pretty grand today. A gorgeous authentic fortified castle dating from the 13th century and cleverly restored in 1986 to retain its considerable characer, while offering every possible luxury for its pampered guests, who may swim in a 20th-century pool and dine in a mediaeval hall. Rooms, furnished with 18th-century antiques, are 350–650f, apartments 700–800f, which I suppose for castle-living is not bad. Menus are 160f and 230f with a modish 'Dégustation' for 300f.

Château de la
Menaudière
(HR)M–L
54.32.02.44
Closed 1/12–1/3
AE, DC, EC, V
Parking

Climb high above the town and river on the Amboise road, and La Menaudière is signposted on the right.

It was originally built at the same time as Chenonçeau and by the same lady, Catherine Brissonet, but has been heavily restored. Now it is a peaceful, comfortable treat for the châteaux-weary, deep in the countryside, away from the tourist hassle but strategically situated for quick sorties to the most popular areas.

The 25 rooms, from 350f to 550f, are all differently styled and well-equipped, with verdant views over the château's park. The personal touch might waver a bit o.o.s. when they tend to be overrun with seminars, but generally this is an efficient and well-run hotel offering considerable comfort for the money.

Food is light, modern, elegant, served in a very pleasant dining-room, warm and intimate with dark beams and log fires in winter. (Allow 200f.) *Demi-pension* is obligatory in high season, at 480–650f.

Map 3G   **CIVRAY-DE-TOURAINE** (I.-et-L.) 2 km W of Chenonçeaux

---

37150
Civray-de-Tour

On the D 40.

Hostellerie de
l'Isle
(HR)M
47.23.80.09
Closed Tues.
p.m. and Wed.
except July and
Aug.; 20/12–20/
1

 hotel

food

This is where I would choose to stay if I needed a base near Chenonçeaux and Amboise. It's a faded *gentilhommière* set down a lane, just off the village centre, in its own wooded grounds, with white chairs dotted about the grass and overlooking the lake.

Not at all grand – the rooms are simple, but in the sense of being rustic rather than without mod cons. Floors are tiled, softened with rugs, rather than deep-piled, the beds have wooden heads rather than nylon button-backs, the bathrooms are white rather than turquoise marble, the furniture is old rather than antiqued. Lovely curling divided staircase, cosy intimate dining-room, good cooking by chef Denis Gandon. Menus 85f, 135f, 175f. Rooms from 210f to 400f.

Not yet in other guides and therefore still with rooms available in hot late June, when Chenonceaux was brimming over.

A real find and arrowed for position, atmosphere and good value.

Map 1I   **CLÉRY-ST-ANDRÉ** (Loiret) 15 km SW of Orléans; 2 km E of Meung-sur-Loire

---

45370

Louis XI is buried in the 15th-century basilica here. For students of the macabre a rare treat – his skull and that of his wife, Charlotte, albeit sawn in twain, are on show in the vault he ordered to be built in his own lifetime. He used to go and lie there, when he had nothing better to do, contemplating death and, one hopes, praying for divine forgiveness for his multiple sins. A cruel and ruthless tyrant was he, so cunning that his own father nicknamed him Le Renard. You have only to study the clever Bourdin marble statue to see the meanness of the man.

However, he was undoubtedly very attached to the place,

originally a shrine to the Virgin Mary, whose statue had been found in 1280 on a nearby route much patronised by pilgrims on their way to Compostela.

On their way to Orléans in 1425, the English had destroyed all but the existing square tower; Charles VII rebuilt the basilica after the war and Louis attempted to bribe the gods by vowing to subsidise it further by his own weight in silver if they allowed him to drive the English out of Dieppe. His wish was granted and he used to visit often, staying in the house, now a school, to the right of the church, hearing Mass in his private and secret oratory (above the Gothic door to the sacristy).

Hostellerie des Bordes
(HR)M–S
9 r. des Bordes
Closed Sun
p.m. o.o.s.;
Mon. o.o.s.; 20/
1–1/3

A funny, old-fashioned, not-at-all-smart, bordering-on-seedy, large, red-brick and stone house, well-situated in its own grounds. Quiet and cheap, it has spacious bedrooms with incongruous frilly bedspreads for 85–250f. Food way above usual hotel standards, as substantial and reassuringly old-fashioned as the building, on menus from 39f.

Map 1K   **COMBREUX** (Loiret) 35 km NE of Orléans

45530
Vitry-aux-Loges

Take the D 9 east of Orléans via Fay-aux-Loges, on the Canal d'Orléans, to arrive at the hamlet of Combreux. The whole area is pure delight. The surrounding Forêt d'Orléans is the largest forest in France. It is exceedingly well organised, with routes for both walkers and cars clearly indicated. North of the moated 16th-century Château de la Rochefoucauld on the D 9 follow the Route d'Étangs to find a series of lakes on which waterlilies proliferate and the necks of recumbent herons protrude like petrified driftwood. Alternatively turn left soon after L'Auberge at the sign 'Étang de la Vallée' to follow the canal to a perfect picnic site by the little white bridge. Continue on this track, past the obsolete 'gare de Combreux' to arrive at the extensive lake, big enough to encompass a bathing area, lots of picnic sites, a dinghy park and seasonal sunbathers.

➤ **L'Auberge**
(HR)M
38.59.47.63
Closed 15/12–
20/1; rest.
closed Mon.
o.o.s.
EC, V
Parking

Exactly the kind of hotel the *FE* readers (and P. Fenn) find to their liking. It is *spéciale*. Small, countrified, with bags of personality and a patronne (glamorous ex-model Chris Gangloff) who knows how important is *l'accueil*.

The rooms are all different. There are some, like the one in which I spent a blissfully peaceful night, in the old vine-covered building, looking out on to a courtyard with ducks and children's swings, far from manicured but green and calm, with tables and chairs for repose or refreshment. The bathroom/dressing-room had beams that made you duck your head, but the mod cons worked; 180f.

Across the road are newer *chalets*, with more modern bathrooms, but always in the appealing unfussy country style that is unusual in France, where the orange vinyl, khaki-carpet-up-the-wall is generally preferred to this subfusc floweriness.

Mme Gangloff is furnishing her precious hotel as she is extending it, little by little, with obvious loving care. She buys antique furniture whenever she can find it and afford it, and will perhaps build some more chalets in due course.

Each of the very pleasant new rooms overlooks a garden – there are four altogether, none of them cared for in the pernickety English style, all a bit ragged round the edges but at the very least green. Some of the rooms have their own terrace, where breakfast can be served; 220f.

There is a smart new tennis court and a little swimming pool, which I found a most welcome refuge after a sticky July day at the wheel.

The beamed dining-room, with log fire, is perfect for dark winter days; the terrace, with sliding windows, a pleasant airy additional option for the summer. In both of them one can choose from menus at 80f, 145f or 155f. I cannot claim the food is gastronomically memorable but it is adequate, verging on good, and certainly better than most hotel meals at the price. I didn't like the obligation to eat in, no matter how many days one spends there, and was cross that I had obeyed the injunction to dine at 7.45 when other less conscientious guests were still arriving at 9. I regretted the feeling

L'Auberge de Combreux.

that the meal should be dispensed with as quickly as possible (four courses in less than an hour) but these are minor quibbles, which I mention only so that readers may know how to deal with the situation.

An arrow for a charming hotel, in a charming situation, with a charming hostess.

La Croix Blanche
(HR)S–M
38.59.47.62
Closed Mon.
p.m.; Tues.

Combreux is twice blessed with hotels. Almost opposite l'Auberge is another country Logis, the delightful Croix Blanche. Its rooms are light and bright and airy, and good value at 175f, with bath. It has a pleasant flowery garden with tables outside. A walk along the almost-adjoining canal path would work up an appetite for M. Jama's cooking; on his 95f menu featured some inventive dishes such as six snails with almonds, and terrine of carp with mushroom mousseline. House wine is 35f.

Map 3G | **CORMERY** (I.-et-L.) 15 km SE of Tours; 10 km E of Montbazon

---

37320
Èsvres

The D 17 from Cormery closely follows the Indre – a very pleasant excursion either to Loches or to Genillé, both with recommended eating places, but Cormery itself is a pleasant little town, renowned throughout France for its macaroons. It is dominated by the ruins of an 8th-century Benedictine abbey.

In the wide tree-lined Grand' Place is:

Auberge du Mail
(R)M
Pl. du Mail
47.43.40.32
Closed Fri.
AE, CB

A nice little old-fashioned restaurant with two small, closely packed dining-rooms and a terrace for summer eating.

Generous menus, 75f weekdays, or 100f, offer terrine, monkfish with saffron, duckling in cider . . . Good wine list.

Map 2H | **COUR-CHEVERNY** (I.-et-L.) 13 km SE of Blois

41700
Contres
Ⓜ *Wed.*

On the D 765.

The village suffers from the château's popularity and always seems to be cluttered with coaches and tourists. The **Château de Cheverny** is on every tour's short-list, partly because of its proximity to the essential Chambord and Blois, and because it represents in its classical severity a striking contrast to those two over-embellished mighties.

More than anywhere else in the Loire, I find the crowds at Cheverny disturbing. Its beauty is of the calm, elegant variety that needs appreciating quietly, unjostled. It is not vast enough to absorb huge numbers unaffected, as Chenonçeau and Chambord do, and the queues at the ticket office and souvenir shops seem an insult to its patrician aloofness. So if you can go early or late or out of season, Cheverny is a treat – probably my favourite – but if not, I would almost say don't bother.

Because it was built in just 13 years, at the beginning of the 17th century (by Count Henri Herrault de Cheverny, whose ancestor, the marquis de Vibraye still lives there), the unity of the architecture is perfect and the first effect of the gleaming white tufa stone façade, topped with grey slate is simply beautiful. As it is a 'private' home, the grounds, understandably, are not open to the public (hence further funnelling congestion) but vistas of parkland, fine trees, and wide alleys, glimpsed from the approach to the house, set the scene perfectly.

Inside the beautifully proportioned rooms (more shuffling round I fear) are fine tapestries, paintings, gilded ceilings, bronzes. Outside (this is prime hunting territory on the edge of the Sologne forest) is a hunting museum, and kennels with a pack of some eighty hounds. It's a fine sight of a misty winter morning to see the huntsmen set off from the château, and listen to the Trompes de Cheverny, the huge writhing brass horns, stirring the blood.

The apartments are open 9 a.m.–12 noon and 2.15–6.30 p.m. (5 p.m. in winter).

Trois Marchands
(HR)M
54.79.96.44
Closed Mon.;
15/1–1/3
AE, DC, EC, V
Parking

Several readers have written to commend this good value hotel. The rooms at 120f–260f are well equipped and comfortable, and the food, on menus from 95f, well cooked and presented. Demi-pension 170–235f.

Map 4E | **CRAVANT-LES-COTEAUX** (I.-et.–L.) 8 km E of Chinon

37500
Chinon

To drive along the little D 21, parallel with the river Vienne, out of Chinon, is to experience another world from that of the tourist-dominated châteaux-land. It's a straight, flat road, with glimpses of the river to the south and, suddenly, the entire northern verge covered in vines. The vineyards slope up as far as the eye can see on that side of the road; even if a stay in Mme Chauveau's delightful establishment is not being considered, a deviation along this stretch brings another dimension to the area's attractions.

▶ **M. et Mme Chauveau, 'Pallus'**
(C)L
47.93.08.94
Open all year

Probably the most comfortable and luxurious of any of the chambres d'hôte that we sampled in the Loire valley. Mme Chauveau has recently added a charming little guest cottage to the ensemble of buildings set around a sizeable swimming pool. Her modern, stone-built house is set high in the middle of the vineyards owned by her husband, with glorious views in all directions. M. Chauveau will show you round his vast caves if you ask him nicely, and no doubt offer a dégustation of the deliciously fruity wine he produces.

The guest house is furnished to a very high standard, in smart rustic style, and it is most agreeable to be part of the ménage, yet as independent as you wish. It has its own bathroom and small kitchen. A superb breakfast arrives on a tray next morning.

The Chauveaux are delightful, friendly hosts and I have no doubt that at some stage during a stay they will welcome the guest-house occupants into their own luxurious home for a chat in English. There are other rooms available there, and when, on a *fête* night, a tired English family arrived on bikes, exhausted from having failed to find accommodation elsewhere, Mme Chauveau never hesitated, but even at that late hour made up beds for them and made them welcome.

With use of that lovely pool, the view, the comfort, the strategic position, the Chauveaux' hospitality, I would rate this one very highly indeed. Perhaps the price – 400f – might seem a lot for a B and B, but you would rarely find this standard of comfort in a hotel for that cost. Arrowed for all the above.

Map 2l **DHUIZON** (L.-et-Ch.) 28 km S of Beaugency

41220
La Ferté-St-Cyr

Take the D 925 and then the D13 from Beaugency.
A village of little appeal, but on the edge of the Forêt de Boulogne, surrounded by the numerous lakes that dot this flat, wooded Sologne countryside.

Auberge Grand Dauphin
(H)S (R)M
54.98.31.12
Closed Tues.
p.m.; Wed.
o.o.s.; 3/1–28/2

A very pleasant surprise, in this area of much interest (near both Chambord and Beaugency) and few reasonably priced hotels, to find this very switched-on little Logis. The bedrooms are comfortable, warm and extremely good value at 98–121f, as it is inexplicably rated only one-star. There is a pleasant salon with dark beams and tiled floor and a most attractive dining-room, opening onto a terrace, well-patronised for summer eating.

The patron M. Rouche welcomes local parties, who know when they're on to a good thing; menus during the week start at 49f. There are others at 65f, 77f, 93f, 112f, 143f, 165f and 195f, which should please most of the people most of the time, since the cooking is more than usually interesting on them all.

Map 2F **DISSAY-SOUS-COURCILLON** (Sarthe) 5 km SE of Château-du-Loir; 39 km NW of Tours

---

72500
Château-du-
Loir

On the N 138.

Château de Courcillon
(CR)M
43.44.10.00
Closed Sun.
and Mon.
o.o.s.; 1/2–20/2

One of my favourites. I cannot think of a happier combination than a visit, perhaps in the evening for *son et lumière*, to Le Lude, followed by a stay here, 24 km away.

Courcillon, dating from the 7~~~~~~~~ry, was bought a few years ago by Mme Claire Ja~~~~~~~~ businessman husband. Mme Jaclard grew to love t~~château and its atmosphere of old grey antiquity so much that she decided, as part-hobby, part-duty, she would share it with as many people as possible by taking in P.G.s. Oh yeah, you might well say, so what about the pay-off?

The pay-off at Courcillon is remarkably modest, because Mme J. wants to keep it that way. 250f buys a room full of character. There are nine of them, all different, some in a tower, some in a 19th-century wing, all spacious, with modern bathrooms and luxurious linen. The most expensive costs 350f. My room overlooked a park sprinkled lavishly with cowslips and violets; it was furnished sparsely, but totally adequately, with antiques, and had an adjoining bathroom the size of many another hotel room.

I could see what Madame meant about the extraordinary vibes. I can only say go see for yourself and I think you will agree that there is a very distinctive, very warm atmosphere here, permeating what could be a cold grey building.

We dined by candlelight in the lovely beamed restaurant, warmed by a huge log fire. Unusually for a *chambre d'hôte*, the restaurant, with talented chef Loïc Lami, is open to the public and stands on its own merits as a gastronomic *tour de force*. All its accoutrements are of the highest standards – the elegant china, glasses, linen – and the food is as reasonable and well-chosen as the rest of this delightful ensemble. A menu of 75f in an establishment of this calibre is a real bargain. I ate a salad of foie gras, skate with mushrooms and a toothsome flaky apple tart. Alternatively, the next menu, at 165f, offered a wider choice and four courses, and there is a good à la carte. The wine list is no slouch either, chosen by Mme Jaclard's son.

Château de Courcillon

Breakfast continues in the same vein; 40f extra but obviating the
need to eat lunch. Egg, bacon, what you will. Mine arrived on a silver
tray and included grapefruit, two kinds of home-made jam, and hot
croissants with different fillings. I enjoyed the treat of having it
served so elegantly in bed, but it could equally well have been on the
terrace overlooking a surprisingly dramatic view. Far, far below is the
valley, with the little river trickling through a panorama of intense
greenness. Look down on the erstwhile moat to the foundations of
the castle, with ancient prisons still facing, to appreciate the
château's ancient history. CLOSED

Notwithstanding the manifold other attractions, for me the prime
reason for a stay here would be the welcome and generous
hospitality of the patronne. I set an unintentional test of her goodwill
by discovering, as she waved me goodbye, that I had lost all my
notes. A year's accumulation of maps and directions, etc. had
disappeared from my car. I could have left them at a dozen different
stops on the way. I knew not where, was late for an appointment,
tired and inclined to tears. Madame, who had her own affairs to
attend to, could have turned a perfectly justified blind eye on the
bêtise of her late-departing guest, but spent an hour telephoning in
an attempt to locate the missing impedimenta, at the same time
consoling the *distraite* and despairing owner. The fact that this book
was ever published is evidence that she was eventually successful.

Here is a winner, for position, comfort, price, food and welcome,
not yet generally discovered. Go soon to my confident choice of
Hotel of the Year. See p. 23.

Map 3C **ERIGNÉ** (M.-et-L.) 12 km S of Angers

49130
Les Ponts-de-
Cé

South of the Loire, with the tributary Louet flowing through the
village.

**Hostellerie le
Château**
(R)M
*41.57.71.95
Closed Sun.
p.m.; Mon.; 5/
1–30/1
EC, V*

A nice old white house, covered in creeper, with lovely garden and
large pond. Inside all is calm and elegant and in pleasant contrast to
the fairly busy road passing nearby. There is an old-fashioned mood
to the dining-room, with lace tablecloths, sparkling crystal and good
china. Interesting menus from 75f.

Map 1J **FAY-AUX-LOGES** (Loiret) 21 km E of Orléans

45450
(M) *Wed. a.m.*

On the D 709.
A little town built around the Orléans–Montargis canal. In its
centre:

Auberge du Poisson d'Argent
(R)S–M
Closed Sun. p.m.
AE, DC, EC
Garage

A solidly reliable little bourgeois restaurant, easily missed because it is attached to a hotel of the same name, but under different direction, which is not nearly of so high a quality (rooms are basic, clean, 67–93f). The restaurant uses local ingredients and serves dishes such as friture de Loire, andouillette du pays, alongside some of M. Mesple's own creations, such as chicken in a cream sauce flavoured with wild mushrooms, on menus starting from 45f. I would counsel the next one up, at 85f, or the 115f, in order thoroughly to appreciate his talents.

Map 2I

LA FERTÉ-ST-CYR (L.-et-Ch.) 13 km S of Beaugency

41220

On the D 925.
   A pleasant wooded area, untramelled by tourists, with the little river Cosson threading through.

Hôtel St-Cyr
(HR)S
15 fbg Bretagne
Closed Sun. p.m.; Mon. o.o.s.; 15/1–31/ 3
DC

A modern Logis, usefully situated. Menus from 60f. Rooms 140–210f.
   'Very friendly couple. She does the cooking, including a very interesting coq-au-vin, apparently made from albatrosses, judged by the size of the bones!' – Dr Peter Sykes.
   More reports please.

Map 2D

LA FLÈCHE (Sarthe) 52 km NE of Angers; 42 km SW of Le Mans

72200
Ⓜ *Wed., Sun.*

Follow signs to the town centre and park in the shade of the trees on the banks of the Loir, where there are pedalos for hire and a lovely view across to the old bridge. Great for picnicking. Take a drink at the bar/restaurant the Auberge du Moulin, built out over the river, through arches of roses, and immediately things will begin to look up, however long and tiring the journey thus far.
   The main tourist attraction is the Prytanée National Militaire – a kind of military Dartmouth-as-it-used-to-be (in that students are accepted at around 13, to follow a normal school curriculum, leading to the Baccalauréat and entrance possibly to the prestigious Grandes Écoles, as well as preparing for a military career). This former Jesuit college is approached by a dusty side street, through a monumental Baroque doorway, which leads into the vast main square, the Austerlitz courtyard.
   During school holidays there are guided tours round the academy and to the 17th-century St Louis chapel, containing the ashes of the heart of Henri IV, who grew up in La Flèche and founded the original Jesuit college, and of his wife Marie de Médicis.

➤ **Le Vert Galant**
(HR)S
*70 r. Grande
Rue*
43.94.00.51
*Closed Thurs.;
20/12–10/1*
EC, V

An old-fashioned very French hotel in the main street. The rooms are a delightful surprise. Nice M. Berger shrugged his shoulders when I exclaimed at their value – 140–180f for a very spacious room; most are furnished with elegant antiques, one or two are unwisely modernised. 'We do not get the Loire tourists here', he said.

The food he serves in his well-tended restaurant is good value too, earning him the coveted red Michelin R. Cheapest menu is 60f.

Arrowed for good value in an underestimated area.

Le Relais Cicéro
(H)M
18 bvd d'Alger
43.94.14.14
Closed 1/1–1/3
EC, V

Mme Levasseur had just taken over this elegant 17th-century house, set back in its own garden from the leafy boulevard, when I spotted the hotel and thought I must have found a winner. I think that first impression will be right, when she has had time to settle in.

The position is ideal, quiet but central, the house is lovely and interestingly furnished with antiques. A comfortable double room with bath fully merits the price of 350f or 380f.

No restaurant but Mme Levasseur recommends Le Vert Galant.

Map 3F **FONDETTES** (I.-et-L.) 5 km W of Tours

37230
Luynes
Ⓜ *Wed.,
Sun.*

On the north bank and then north on to the D 3.

A pleasant surprise to find village atmosphere so near the Tours agglomeration.

➤ **Manoir du
Grand Martigny**
(C)L
47.42.29.87

A brave man, M. Henri Desmarais, to recognise the potential in this crumbling 16th-century manor house and not to lose heart and patience over the two years it has taken to restore it to its present state of comfort and attractiveness. Until he showed me (in May 1988) the old salon and dining-room, paint peeling, mirrors scarred, damp prevailing, chill, dark, and assured me that these two horrors would be alive and well by August, I had not realised the intensity of his dedication and determination.

Having slept in an utterly charming room, all blue and white Toile de Jouy over walls, curtains, bed canopy, with polished wood floors, antique furniture, skilful lighting, luxurious bathroom, I had no idea of what he had achieved in just two years. The six other rooms are all different, all delightful (though I liked mine best); they are furnished with bits and pieces that his wife Monique has painstakingly collected from the auctions she attends every week and then patiently restored. With the help of their two sons, she has done all the sewing, he has done all the decorating; together they frame pictures, reincarnate furniture from junk to treasures.

The emphasis is and always will be on a friendly atmosphere. They particularly like having families to stay – there are two family suites, with two rooms and a bathroom apiece, for 600f, including four substantial breakfasts – and they point out that, with good and reasonable restaurants five minutes down the road, there is no need to go into Tours for an evening meal, nor obligation for Monique to cook.

Little by little, the outside of the house, the gardens, the ancient dovecot and tower, and the rotting hothouses will get the Desmarais treatment. Even before that happy ideal state of affairs, here is a very good deal (and arrowed accordingly), so near Tours, easily accessible from the main road but apparently in deep countryside, with friendly and efficient hosts. My room was 430f; others are less.

| Map 4D | **FONTEVRAUD-L'ABBAYE** (M.-et-L.) 16 km SE of Saumur; 21 km W of Chinon |

49590
(M) *Wed.*
Sun. a.m.

A must on any English tourist's map should be a visit to this village, in whose abbey, dubbed the Westminster of the Plantagenets, lie four famous effigies, Henry II of England, his wife Eleanor of Aquitaine, their son Richard Coeur de Lion, and Isabelle of Angoulême, second wife of their son, John Lackland. Isabelle is the only one carved in wood rather than tufa stone. All most moving, painted in faded blue and red, all individuals, reading a book (Eleanor), asleep (Henry), dignified and aloof (Richard) and romantically forlorn (Isabelle).

But these astonishing Plantagenet reminders are not the only reason for a visit here. Remarkably underpublicised is this largest and virtually complete ensemble of mediaeval monastic buildings in France. A whole village, in fact, within a village. You can take an excellent guided tour round the ensemble from 1/4 to 30/9, 9 a.m.–12 noon and 2–6 p.m. (4 p.m. rest of year); closed on Tuesdays and *fêtes*.

The architecture varies from 11th to 16th centuries and includes abbey church – late Romanesque, pale and light tufa – two sets of cloisters (one for the monks and one for the nuns), infirmary, chapter house, refectory, and the only Romanesque kitchen to be conserved, vast and fascinating.

There are tremendous works of restoration going on throughout the complex and a huge sum has been allocated to place Fontevraud in the place it merits – one of the top tourist attractions not only of the Loire but of France. Meanwhile the diggers and excavators and the dust overall do not make for tranquillity. The authorities have seen fit to allocate one whole wing to a conference centre with bedrooms. Pity it wasn't a hotel.

St Michel, the parish church, is also worth a visit in its own right. Originally Romanesque, with typical Plantagenet vaulting, it was enlarged in the 11th and 15th centuries, and had an 18th-century gallery. Invest 1f for the recorded music and lighting to enhance the many treasures, carvings and paintings the little church contains. The gilded high altar comes from the abbey and was commissioned in 1621 by Henry IV's daughter, Jean-Baptiste de Bourbon.

Fontevraud is well served for hotel and restaurants:

Croix Blanche
(HR)M
*7 pl.
Plantagênets*
41.51.71.11
*Closed 14/11–2/
6; 16/1–4/2*

A nice little Logis right opposite the abbey, light and bright and cheerful, with friendly owners.

It's all very French and absolutely typical of the genre of small country hotels, family-run and popular locally. Everyone sits down to eat early, jeans, sweaters and T-shirts are *de rigueur*, pour your own wine, generate your own atmosphere, concentrate on the nosh. The lighting is too bright, the flowers are plastic, the food is no-nonsense, good quality, plenty of it and not expensive. Nothing wrong with the 50f menu, or you can go mad on the 85f version.

Most of the rooms unexpectedly look out over a courtyard and are consequently tranquil, pleasantly furnished in mock-rustic style, comfortable, with bathrooms, at 285f. Other smaller rooms overlooking the road are 145f.

➤ **La Licorne**
(R)L
*Allée St-
Catherine*
41.51.72.49
*Closed Sun.
p.m. and Mon.
except fêtes;
30/8–7/9; Jan*
AE, EC, V

In the running for the best restaurant in the region. Patron Jean Criton is definitely not in the business of cashing in on the tourist trade and does not go out of his way to make his little restaurant eye-catching. It is tucked away in an alley behind the church, in an 18th-century house, not large, not ostentatious. It has a pleasant magnolia-shaded garden for summer drinks, and a mere half-dozen tables inside.

Young chef Michel Lecomte brings all the skills of his *stages* at Taillevent and Robuchon to Fontevraud, and a meal here, even with no menu and an à la carte bill of around 300f, must be a bargain.

Try some of his creations, such as a terrine of hare with a creamed cauliflower sauce, or beef with a Champigny sauce and marrowbone, and see if you don't agree with me.

Arrowed for truly outstanding cooking.

Abbaye
(R)S–M
8 av. Roches
41.51.71.04
*Closed Tues.
p.m. o.o.s.;
Wed.; 10/2–28/
2; 7/10–31/10*
CB

Or for the penny-wise try this little auberge, well-known to Abbey pilgrims. Excellent value (red R in Michelin) on menus that start amazingly at 50f including wine; others at 54f, 85f and 92f all equally commendable and an excellent local wine list.

What is more, it's open on the dread Sunday p.m. and Monday.

Map 4G | **GENILLÉ** (I.-et–L.) 11 km NE of Loches

37400

A pleasant drive through the Forest of Loches on the D 764, or along the valley of the Indrois via the D 10.

➤ **Auberge Agnès
Sorel**
(H)S (R)M
47.59.50.17

This nice little village-centre house, named after Charles VII's popular mistress, is generally listed as a restaurant, but it was the bedrooms that particularly impressed me. They are quite charming, furnished in simple country style but in excellent taste. No. 2 I especially recommend. With bathroom en-suite, it costs 160f for two people, which is top value in this area. If you're happy with a shower, there are two others, even cheaper at 140f.

The restaurant is charming, small and very popular, so book.

The owner, Daniel Hautz, comes from Alsace but there is nothing heavy about his sauces or dishes, such as poached river fish with a watercress sauce, or saddle of lamb with garlic purée.

Agnes Sorel, Genillé

The prices – 100f, 130f, 170f and 230f menus – might seem to be on the high side perhaps for such a seemingly simple spot, but the quality is there both in the cooking and the accoutrements, and I think this could well become a *French Entrée* favourite – small, quiet, well situated for sightseeing, friendly owners and an excellent house cooking. Arrowed for all these.

Map 3D   **GENNES** (M.-et-L.) 15 km NW of Saumur

49350

 Tues. a.m.

On the south bank of the Loire.

The drive from south to north along the river takes on a completely different character around here. The red routes on the map turn into yellow, edged with green. Commerce seems to peter out and a more gentle relaxed atmosphere prevails. Those who abhor hustle and crowds should consider heading this way, to any of the little fishing villages strung along the banks.

Most tourists usually stop short at Saumur, and do not even bother to look for the dolmens, menhirs and historic churches of the region, so overwhelmed are they by the more obvious riches further east.

Gennes is one of the largest villages, almost a town, built on the slopes of a steep knoll and straggling down to the river. Good picnicking abounds, either on the banks or high up by the deconsecrated church, where lie the graves of the Saumur Cavalry School cadets who so bravely and hopelessly defended the valley from this point in June 1940.

Aux Naulets d'Anjou
(HR)M
18 r. Croix de Mission
41.51.81.88
Closed Mon.;
Jan.; Feb.
EC, V
Parking

First impressions disappointed, as I drove up the hill and found a very modern building, with dark-suited businessmen carrying briefcases just leaving. Not my kind of scene, I thought. But nice M. Paul Maudonnet, chatting to a guest on the steps, spotted my hesitation and asked if he could help, so I was trapped. And very glad I was that this should have been so. (I must learn to overcome these prejudices.) The hotel perhaps lacks instant charm, but once inside the vibes are right and I would stay here most happily.

Paul is an artist, and a very good one, with a studio below the hotel, where guests can look and learn and perhaps buy one of his lovely watercolours of local scenes, or at least some postcards. His wife, Colette, is the chef.

They stress it is a family hotel, and children are encouraged and made most welcome. There is a big flowery garden, and tennis court, and the restaurant, with its panoramic windows, has a good view far below.

The well-equipped rooms are determinedly and rather refreshingly modern, not the usual mock-rustic, with bright clear colours and lots of light. Some have French windows, opening on to the garden, where it is good to sit soaking up the peacefulness after the day's sightseeing. They cost from 200f to 250f.

Food is said to be *familiale* but, if so, it's of a very high-class family. Colette cooks dishes such as escalope of salmon with sorrel, grenadin of veal with wild mushrooms. Menus 80f, 120f, 160f and 210f.

Hostellerie de la Loire
(HR)M–S
Av. des Cadets de Saumur
41.51.81.03
Closed Mon. p.m.; Tues; 28/ 12–10/2

Down in the town, nearer the river, an older hotel, well-known to many a generation of English visitors. The patron, M. Reynier, is a very active member of the Association of Logis de France, and always very much in evidence. His rooms cost from 130f to 290f, and it is wise to ask for one overlooking the garden rather than the busy road leading to the bridge.

The food is excellent, with the 88f menu meriting a red R in Michelin. Other menus at 130f and 190f.

Map 1K

GERMIGNY-DES-PRÉS (Church) (Loiret) 3 km SE of Châteauneuf-sur-Loire

---

Between Châteauneuf-sur-Loire and Sully, the Loire convolutes in two bulges, which the D 60 avoids. It passes instead through the sleepy hamlet of Germigny-des-Prés, on the Bonnée stream, unremarkable except for one outstanding feature – the claim to have the oldest church in France. Restored some of it may be, but there is no doubt that the east apse at least is genuinely 9th century, unique.

I care not what the experts say. For me it was an unforgettable experience to discover the clarity and simple beauty of the tiny church. From outside, through a screen of tamarisks, the ancient stones seem bleached pale by the sun of the Midi rather than misted with the moistness of the Loire; one could easily be in the South – Italy, Greece. So the sight of the golden mosaic apse ceiling seems perfectly fitting.

In fact the style is unmistakably Byzantine, and the architect, Odo of Messina, was an Armenian, whose whim it was to reproduce in part the plan of a famous cathedral from his native land in the French countryside. The mosaic, then already at least 300 years old, was brought from Ravenna by Theodulf, an abbot of nearby St Benoît, who built this as his personal oratory in 806.

The stunning ceiling was discovered in 1840, when the ruined church was restored. Charlemagne, who often came to visit Theodulf here in Germigny, must have looked up at the gold and silver cupola nearly 1200 years ago.

The pale stone inside has been effectively cleaned and the whole building shines. I love, too, the wooden statues, particularly that of the Virgin as a little girl being taught to read by her mother, St Anne, depicted as a local peasant woman, and the moving Piéta, with Mary's arms folded in resignation at her son's fate.

Do go and visit Germigny-des-Prés. A table outside the Relais Routier café on the corner (menu 60f) would make a good guide-book-homework vantage point.

Map 2L

GIEN (Loiret) 64 km SE of Orléans

45500
(M) *Wed. a.m.*

Gien should be proud of its post-war reincarnation. Few visitors today, unaware of the devastation wrought in 1940 when the Germans bombed the town for three days, and again four years later when it had to suffer Flying Fortress bombardment, would guess that the centre had been almost entirely reconstructed.

The 14th-century *dos d'âne* bridge spanning the river was so skilfully – one might say sympathetically – breached that just one arch had to be renewed after the war. The fine old stone quays above and below the bridge are intact, the church of Jeanne d'Arc, left with only a 15th-century tower standing, has been elegantly rebuilt to a new design with splendidly pink local bricks, and miraculously the château, which dominates the town and riverscape, was spared by a heaven-sent shower of rain that put out the encroaching 1940 flames just as they reached the summit of the town.

Drive up to the château's escarpment, a good place to leave the car, and look down at the fine view along the river.

Gien's claim to be The First Château on the Loire is based on the fact that the original château was built here by Charlemagne. The present castle dates from the end of the 15th century, built by Anne of Beaujeu, favourite child of the sexist Louis XI, who described her as *la moins folles des femmes* (the least stupid of women); he went on to add insult to this injurious faint praise: *de sages il n'y en a point* (wise women don't exist). It now houses the remarkable Musée International de la Chasse, open 9.15–11.45 a.m.; 2–15–6.30 p.m. (5.30 p.m. in winter).

Whether or not you approve of hunting, there is much of interest here in the international collection of weapons, tapestries, faience, paintings, sculpture and the falcon gallery. I particularly like the fact that the tour is unguided, so you can skip the bits that bore.

The town is very proud of its pottery industry, founded in the early 19th century, and uses local faience to great advantage in street signs and in church, where plaques of the Stations of the Cross are set in the walls, and the capitals of the pillars are coloured Gien earthenware. Many of the shops stock a range – the blue and white Nevers style, the *vieux grès* glazed earthenware, and the many-coloured scenes of birds, animals and hunting scenes which are typical of Gien and very attractive. The museum of Faïenceries de Gien in the place de la Victoire is open every day, and the factory with its seconds shop from Monday to Friday by appointment with the Syndicat d'Initiative in the rue Anne de Beaujeu.

➤ **Le Rivage**
(HR)M
1 quai Nice
38.67.20.53
Closed 8/2–2/3
AE, DC, EC, V

Turn right after crossing the bridge, along the quay, to find Le Rivage, with just the road between it and the river.

First sight of the dining-room may be disappointing – it's large and characterless – but the air of professionalism is unmistakable and the fact that it's always full is indicative of the high standard.

The service, from receptionist, to waiters, to *sommelier*, to patron M. Gaillard weaving amongst his customers, chatting, checking, is impeccable. His 75f menu is the perfect example of how the cheapest menu in a good restaurant is better value than the top price in an inferior one. There are two others, equally commendable, at 125f and 145f, both admirably short and to the point, with local specialities such as a feuilleté of snails in Sancerre, Loire sandre (zander) with asparagus, beef with a sabayon flavoured with Bourgueil, and I look forward enormously to sampling them, but meanwhile I was more than happy with my bargain 75f-worth, especially as there was never a hint of nose-turning-up and the service was just as caring as that given to the big spenders. Mushrooms à la Grecque, a terrine of pike with beurre Nantais, and a fresh orange cream made a perfect lunch, washed down by a delicate and very pretty Giennois rosé wine from Cosnat-sur-Loire, 15 kilometres away.

The hotel rooms are gradually being refurbished and improved; some luxurious new ones were being built while I was there. At the present price of 230f for a double with bath the existing pleasant and high-quality rooms are excellent value. They, with the outstanding food and good position, earn Le Rivage an arrow.

Hôtel Beau Site Restaurant La Poularde (HR)M
13 quai de Nice
38.67.36.05
Closed Sun.
p.m.; 1/9–7/9; 1/
1–15/1
AE, DC, V

A few doors along the quay, and obviously aware of the competition, is the nice old-fashioned façade of the Hôtel Beau Site, with, across the courtyard, its more modern restaurant, La Poularde. Prices neatly undercut those of Le Rivage. The cheapest menu is a bargain 62f for four courses; it too has 10 very pleasant flowery rooms, at 205f. It too seems arrow-worthy, but as I have not yet tried it out I must wait readers' confirmation.

Map 3C   **GOHIER-BLAISON** (M.-et-L.) 15 km SE of Angers

49320
Brissac-Quincé

Cross the river, take the D 751, turn left onto the D 132 through St-Sulpice and follow the signs to the village, which in fact is only a kilometre or so away from the river. It's a delightful rural ride through vineyards and sleepy hamlets.

Le Château de Chéman, Mme Antoine
(C)L–M
41.57.17.60

The approach to the château is through a cobbled courtyard encircled with barns and enlivened with a few scratching hens. All round are the slopes of the vineyards, from whose grapes are made the excellent and unique Cabernet d'Anjou wine named after the château. Mme Antoine poured me out a glass by way of Hello. It's an extraordinary colour; a very pale golden rose is as near as I can get to describing it – ambre gris. Quite delicious, fresh and fruity with a bit of body. You can buy it for around 20f a bottle and it's worth every sou. Other home-grown rosés and reds are on sale in the château.

'Château' is a bit of a misnomer; this is part farm, part country house, full of old beams, steps up, steps down, winding stone staircases, massive worm-eaten doors, crumbling stone façade, impossible to photograph, impossible to pigeonhole.

I found it hard to believe that Madame is 80 – 15 years younger would have been my guess, so sprightly and so enthusiastic and knowledgeable about her wines she is. Nothing is too much trouble for her, as evidenced by her new project of taking in PGs. She accommodates them in three luxurious suites, with bedroom, sitting-room and bathroom apiece, 380f a night, 1,200f a week. There is a kitchen corner in the sitting-room, so knocking up your own breakfasts and picnic lunches would save some of the rooms' cost.

Downstairs, guests are welcome to be part of the family and make use of the salon, over-furnished, perhaps, in the old style, but with a wonderful antique stove throwing out lots of comforting warmth.

Certainly an intriguing stop for those who want absolute peace and quiet, with the interest of a working wine château, very near the tourist belt, with comfortable rooms, presided over by a kindly hostess.

Map 3B	**LA HAIE LONGUE** (M.-et-L.) 16 km S of Angers; 7 km E of Chalonnes

49190
St-Aubin-de-
Luigné

Here is a uniquely attractive patch of countryside, self-contained, untroubled by tourists, unremarked by guide books, quite unlike anything else in the area, encompassing high cliffs around which a corniche road snakes, revealing the islanded water far below; in between are marshes, sloping vineyards and hill-top mediaeval villages. Through it threads its way into the mighty Loire the little river Layon, which gives its name to the delectable and relatively unknown honeyed wines of the Côte du Layon.

On this safe, gentle, green river, so different from its impatient neighbour, you can hire a little motorboat and phut-phut past the black flat-bottomed punts from which the fishermen pull in the shad and carp, the eels and the pike, into a different world of overhanging trees and perfect picnic sites; all this is within 17 kilometres of the hustle of Angers.

Look for this little area on the map, on the south bank in the square between Rochefort and Chalonnes, the D 751 and the D 125 to St-Aubin.

Auberge de la Corniche
(R)S
41.78.33.07
*Closed Tues.
p.m.; Wed.*

On a bend high in the corniche road, with a terrace taking full advantage of the view over the vineyards. It's a simple little restaurant sensibly concentrating on Angevin specialities and suggesting a glass of local wine as an aperitif.

For lunch, looking out over that peaceful panorama, I had just a plateful of friture d'anguilles – fried baby eels in crispy batter, wonderfully garlicky. A three-course meal costs 40f or 70f, including pike with beurre blanc. The cosy little restaurant through the bar is fine too in bad weather, except for the dreaded pop, so particularly inharmonious in this situation.

Map 2G	**HERBAULT** (L.-et-Ch.) 16 km W of Blois

41190
(**M**) *Thurs.*

An undistinguished village on the D 766, with a big market-square.

Auberge des Trois Marchands
(HR)S
54.46.12.18
Closed Mon. p.m.; Tues.

Included really because of its prices. The rooms are very basic but there are not many hotels in this area that charge only 78f for a double!
   Food likewise – excellent value on a 45f menu, cooked by patron M. Cuvier. At lunchtime the glassed-in verandah is full of locals, napkins tucked in, enjoying the quantity and quality. A rebuttal in fact to the view that a holiday in the Loire valley *has* to be expensive.

Map 4E	**L'ÎLE-BOUCHARD** (I.-et-L.) 17 km S of Azay; 15 km E of Chinon

37220
(**M**) *Tues.*

From Azay by the D 757; from Chinon by the D 8.
   The little town, which spreads out over both banks of the river Vienne, gets its name from the midstream island, where a 19th-century M. Bouchard once built a fortress. Until the 19th century the ancient settlement used to be an important river port, linked with the Loire traffic, but now it is a disappointingly dull place, failing to profit from its interesting setting.

Auberge de l'Île
(R)M–L
3 pl. Bouchard
47.58.51.07
Closed Sun. p.m.; Mon.; 15/ 1–28/2
AE, CB, EC

A wide terrace directly overlooks the river from the south bank and a summer lunch here would no doubt be an agreeable interlude. The food is well cooked, using prime ingredients, but, I feel, expensive. The 150f menu is lunch midweek only, otherwise it's going to be 250f on the carte.

Map 1C	**LA JAILLE-YVON** (M.-et-L.) 39 km N of Angers

49990
Le Lion
d'Angers

By the N 162 and D 189.
   This area of lushest green, threaded by the river Sarthe, on which delightful meandering boat trips can be enjoyed, seems a long long way from the commercialism of the Loire; in fact Angers *et al.* are only an easy drive away, and the situation 55 kilometres south of Le Mans makes an overnight stop here tactical good sense. Try and make it longer though.

▶ **Château Le Plessis** 🏠
(C)L
41.95.12.75
Closed 15/10–1/ 4

My guess is that once established under Mme Benoist's hospitable roof, it would be hard to move on. The place exudes restfulness.
   It is still very much a home, not a hotel. When M. Benoist had to retire from his high-powered oil job a couple of years ago, decisions had to be taken. To sell their 16th-century family home would have been a tough one. Their daughter persuaded them overnight to settle for another alternative – to rearrange the manoir's rooms to accommodate PGs. Now each of the six bedrooms has a private

Le Plessis

bath; all are furnished with old family furniture, some with twin beds, some with doubles, all cheerful and comfortable, all looking out on to aspects of greenery.

Mme B. was sitting on a tractor, cutting some of it, when I arrived one sunny afternoon, hot and fusty from too much car; she took in the situation at a glance and in no time ministered with a soothing cuppa in her nice drawing-room. The sun danced off the polished boards, lilac perfumed the room, the tea and little hot croissants, conjured up from nowhere, did their work and all soon became very well with my world.

Mme B. is a good cook and her guests can enjoy her table d'hôte in the evenings, at 150f a head, including as much Anjou wine as they wish. The rooms are 450f and 550f and their comfort, the position, and hospitality merit an arrow.

| Map F3 | **JOUÉ LES TOURS** (I.-et-L.) 6 km SW of Tours, by D86 |

37300

I got hopelessly lost in the Tours suburbs trying to find Joué. There are various approaches, and I suggest you get clear instructions before venturing.

Having arrived in the quiet steep lane that leads up to the château, all is amazingly rural and peaceful, and although the view from the splendid terrace is towards the skyscraper blocks of flats and offices of the city, this would make an excellent peaceful location for a stay very near, but not absorbed by, Tours.

Château de Beaulieu
(HR)M–L
1 rte Villandry
47.53.20.26
Open every day
year round
CB, EC, V

A lovely old stone manorhouse dating from the 18th century, with extensive grounds, a fountain and flowery terraces.

It has 19 very comfortable rooms, furnished with dignity in period style, and the prices are not excessive for this standard and situation – 300–520f. The restaurant is a delightful room with a good view. Menus 145f, 185f, and 250f. The cooking by J-P. Lozay, a *maître cuisinier de France*, is in the classic style, backed up by a long and impressive wine list.

All very popular, so book.

Arrowed for good value in a useful situation.

Map 1l | **LAILLY-EN-VAL** (Loiret) 5 km E of Beaugency

45190
Beaugency

On the D 19.

Auberge de Trois Cheminées
(HR)S
Closed Wed.
o.o.s.; 8/2–1/3

On the crossroads of the main Blois–Orléans road, the D 951, an unassuming Logis de France, recommended generally as 'where the locals, not the Beaugency tourists, eat'. Rooms cost 90–230f. Menus from 69f to 180f.

'Six rooms – those on the front rather noisy, but some over a pleasant little courtyard at back. Very good food, like brochets cooked over wood fire in dining-room.' – Dr Peter Sykes.

Château de Beaulieu.

Map 3E   **LANGEAIS** (I.-et-L.) 25 km W of Tours

37130
 Sun.

On the north bank of the Loire.

A busy dusty stretch of the route nationale passes through the town immediately beneath the castle. Park the car by the information bureau and walk back to the drawbridge entrance. And walk back you should because Langeais, outwardly daunting, is one of the most interesting of the Loire châteaux. It is exceptional in that it stands today complete and exactly as it was on its completion in 1467. Louis XI had it built in only six years, so, apart from the keep, it is all in the same style.

The tours are guided and if you have to wait for one to start walk around the gardens and up to the ruins of the keep – the oldest in France. It was built by Foulques Nerra (see p. 000) at the end of the 10th century.

Once inside the yard, past the massive fortifications, the aspect is more of a grand residence than a fortress. Here is a case where it is well worth taking a guided tour – the guides are highly knowledgeable and multilingual (but there is a written text in English too).

The last owner, M. Siegfried, painstakingly furnished the whole castle in 15th-century contemporary style before handing it over to the State in 1904, and there is much to admire in the way of

Langeais

tapestries, four-poster beds, chests . . . with a high spot in the room where the puny Charles VIII and his child-bride, Anne of Brittany, celebrated their marriage. The waxwork figures cleverly indicate the politics involved, with the young couple totally ignored by the power-seeking prelates, lawyers and aristocrats signing the fateful documents of their alliance. The gleam in the glass eyes speaks volumes.

The watchpath, where the tour concludes, is just that, with an eagle's eye preview of any possible predators up and down the Loire.

Another very good reason for stopping in Langeais is the pastry shop opposite the château – the best I came across in the area.

Hôtel Hosten
(H)M
Restaurant Le Langeais
(R)M–L
2 r. Gambetta
47.96.70.63
Closed Mon.;
Tues.; 20/6–10/
7; 10/1–1/2
AE, CB, DC

This old hotel on the main road has been run by the Hosten family since 1904. For the last two years the youthful Jean-Jacques has taken over from his father in the adjoining restaurant and made it one of the top local gourmand stops. It is a serious well-heeled kind of place for serious well-heeled diners. The food is classically orientated – fillet of beef with red wine sauce, grilled turbot, and very good hot crêpes with blackcurrant sauce. Menu 120f, à la carte 250–300f.

Rooms are comfortable, nothing special, at 240–310f, but breakfast (another 33f) is unusually good.

Crêperie du Château
(R)S
2 r. Ann de Bretagne
47.96.59.56
Closed Mon.

For a quick cheap snack, here is a variety of galettes and crêpes, served in simple surroundings, in the lee of the château.

Only boring ice-creams for dessert (black mark in strawberry season), so I nipped across to the *pâtisserie* and bought a wonderful chocolate and lemon confection to eat with my coffee. They didn't seem to mind.

Map 4G **LOCHES** (I.-et-L.) 41 km SE of Tours

37600
(M) *Wed.,*
Sat.

If time allows, abandon the obvious route from Tours on the N 143, and meander instead from Cormery down the D 17, following the valley of the Indre, stopping perhaps at Azay-sur-Indre, a pretty village, good for a picnic by the river. Return by the forest of Loches, cutting through one of its straight rides, or driving up to Genillé, thereafter taking the D 10 along the Indrois. All very gentle rural stuff, preparing the mood for the delights of this charming mediaeval town – an essential excursion from the better-known Loire valley.

Here on a hill spur is a citadel enclosed within its ramparts. A walk around them is a splendid way to view the countryside, the town and the castle, but be warned – it's a full 2 kilometres around, with no short cuts.

All the town is pretty, with its river and gardens, but once within those walls, through the turretted Porte des Cordeliers, you enter another world, of quiet echoing cobbled streets, narrow, shaded, dominated by the towering giant of a castle.

It's quite a puff up to the 13th-century Porte Royale and a further puff from there to the **Musée du Terroir**, housed in one of the towers in front of the **Lansyer Museum**, (open 9-11.45 a.m., 2–6 p.m. (5 p.m. Mar.–Oct., 4 p.m. Nov.–Mar.), closed Fri.), which was the home of one of Delacroix's painter friends, M. Lansyer. Lansyer's work, especially of local scenes, is well worth viewing, along with Delacroix' sketchbooks. Anyone interested in the craft of drawing should not pass by. And there's a fine view over the town's rooftops from the terrace.

As indeed there is, in the opposite, southwards, direction from the terrace of the château itself. Guided tours 9 a.m.–12 noon, 2–6 p.m. (5 p.m. from 1/10 to 14/3), no lunch break in July and Aug., closed Wed. o.o.s. and Dec. and Jan.

In the 13th-century tower named after her in the 16th century, lived Agnès Sorel, mistress of Charles VII, having retreated from Chinon, where she had been insulted by the Dauphin. She died, possibly of poison, in 1450, at the age of only 28, leaving a legacy to the Convent of St Ours where she wished to be buried. The statue on her tomb was ritually desecrated during the Revolution under the misapprehension that it depicted a saint not a sinner, but was repaired (with a plaster nose) and is now to be seen in the Charles VIII Room. The two rams at her feet can be taken as an acknowledgment of her name, Agnès, or as a comment on the sexual proclivities of her king!

She was criticised for her extravagance and morals but her reign at Loches seems to have been a happy time, and her image remains one of good humour, a favourable influence on the king and an enchanting personality. The number of restaurants and hotels named after her in the area is a good testimony.

The building of Loches castle is in two distinct parts, the Vieux Logis built in the 14th century and the Nouveau Logis under Charles VIII during the Renaissance. To the great hall Joan of Arc came in 1429 to persuade Charles VII to accompany her to Reims.

The 11th-century square keep (*donjon*) was built by the powerful Foulques Nerra (see p. 33) to defend the fortified town from the south. Climb to the top for a fine view.

Those with a taste for the macabre will get their money's worth here. Torture chambers and dungeons galore, with gruesome tales recounted with relish by the guide.

Le Georges Sand
(HR)M
39 r. Quintefol
47.59.39.74
Closed 7/12–27/12
CB

The most favoured position in a favoured town, flower-hung balcony jutting over the Indre, in the lee of the château. Very pleasant to sit on the terrace of the 17th-century inn and listen to the fast-flowing ripples. In fact we sat so long on a busy Easter Sunday, when we should have known better, that we were too late for a table. No grave matter, since our picnic by the river in the public gardens could not have been more agreeable, but I missed the chance to report at first-hand on the cooking (so readers' accounts particularly welcome).

Certainly it seemed that the wise burghers who had reserved places in the two dining-rooms were enjoying their tucker. As it was a *fête* day, menus started at 130f, but normally there are 60f and 85f versions.

The rooms are well equipped, furnished with repro. antiques, from 190f to 280f. When all 17 are full, M. Fortin sends the overflow to his comfortable *chambre d'hôte*, 3 kilometres away.

Hôtel France
(HR)S
6 r. Picois
47.59.00.32
Closed Sun.
p.m.; Mon.
a.m.; 4/1–8/2; 2/
5-8/5
CB, EC, V

Near the main square, the place de la Marne. Simple good value at 120–240f for a room, 56f for the cheapest menu.

Map 2E | **LE LUDE** (Sarthe) 20 km SE of La Flèche; 4 km S of Le Mans

---

72800
(M) *Thurs.*

A small town on the south bank of the Loir, famous for and dominated by its wonderful château. The *son et lumière* programme here was the first and is still one of the best, partly because the site, with wide terraces overlooking the river, lends itself so perfectly to the manifestation, and partly because the building of the château

Georges Sand , Loches

encompasses so many fascinating periods of history – over five centuries, from the 100 Years' War up to the end of the last century, including the Renaissance, the visit of Henri IV and Mme de Sévigné, the elegant 18th century, Napoleon, and the Second Empire. The whole town is involved, with the locals supplying many of the 350 cast, colourfully attired in period costumes. The performances last 1¾ hours, June and July, Fri. and Sat. at 10.30 p.m.; Aug.: Fri., Sat. and some Thur. 10 p.m.; Sept.: Fri and Sat. 9.30 p.m. Fireworks Fri. and Sat. Unforgettable.

I would rate the château too very highly in the pecking order of obligatory châteaux visits. Part of its charm lies in the fact that it is still inhabited by a young and lively family, and although it is undoubtedly a very impressive building, its atmosphere is more home than monument.

Built round a central courtyard, the contrasting façades somehow manage to be totally harmonious. That of François I, loomed over by huge fortress towers, is a rare combination of a severe feudal style, softened by Renaissance decoration. Overlooking the river is the Louis XVI wing, in classical style, very elegant in white tufa stone. The north wing is early 16th century, rearranged in the 19th century, when the stone balconies were added.

The vast rooms are furnished with treasures collected over the centuries to be lived among and used rather than treated as museum pieces. In the Louis XII wing is a ballroom, restored in the 15th century; in the 18th-century wing is a suite of lovely salons, opening one from another, with gorgeous gilt mirrors and family portraits. But just when the ensemble convinces you that this is just a family house at heart, you come across the salamander and ermine carved over a vast chimneypiece, reminders of the previous royal connections.

Maine
(HR)M–S
24 av. Saumur
43.94.60.54
Closed Mon.
lunch in winter;
11/9–22/9; 20/
12–20/1
AE, DC, EC, V

A good-value base from which to explore the château, with rooms from 110f–250f, and extra good cooking from the patron, earning a red R in Michelin for his 65f menu. Others up to 140f.

Map 3C	**LUYNES** (I.-et-L.) 13 km W of Tours

37230
(M) *Sat. a.m.*

On the north bank of the Loire.

Domaine de Beauvois
(HR)L
Rte de Cléré
Closed 15/1–15/3
EC, V

Just 4 kilometres north west of Luynes and ideally situated for the central châteaux, yet in deepest countryside, approached from the noisy north bank by country lanes, the D 49 or the D 126, through the pretty ancient village of Vieux Bourg.

The Domaine stands high above a vast and murky lake, remote in 140 hectares of land, with a new swimming pool built on a platform overlooking the lake. The oldest part, the tower, was built on the 12th-century ruins in the 15th century. Most of the rest dates from a century later.

The rooms and apartments are all different in style, size and price, the most dramatic being the Chambre du Roi, on the first floor of the tower, with impressive chimney, surmounted with the arms of the Beraudière family, who owned the château until 1887, and a colourful ceiling decorated with red and gold beams. The Americans love it but, like me, probably forget to ask 'Which king?'

Rooms cost 495–1,195f and apartments from 1,290f to a kingly 1,785f. The cooking is among the best of the Loire Relais et Châteaux – modern without exaggeration. Langoustines sautéed with a touch of ginger and a roulade of fresh haddock are new ideas of chef Daniel Tauvel, while old favourites such as a variety of Loire fish simply cooked are not neglected. Menus are 135f and 195f (lunch only) and 215f. Pleasant, helpful management and a high proportion of young customers, several of whom told me they were regulars, make for a most agreeable unstuffy atmosphere.

Map 3L	**MENETOU-RÂTEL** (Cher) 9 km NW of Sancerre

18300
Sancerre

An attractive drive along the D 923, climbing high above the vineyards and the goats-cheese-dominated Chavignol. Menetou-Ratel itself is nothing much, and the road flattens out thereafter.

Maillet
(R)M
Rte de Sancerre
48.79.32.54
Closed Mon.;
22/12–10/1; 2/3–16/3; every evening

A delightful little bar/restaurant on the crossroads, much more attractive inside than one would suppose from the nothing-special exterior, with an immensely friendly welcome.

Lunch only, alas, but worth making a diversion to eat honest French food, well cooked and served in copious portions. Menus from 80f to 150f may sound expensive for such an apparently simple restaurant but the quality is there.

Map 1I	**MEUNG-SUR-LOIRE** (Loiret) 6 km NE of Beaugency; 18 km SW of Orléans

45130
(M) *Thurs. p.m.*

On the north bank of the Loire.

An unexpectedly charming little fortified village, squeezed between the frantic Orléans–Blois highway and the river. It is built

101

around the river Mauve, whose tributaries and channels interlace the lower part of the town, les Marais. There are lovely walks along the banks, dotted with watermills.

Pleasant strolling too along the quai du Mail to the quai Jeanne d'Arc (she lodged here in 1429, gathering strength before wresting Beaugency from the English next day), passing the house where the painter Ingres lived for several years, on the corner of the street named after him.

But it is the other higher end of the town, les Monts, which is the really old, history-steeped part, centred round the place du Martroi, on the corner of which is a fine Romanesque church, dedicated to St Liphard – he who in the 6th century set out to convince the heathen villages, by killing a dragon that lurked in the Mauve, that Christianity would be good for them too.

Beside the church is the **château**, given short shrift by the green Michelin guide, but in fact one of the more interesting and atmospheric châteaux of the region. Part of it, built in the 18th-century, is still occupied by its owner and his covetable collection of furniture, including some English Chippendale.

In contrast to this elegance and civilisation, the horrors that lurk below are all the more potent. Here is the *oubliette*, a cone-shaped well into which prisoners were lowered, to spend the rest of their lives on a narrow shelf, forgotten (*oublier* = to forget). Perhaps even this fate was looked forward to as a respite from the preliminaries – a spell in the mildly named Salle de Question, the questions being posed during torture. I doubt if many could manage the hollowest of laughs to see the sign *Cachot d'accueil*.

It was the Bishops of Orléans who for 500 years dispensed 'justice' here. Their best-known prisoner was François Villon, in 1459, who, fine poet though he may have been, undoubtedly mixed in dubious company. After his turn of 'questioning' and the *oubliette*, he was more fortunate than most of his fellows in being granted amnesty by Louis XI, who passed through Meung during his coronation celebrations. How Villon managed to write his famous 'Épître à mes Amis' under such conditions one cannot imagine, but he was obviously a man of many parts – no sooner did he return to Paris than he committed both burglary and murder!

Auberge St Jacques
(HR)S
R. Gén. de Gaulle
38.44.30.39
Closed Mon.
o.o.s.; 15/1–31/1
AE, EC

A simple little restaurant, serving good-value meals, and the 65f menu earns a red Michelin R. There are 12 rooms too, which I have so far not managed to inspect, so reports would be particularly welcome.

Le Rabelais
(R)M
38.45.11.55
3 r. du Docteur
Henri-Michel

Truly Rabelaisian the 100f buffet on offer here, in this *maison bourgeoise* near the castle. In a jolly, slightly scatty, atmosphere, you help yourself to as much as you want, as many times as you wish, from a groaning table loaded with more than the all-too-common buffet food of baked beans and tinned sweetcorn. A good place to take the kids, with a nice terrace on which to soak up the sun.

Map 2H   **MOLINEUF** (L.-et-Ch.) 8 km SW of Blois

41190

On the D 766.
    The valley of the river Cisse is a charming route to follow, intensely rural. At the pretty flowery village of Molineuf the bridge crosses the rushing waters and, appropriately enough, on the river bank is:

Hôtel du Pont
(HR)S
1 r. du Gué
Tarreau
54.70.04.26
Closed Jan.;
rest. closed
Mon.

The hotel has a terrace across the village street, directly overlooking the river – a very pleasant place to take a simple meal of fish straight from its waters.
    The du Pont is a modest, one-star hotel, run by the same family for over a century. The bedrooms are clean and wholesome and would suit very well those on a tight budget who seek rural tranquillity not far from the high spots of the Loire. They cost a mere 100–120f for a double, with shower; 6 of the 14 overlook the garden.
    M. Laigret cooks very well on menus from 49f, so altogether this is a recommended bargain stop, but please don't write and complain that the rooms are not luxurious.

Map 3F   **MONTBAZON** (I.et-L.) 9 km S of Tours

37250
Ⓜ *Tues.*

A spaghetti junction of routes nationales, autoroute, and minor lanes and byways. Get away from the main roads a.s.a.p. and tranquillity is not far away.

Moulin Fleuri
(HR)M–S
5 km W by N 10.
D 287 and D 87
47.26.01.12
Closed Mon.
except fêtes;
15/10–30/10

First impression is a disappointment. *Moulin* once yes, *fleuri* in parts, but not the picturesque, remote watermill I had imagined. This is now a modern rectangle of a building, with only vestiges of its old rôle to lend a little character.
    However, the site is undeniably attractive, with terrace overlooking the river Indre, offering a peasant's view of the splendid Château d'Artigny just opposite. All very green and peaceful, and not exploiting the situation, as is so often sadly the case, with poor tourist-orientated food.
    Here at weekends and holidays the sizeable restaurant is rushed off its feet with locals profiting both from the fresh ingredients in dishes such as a marinade of local fish, or young hare with prunes, and from the spectacular list of Loire wines. Go for the 94f menu.
    The 12 rooms are being successively modernised and redecorated, so prices might increase. Currently they are a very reasonable 143–203f. Understandably, with these prices, in this situation, both hotel and restaurant are very popular, so book ahead and avoid busy times.

Château
d'Artigny
(HR)L
Rte Azay-le-
Rideau
47.26.24.24
Closed 28/11–
9/1
All credit cards

Many moons ago, when you and I, my dears, were young and
innocent, there was held a competition to write about the liqueur
Cointreau, made at Angers in the valley of the Loire. The prize was to
stay at the most luxurious of all the château hotels, perhaps the best.
I knew nothing about Cointreau, very little about the Loire and
absolutely nothing at all about the top hotels in Europe. So of course
I entered. The winner 't was I, and the prize two nights at the Château
d'Artigny.

I do remember driving up a wide tree-lined avenue, which
suddenly revealed a sugar-icing, fairy-tale château set between
formal gardens and teetering on a precipice high above that
legendary and previously unvisited river, the Loire. I do remember
being led, an honoured guest, up a gloriously sweeping staircase, all
of polished white stone, to a glorious suite overlooking that river.
The bed was vast, four-postered, satisfyingly draped with the kind of
rich hangings I had always imagined came as standard with château
bedrooms, the bathroom was as big as any bedroom, the bath was
marble, the taps were gold, and there was not only one washbasin at
normal height but another, strangely shaped, at lower level, at
whose function I could only dimly guess.

I do remember a circular salon somewhere, with a *trompe l'œil*
balcony, painted with a crowed of characters revelling at a masked
ball, whose names – Diaghilev, Edwige Feuillère, François Côty – I
had never heard before, or perhaps had relegated to a youthful,
overcrowded Filofax way back in the recesses of an unformed mind.
Not too youthful, or unformed however to disregard the food served
in a curved drawing-room, all pillared and green and gold, with
glittering chandeliers and suave waiters helping me to dishes as rich
and rare as the décor.

In the intervening years the territory has become familiar and the
geography better orientated and many's the time those authoritative
signs 'Slow down – Château d'Artigny' have been passed by. Once,
intent on impressing my family, I persuaded them to drive smartly up
to the front door, and smartly out again, boggling the while.

So, you will understand that while *FE* has provided me with many
a unique opportunity, none has been so keenly anticipated as the
chance to stay again at the Château d'Artigny. Older and somewhat
wiser about the relative merits of hotels from L to S, more sceptical,
less readily impressed, I obeyed the sign and, antennae a-quiver,
turned into the drive.

It was even longer than I recalled, cleverly confusing the sense of
direction, so that although the château is directly above the road, by
the time you've twisted and turned through some of the 25 hectares
of park and arrived at the other side, it seems far, far remote from the
plebeian world below.

The gleaming façade was just as impressive, though now I
recognised that, far from being fairy-tale, it was a 20th-century
construction built from the proceeds of the Côty perfume empire and
transformed into a hotel 30 years ago by René Traversac, the Parisian
industrialist.

I found that, surprisingly, the interior had changed very little from
what I remembered and perhaps had fantasised upon. The staircase

was just as grand, the salons just as gilded, the view down to the river just as dramatic and the rotunda *trompe l'œil* even more interesting now that I had heard of some of the characters.

What had changed was my status. Instead of the four-poster suite I got an attic bedroom, dark and hot, up in the mansard roof, with only a small porthole, too high to capitalise on the view. The bathroom was cramped and functional. At 750f I wasn't impressed, but I did now know what the second 'washbasin' was for.

A great relief therefore next day to see other rooms, quite as beautiful and grand as I had hoped. The message is obvious. Do not think of staying at the Château unless you can afford the best. And the best costs around 1,000f, which, for what's on offer, is not bad. There is still my four-poster, or Corinthian Columns, or country-house chintzes; some rooms are very formal, some are relaxed; marble bathrooms galore.

The dining-room is still green and gold, and if you're lucky (or famous or mega-rich), you'll get a table in the bay overlooking the Loire. However, the food must be very different from those far-off carefree days when cream and butter and red meat were not sinful. Nowadays it is light and fresh and flavoursome and costs 210f or 255f for the menus, around 400f à la carte, and does clever things with pigeons and vegetables rather than roast beef and six other courses.

Equally modern is the emphasis on sporting facilities – a golf course, swimming pool and tennis courts, and the flavour of the day customer-wise is Japanese and American rather than European. What Gault et Millau describe as a *clientèle fortunée*, arriving insouciantly by helicopter.

If I were ever to stay in d'Artigny again, I would choose one of the famous winter *weekends musicaux*, when the stately rooms reclaim the elegance that goes with moneyed leisure and refinement. Then the combination of superb food, wine and music must be a treat indeed.

► Domaine de la Tortinière
(HR)L
47.26.00.19
Closed 16/11–
15/3; rest.
closed Wed.
lunch; Tues.
o.o.s

Turn off the N 10 south of Montbazon on to the D 287 and look out for discreet signs to La Tortinière. What's good enough for the Earl and Countess Spencer would definitely be good enough for me. They had just vacated the lovely suite of bedroom, bathroom and salon built into a turret of the château (1,300f a night) when P. Fenn arrived to inspect, and she would have been very happy to have taken over.

La Tortinière is a small château/large house, set in quiet substantial grounds above the river Indre. What you pay for, apart from the rooms (370–700f), are the views down the terraces, the swimming pool, and the country calm that must merit a considerable premium in this sometimes frenetic area.

The bedrooms are lovely, the service is suave and the public rooms a delight. The restaurant has a Michelin star and features such seemingly simple dishes as clafoutis (a kind of Yorkshire pudding with seasonable fruits embedded) alongside truffle-studded hare and salmon cooked in a coarse salt case; local wines predominate. Allow 250f à la carte.

Arrowed for supreme luxury.

> **La Chancelière**
(R)L
*Pl. des
Maronniers
Rte de Monts
47.26.00.67
Closed Sun.
p.m.; Mon.; 16/
11–30/11*

Somewhat unhappily sited on a very busy corner of the minor road that crosses the N 10. It's an outwardly simple village house, covered in creeper, but step down inside and it's an altogether different story. Clever decorators have lightened the old beams, chosen tables of glass set on ornate gilded bases, on which the crystal glasses reflect and sparkle, used cane chairs, painted the walls soft caramel and altogether succeeded in creating an atmosphere of sophistication and luxury without any hint of o.t.t.

The food, cooked by a young chef, Michel Gangneux, is in similar vein – tastefully presented, contrived from no-expense-spared ingredients – no doubt to attract clients from the palaces of luxury down the road, the Château d'Artigny and La Tortinière. Ravioli stuffed with oysters in a champagne sauce, duck liver sautéed with figs, and masterly desserts, such as hot blinis souffléed with orange butter, show a very skilled and professional touch.

For this quality of cooking, in this setting, the 130f menu is a bargain. So is the 156f, and it would be foolish not to take advantage of them; if you eat à la carte you must expect a bill of around 400f.

Arrowed for superb cooking, at realistic prices.

Map 2D

MONTGEOFFROY (LE CHÂTEAU) (M.-et-L.) 26 km E of Angers

By the N 147 and then north by the D 74. Open 15/6–15/9 from 9.30 a.m. to 12 noon; 2.30–6.30 p.m.

Try and make the short diversion to Montgeoffroy in order to see one of the few châteaux along the Loire to retain its original furnishings. It has been lived in by the same family since it was built in the 18th century and the atmosphere of a home rather than an institution is pervasive and very heart-warming.

The two round towers flanking the main buildings, the chapel, and the moats are all that remain of the original 16th-century building; the rest is designed to a single and harmonious pattern. Enjoy the beautiful furniture, still occupying the place for which it was originally designed.

Map 3G

MONTLOUIS-SUR-LOIRE (I.-et-L.) 12 km E of Tours

37270
Ⓜ *Thurs.*

Take the D 751 from Tours.

Squeezed between the rivers Loire and Cher, the vineyards of this village, riddled with caves in its tufa cliffs, produces some of the finest white wine of the region.

> **Roc-en-Val**
(R)M-L
*4 quai Loire
47.50.81.96
Closed Mon.;
Sun. p.m.; 15/
2–10/3*

Facing the river, an old family house, transformed in 1986 into a luxurious and charming restaurant by the young Thierry Regnier and his sister Laurence. The terrace, overlooking the water, is a particularly happy choice for summer dining, under the shade of a 300-year-old tree.

Chef Frank Graux trained with some of the great French chefs – Marc Méneau, Michel Guérard, and Alain Chapel, so it is no wonder that here you will find some of the best cooking in the region. His background tends towards *nouvelle cuisine* but his intelligence leads him back to the traditional dishes of the region, such as a carrée of lamb, a definitive oxtail stew, bass with orange juice. New ideas include a subtle coconut tart accompanied by a thyme and lemon sorbet.

This is an example of luxury cooking at bargain prices, so long as you stick to the cheapest menu. For 145f (not *fêtes*) you can see what I mean.

La Cave
(R)M
47.45.05.05
Closed Sun.
p.m.

OK, so it is a big tourist attraction to eat troglodyte style, but it's also great fun to sit in this tufa cave, in the cosy restaurant built around the central fireplace, and to eat Michel Antier's charcoal grills. I wouldn't waste a beautiful day there, but if it's a touch miserable outside, this is the place to forget the blues. Allow 120f.

Map 3G   **MONTPOUPON** (I.-et-L.) 11 km S of Chenonçeaux

11 km south-east of Montrichard on the D 764.

Le Château de
Montpoupon
(C)L
47.94.23.62 and
47.94.30.77

You can't miss the château, whose 16th-century gateway opens directly on to the road which was once the main pilgrim route to Spain; its stubby grey towers, all that remain of the 13th-century fortress, dominate the wooded valley below.

Montpoupon describes itself as a *Demeure de gentilhommes chasseurs*, and hunting and its accoutrements form the most important part of the lives of its owners, including the present *châtelaine*, Mlle de la Motte-St-Pierre, who still hunts the wild boar, stags and deer in the surrounding forests as avidly as did her ancestors throughout the centuries. In one of the stables is set up a hunting museum, showing some of the château's trophies, costumes and trappings of previous de la Motte-St-Pierres.

The equipment of the ancient kitchen too has been preserved, and the guided tour, from 15/6 to 30/9, includes a visit to admire the copper pans and beautiful linen and lace, dating back to an age when an estate like this was a self-contained village of servants and retainers.

Nowadays Mlle de la Motte-St-Pierre lives and works with a skeleton staff, and she herself helps out with guiding, maintenance, and cooking for the three bedrooms she lets out. Not your common or garden bedrooms these. Mine, the size of six hotel rooms, had an imposing four-poster bed (surprisingly comfortable) with venerable tapestry hangings that I nightmared would tumble on top of me if I so much as sneezed.

Priceless antique family heirlooms provided furniture and pictures on the walls. The bathroom was a fascinating period piece. I started running the bath, unpacked and wrote up my notes for the day, and returned to find it still only half full. I feared at first that loos had still to be invented in the castle's time scale, until I touched a bevelled corner panel and it swung open to reveal a mighty mahogany throne.

Mlle and I had the whole château to ourselves that night, she in her small corner (the north wing) and I in mine (the east). Footsteps echoing down stone-flagged corridors and winding staircases announced my coming down for dinner, giving Mlle time to get *un petit whisky* all ready. I confess to a case of the giggles as we sat at opposite ends of the dining table in the impressive dining-room, with my hostess popping out into the kitchen every so often, to reappear with an omelette pan. (But I had sprung my visit on her and when there are more visitors she does have a cook and the meal is much more sophisticated.)

She also owns a little restaurant in the grounds of the château, Le Moulin Bailly, where visitors can eat simple grills and crêpes. Open to the public from Easter to 15/6 and in October at weekends and *fêtes* only, and from 15/6 to 1/10 every day.

Definitely something different. For those who want a first-hand experience of how the landed gentry of France live now, and the chance to sleep in the grandest possible style, the charge is 500f a night for two.

Map 4H **MONTRÉSOR** (I.et-L.) 34 km S of Montrichard

37460
(M) *2nd, 4th, 5th Tues. of each month*

Once south of the river Cher, the countryside reverts to its original unspoilt, un-tourist-ridden delightful state and small sleepy villages, lost in time-warps, abound. Drive through Céré-la-Ronde on the D 81 and from Orbigny follow the little river Olivet on the D 11 to see what I mean.

Montrésor's boast is that it is *le plus beau village de France*, which may be pushing it a bit, but certainly it would be a contender for the most attractive village in the region, tumbling round the mighty château that dominates the valley, as it has done since time immemorial.

The château *is* the village, the reason for its existence. From its mighty doors down to the church runs a narrow cobbled lane, lined with old stone cottages, window-boxes aflame. On Ascension Day I walked along it with the castle's *châtelaine*, la Comtesse de Rey, on her way to mass. Small boys emerged along its route and were embraced – ('my grandsons'), a young woman joined us ('my daughter-in-law'), and at the church door a young man crossed the street and solemnly performed the ritual two cheeks' greeting ('my nephew'). Inside the 16th-century church, Mme pointed out to me the tombs of its founders, the Basternay family. There lie the Lord, his wife and son, lying in marble incarnation, hands clasped on bosoms, regardless of the villagers clustered around, swapping local gossip before the service begins. All round the walls are imposing portraits of important local families. The good folk of Montrésor have plenty to look at if their thoughts should stray during their religious observances. It's a lovely, light interior, thanks to the white tufa, and particularly interesting as a transition from the Gothic to the Renaissance.

Our exit was a lengthy one, prolonged by the necessity for Mme to greet every member of the congregation in varying degrees of intimacy, from handshakes to hugs. How lucky they all are to be part of such a close extended family. I left her at this point and set off to visit the hotel and take *un petit verre* outside in the sunshine. When I did drive back through the village, there was Mme still happily chatting away to her less aristocratic neighbours.

Smashing. Can't see it happening in England.

Le Château de Montrésor is another Foulques Nerra (see p. 33) 11th-century fortification. He certainly knew how to pick all the best sites. It stands proud above the valley surprisingly far below, original curtain walls and crumbling tower still standing. From the south it appears picturesque, from the north totally intimidating. Within the walls is a surprise – a pleasant leafy overgrown garden. No hint of aggression here – double wisteria curtains the walls, roses ramble unrestrained and borders of annuals show tender loving care. It's all very agreeable and peaceful to walk around the walls, colourfully bedded out on the valley side, hazardous and bleak to the north.

Mme lives in the nice 16th-century grey stone house to the right of the entrance; the château itself, opposite, was restored by her ancestor, a Polish nobleman, Count Branicki, in 1849 and the furnishings within have not been changed since his time.

The walls are hung with his souvenirs from battlefield and hunt; there are 19th-century Polish and French paintings and some Italian primitives and carvings. The Count and his family might have moved out yesterday. His ancestors are just across the courtyard.

An interesting château to put on the visiting list, full of character, and definitely different.

Montrésor

➤ **Hôtel de France**
(HR)S
47.94.20.03

Grandly named, misleadingly. This is a modest little establishment, located by following the noise emanating into the street from those villagers who preferred to celebrate Ascension in the bar. In order to eat in the pretty little restaurant, overlooking the rear garden, you must run the gauntlet of smoke, pin machines, curious proprietory eyes. It's worth it – the food on menus from 48f is way above average for a village pub. They say that ever since the chef/patron was squashed against the wall by a lorry the cooking has never been the same, but all I, a parvenu, can say, is that it must have been superb before the crumpling, because it's pretty good now.

The rooms likewise. 135f (180f for three) buys a pretty, countrified rear bedroom with bath, overlooking the courtyard wherein summer meals are served. No bathroom – 85f. Beat that!

It's all very charming, with decorations of costumes, dolls and dried flowers, and totally unpretentious. This rare combination of comfortable village rooms, good cooking, and the bonus of the surroundings of Montrésor earn it an arrow.

| Map 4D | **MONTREUIL-BELLAY** (M.-et.L) 16 km S of Saumur |

49260
Ⓜ *Tues.*

On the N 147.

A most attractive village, thanks to its site high above the river Thouet, almost surrounded by 13th-century fortifications, and the imposing castle that dominates the town and reflects its turrets in the water far below.

The original was built by Foulques Nerra (see p. 33) early in the 11th century and razed by Geoffrey Plantagenet a century later. The moat, ramparts and gateway were built on its foundations. Once over the fortified gateway, the fortress aspect mellows into a gracious 15th-century house. Beside the gate is the 'new' castle built at the same time, a narrow spiky building with a lovely turreted staircase.

Guided tours from 1/4 to 1/11, 10–11.30 a.m. and 2–5.30 p.m. Closed Tues. In the summer, at Easter and Ascension you can sit in the gardens created in the moat and listen to a recording of the château's history.

Hôtel Splendid
(HR)M–S
Annexe
Le Relais du Bellay
(H)M
41.52.30.21
Closed 14/1–30/1; rest. closed Sun. p.m. o.o.s.
EC, V

A nice little Logis de France built into an old house in the town centre, approached via a courtyard with pond, with tonight's supper (trout, eels) swimming therein.

The rooms are good sized and comfortable, and on a dark and dirty night I chose to stay in one of those instead of the rather grander versions in the new annexe, Le Relais du Bellay, a good five minutes' soaking walk away.

A pity, because in fine weather Le Relais would probably be first choice. Although further away from the château it has a better, uninterrupted view of the magnificent pile rising above the roof-tops. And a swimming pool, though that too failed to attract in the face of such general dampness. Its rooms are more upmarket altogether, with mock antique furniture and a good deal of gilt. Good bathrooms.

Whether you choose to stay in the main hotel where rooms are 120f or in the annexe at 230f, you will be getting very good value.

Both hotels share the restaurant in the Splendid, which is really quite smart, with wine-coloured cloths and napkins, massive old beams, and a very French feel about it. I cannot say the food merits a detour, but as long as you stay simple it's fair enough. Perhaps I was unfortunate to pick an evening when there was something special on the TV. To see the chef settled down in front of it when I felt he should have been supervising my dinner, was not encouraging. He certainly hadn't concerned himself with my asparagus, which were in sad shreds and drearily oozing cooking water, nor yet the veg. – which had been ready a long time before I was ready to eat 'em, but the beurre blanc with the zander was good and the faux filet tender enough. Best value is the 50f menu – a gratin of seafood, entrecôte, pud. With a bottle of Beaujolais at 36f you can set out feeling very satisfied, with a modest bill.

Hostellerie Porte-St-Jean
(R)M
432 r. Nationale
41.52.30.41
Closed Mon.
p.m.; Tues.; 23/
6–30/6; 15/10–
30/10; 15 days
in Jan.
CB

If the chef at the Splendid is still glued to the telly, you would do well to retreat down the road to the little restaurant that takes its name from the old gateway out of the town. Chef M. Corbin cooks interesting local food – ravioli stuffed with eels in a Layon wine sauce, a boudin of pike with a red wine sauce, and a 'panaché' of zander and salmon. Excellent local wines. 65f lunch menu is a bargain; otherwise it's 100f.

Map 3H   **MONTRICHARD** (L.-et-Ch.) 43 km E of Tours; 33 km S of Blois

41400
(M) *Mon.*

A long narrow town, squeezed between the north bank of the Cher and the crumbling keep of Foulques Nerra's 11th-century castle, built on the edge of the cliff. Around the church are some picturesque old mediaeval houses.

Bellevue
(HR)M
Quai du Cher
54.32.06.17
Closed Mon.
and Tues.
o.o.s.; 15/11–
21/12
AE, DC, EC
Parking

Modern hotel with only the road between it and a pleasant river scene. Panoramic view from the restaurant, where menus start at 78f. Allow 210f for an à-la-carte meal. Bedrooms well accoutred, 140–260f.

Tête Noire
(HR)M
R. de Tours
54.32.05.55
Closed Fri.
o.o.s.;
2/1–7/2
V
Parking

One street back from the river, on main through road. Modern again and lacking a great deal of character, but well maintained and comfortable. The rooms, equipped with all mod cons, are 170f–220f and the restaurant, though lacking the view of its rival the Bellevue, probably has better food. Menus from 70f. À la carte allow 210f.

Le Bistrôt de la Tour
(R)S
6 r. du Pont
54.32.07.34

A recently opened little bistro facing on to the vegetable market place. A friendly, young, informal atmosphere and very popular at lunchtime; menus starting at 44f.

Le Grill du Passeur
(R)M
2 r. du Bout du Pont
54.32.06.80
Closed 5/12–15/3

A very old building indeed, actually on the bridge, on the Faverolles side, with the water lapping its grey stones. Inside all is resolutely rustic, with a vast hearth where chef M. Daros grills prime meat and fish.

A good stop if you yearn for simple food, simply cooked, and are prepared to pay 160f–180f à la carte.

Map 4D | **MONTSOREAU** (M.-et-L.) 11 km SE of Saumur; 18 km NW of Chinon

---

49730
(M) *Sun. a.m. 1/4–30/9*

On the south bank of the Loire.

A pleasant little town, at the junction of the rivers Loire and Vienne; the resulting wide stretch of water flows between small sandy beaches and marshy banks. Parking is easy down on the quays, where a few fishing boats are still tied up and the general feeling is much more relaxed than the next stretch of the Loire, up to Saumur, where the busy road on the southern bank is shadowed by high tufa cliffs, riddled with troglodyte dwellings. Even on a sunny May *fête* day I found a vacant table outside the café on the parade, relished the calm after a long journey, watching the river and my fellow imbibers.

Rising sheer from the road is the château. The road used to run behind it so that the river lapped its walls, but its fierce repelling bastions are still reflected in the water. Not of prime interest to visit except perhaps for its good view downstream. It owes its renown to Alexandre Dumas, who used it as the setting for his novel *La Dame de Montsoreau*.

I am ashamed to say that I had never bothered to explore any further, assuming that the village consisted only of the narrow stretch along the quays; only by investigating Le Bussy (see below) did I discover a charming flowery mediaeval village scrambling up the hill behind it.

All in all, I would recommend Montsoreau as a most agreeable place to stay, well situated for visits to some of the most interesting Loire treasures, but intrinsically calm. And you can take boat trips along the river Vienne towards Chinon from its quay.

Le Bussy 🏨
(H)M
41.51.70.18
Closed Tues.
o.o.s.; 15/12–
31/1

Under the same management as the restaurant Diane de Meridor (see below), and known as its annexe. As it's 250 yards up a steep hill, in the village, I would call it a totally independent hotel, charmingly converted from an old house, built into the tufa walls.

What good value it all is – a unique view of the river over the roof-tops and around the tower of the château and the peacefulness of the charming village. The 16 rooms are pleasant and comfortable, at 90–250f. No hardship whatsoever to stroll down the hill to eat at:

Diane de 🏨
Meridor
(R)M–S
41.51.70.18
Closed Mon.
p.m. o.o.s.;
Tues. except
July and Aug.;
15/1–31/1
EC, V

A few doors along the river road from the castle, the restaurant has a good view over the water and is very popular, so make sure of a reservation.

Patron William Winffel, from Alsace, is a popular character anu has gathered together a regular clientele, quite a few of them English, who enjoy his *bonhomie* and excellent cooking. He specialises in fresh river fish, served in the pretty rustic dining-room, all cane chairs, red checked cloths, low lamps and a good fire in winter. Menus from 65f.

These two make up a deservedly popular combination, well situated and good value. Arrow.

Atelier Maridor
(C)M
Le Chapitre
(R)S
Quai A. Dumas
41.51.75.33
Open all year

A well-organised combination, with restaurant across the courtyard from the *chambre d'hôte*. Clearly indicated from the river-bank road, near the château.

Le Chapitre is particularly attractive on a miserable day, since it is built into a cave and seems warm and cosy compared with the external elements, or one of those sultry midsummer lunchtimes when its dim coolness soothes away the stress of a long, hot, car journey.

Food is simple but good – à la carte grills mostly – and candlelit suppers, from 37f to 78f.

The Maridor used to be part of the castle. Its rooms are well equipped and cost 230–270f for a double, including breakfast, taken in the pretty courtyard on fine days.

Map 3G   **NAZELLES** (I.-et-L.) 7 km NW of Amboise; 25 km E of Tours

37400

From Tours take the pleasant little D 1 through Vouvray and Vernou-sur-Brenne, and turn left just before the village of Nazelles towards Vaugadeland. From Amboise cross the bridge, turn left and follow signs to Nazelles-Bourg (not Nazelles-Negron).

Either way, having turned off the D 1, the lane climbs steeply up the valley, with glimpses of a rushing stream down below. The birdsong starts to become noticeable, the greenery grows more intense, and I guarantee that by the time you turn into the drive you'll be mentally rubbing hands, gently prepared for all the peace and tranquillity on offer at:

La Huberdière
(C)L–M
47.57.39.32
Open all year

It's a faded grey stone ex-hunting lodge, set in 20 acres of woodland, its wide terrace facing a great lake. The cowslips around here know when they're on to a good thing. Unpesticided, they tumble riotously down the wide clearing cut in the hill facing the château, down to the border of the lake, showing their appreciation of the lushness by growing bigger, taller, brighter than any cowslips heretofore. One could pick an armful before breakfast. One did.

Châtelaine Mme Sandrier, or someone in her amorphous household of students, guests, children and au pairs had picked a basketful and placed it on the Easter breakfast table. An extended family of ten PGs, assembled from different parts of France for the holiday weekend, had spread their generous Easter offerings to one another around the places laid with giant pottery coffee bowls and elegant Breton cafetière. The big children got chocolate eggs, the small ones Easter bunnies, and the parents elegantly wrapped boxes of expensive chocs.

They were sampling *chambre d'hôte* hospitality for the first time, and, like me, relishing the difference between the laid-back relaxed family approach of Mme Sandrier and her team and the rushed impersonality common to many hotels on a busy weekend.

La Huberdière

Mind you, they had struck lucky here. La Huberdière is a stunning place. Mme Sandrier's parents bought the originally 17th-century château (with bits of 18th and 19th too) when she was a baby; she grew up here, loved the place and in order to maintain it takes in PGs. It's a rambling grey pile, with wooded grounds, dotted with violets and daffodils as well as the prolific cowslips. Amboise, 7 kilometres across the river, had been traffic-jammed and very noisy the night before, so this green and secret hideaway just over the bridge was very heaven. Oh to be in England, but not necessarily so.

It's all enough to make a property developer's eyes shine. The out-buildings, the barns and pavilions and the grounds could support many an interesting development.

Our bedroom could easily have been chopped into four neat little Identikit plastic cubes for a chain hotel. The bed was brass, high and deep, hard to leave in the morning even when the sharp spring sunshine shafted through the tall windows backed by peeling white shutters. The pale blue curtains had been faded by many a summer, as had those on the canopy over the bed, and the figures on the blue-and-white Toile de Jouy wallpaper had almost merged into the background, so delightfully attuned were they to the period of the room, where nothing was newer than the 50-year-old radiators. Most of the furniture throughout the château is antique, and must be very valuable. In here were a fruitwood armoire, a gorgeous chaise-longue and some very good family portraits. The bath was modern, but still took half an hour to fill.

That evening Mme Sandrier, jolly, sociable and speaking perfect English, was calmly preparing dinner for 25, with the assistance of an army of au pairs of all nationalities, who seem to get a good deal of fun out of their stay at La Huberdière. She said that as she was particularly busy over Easter this would be a simple meal – soup, turkey escalopes with cream and mushrooms, salad, cheese, fruit. Including unlimited wine, this would cost 95f. I suspect that most guests would wish to eat in at least once, to decide if the company and food suited them; if not, there is absolutely no obligation, and Mme S. has plenty of alternative nearby suggestions.

Prices of rooms vary drastically, as do the rooms themselves. All include breakfast for two people. Small attic rooms cost 210f. One with three beds costs 290f. Our room, which I believe was the best, was a well-spent 380f.

By B and B standards not cheap perhaps, but for me a winner, by virtue of its atmosphere, owner, lovely bedroom, and position so near the sights, so far from the aggro. Arrowed accordingly.

Map 2G | **NEUILLÉ-LE-LIERRE** (I.-et-L.) 16 km N of Amboise; 26 km NE of Tours

---

37380
Monnaie

Local people feel very badly about the ruination of the valley, but the great gods autoroute and TGV must have their way and pay no heed to the scars they leave behind. The new straight-as-an-arrow's-flight railway line cuts right through what was once lovely unspoilt rural scenery, so near in miles to Tours and the Loire hordes, yet so far in spirit. Currently it is hard to appreciate the little roads like the D 46 north from Vernou-sur-Brenne, with mountains of newly excavated earth obtruding, but perhaps when the railroad is built and the verdure of the countryside takes a hold, it will regain a little of its former pastoral beauty.

Auberge de la Brenne
(R)M–S
Le Bourg
47.52.95.05
Closed Tues.
p.m.; Wed.
o.o.s.; 20/10–
26/10
AE, CB

Whatever the scenery, a drive here is warranted to eat at this unpretentious little roadside inn, where Nelly, wife of the patron, presents simple straightforward dishes such as fish from the Loire and home-made *charcuterie*. The 54f weekday menu is a snip and earns a red R in Michelin but at weekends the 94f and 124f versions are also deservedly popular, so book.

Map 4H **NOUANS-LES-FONTAINES** (L.-et-Ch.) 18 km S of St-Aignan

---

On the D 675 from St-Aignan.
   A boring village at the end of a green and pleasant drive from Tours, skirting the forest of Loches, on the D 760.

Le Lion d'Or
(R)S
47.92.62.19
Closed Tue.
p.m.; Wed.

The kind of focus spot to be found in every French town, spotted usually by chance or personal recommendation. The Farleys (see p. 174) propose Le Lion d'Or for any guests who want simple, good food cooked *à l'ancienne*. Menus at 80f.

Map 3H **NOYERS-SUR-CHER** (L.-et-Ch.) 37 km S of Blois

41140
(M) *Sun. a.m*

2 kilometres north of St-Aignan on the north bank of the Cher.

Hôtel de la Gare
(HR)S
54.75.16.38
Closed Sun.
p.m.; Mon.
except fêtes

Don't think I'd like to stay here – on the corner of a busy main road facing the little station of Noyers (the rooms cost 82–124f) but it is undoubtedly a good place in this tourist-geared area to come for copious, honest cooking. It was well into a *fête* afternoon when I called in and the large dining-room was still full of perspiring, red-faced worthies at the stomach-patting stage. Satisfied repleteness all over the place. The cheeseboard – always a good test – looked magnificent even then. Menus from 52f.

Relais Touraine
et Sologne
(HR)M
Le Boeuf
Couronné
54.75.15.23
Closed Tues.
p.m.; Wed.
o.o.s.; 4/1–20/2
AE, DC, V

Just across the bridge from St-Aignan, on the crossroads of le Boeuf Couronné, sheltered from the two busy main roads by a courtyard.

Jovial patron Maxime Robert cooks freezer-free ingredients in traditional but inventive style on menus from 85f. Very popular for local blow-outs at weekends.

At lunchtime all the staff were fully stretched and I didn't have the nerve to ask to see the rooms, so reports particularly welcome.

Map 1J   **OLIVET** (Loiret) 4.5 km S of Orléans

45100
Orléans

Orléans is not a city in which I would choose to stay during a tour of the Loire area, but I thought I'd better see what I could find to make me change my mind. The result was as half-anticipated – frustrating, with the obvious hotel scene unexciting, and I didn't hear about what would seem to be the most promising one, the Auberge de la Montespan at St-Jean-de-la-Ruelle, until I had left the area (reports please). Little daunted I was still confident that the outskirts of the city, with all that water on whose banks to build, would yield the best crop of both hotels and restaurants, but Olivet, with all its possibilities, proved a disappointment too.

We had lunch at a little Logis de France, Paul Forêt, on a charmed site on the willowed bank of the Loiret, sitting on the terrace watching the oars of the local sculling teams dip into the splintered surface; the potential is unlimited and I hope very much that the young owners will eventually capitalise, but on our visit the food was indifferent and the rooms too shabby and bare for even an S recommendation.

Moving on to the more upmarket range across the river on the north bank, we considered La Reine Blanche and Le Rivage and found that the advantages of the perfect site, so calm, so green, on the water's edge, so near Orléans, did not outweigh the arrogance of the management, so off-hand, nor the poor value of the rooms with compulsory *demi-pension* in season.

The conclusion is to make hastily for the one good deed in this wicked world, at St-Hilaire-St-Mesmin (see p. 138), but not before making a visit to the Floral Park of La Source, which puts Olivet on the *French Entrée* map.

74 acres of the park are dedicated to a spectacular flower display, which changes throughout the seasons; not even in winter does the colourful palette entirely lose its impact. The flower and tree species are well marked and any garden-lover would undoubtedly learn a lot throughout a pleasant tour here.

The infirm can take advantage of the little train that draws its load of passengers throughout the gardens and along the 'Miroir', a half-moon basin, and past the bubbling emergence of the source of the Loiret (it actually starts in St-Benoît and reappears in the park). Along the route can be spotted flamingos, cranes, emus and deer.

The park is open 1/4 to 11/11, from 9 a.m. to 6 p.m.; the rest of the year from 2–5 p.m.

Map 2H	**ONZAIN** (L.-et-Ch.) 16 km SW of Blois

41150
Ⓜ *Thurs.*

On the D 58.

The north bank of the Loire from Amboise to Blois is a good road, affording many views of the river and opportunities to get down to the water, via old gravelworks' ramps, but it is the main road and consequently very busy. The D 58 runs parallel, a couple of kilometres inland, and, sometimes, if the *camion* fumes outweigh the river views, it's not a bad idea to use this slower but calmer alternative. Onzain is a sizeable village, useful for picnic stocking-up.

Château des Tertres
(H)M
Rte de Monteaux
54.79.83.88

1½ kilometres west of the village on the D 58 you will come across the sign to this old grey *gentilhommière*, covered with Virginia creeper. It's set high in its own grounds, a very peaceful base for an assay on Blois.

The 14 rooms are pleasant, unsophisticated and cost a reasonable 210-320f. No restaurant, but the very friendly receptionist has lots of local eating ideas.

'When you cover this area of the Loire, this should feature at the top. Family run with no restaurant, beautiful setting and totally unpretentious; at the same time a very comfortable room which looked over to the Château de Chaumont.' – Nicholas Kramer.

Domaine des Hauts de Loire
(HR)L
54.20.83.41
Closed 1/12–15/ 3
AE, CB, EC

This is an area where members of the Relais et Châteaux group would be ten-a-penny, if that were not so ridiculous a claim for these unrepentantly expensive bolt-holes. There are some, it has to be admitted, which undoubtedly cash in on the prosperity of the region and its clients, and its ease of access for Paris. There are some geared to easy transatlantic custom, telephoning from château to château to book the next soft bed for these pampered birds of passage. And there are some, like the Domaine des Hauts de Loire, which are so excellent in everything they set out to do, and that includes the *accueil*, that they set the standards for all other hotels, and I for one am not ashamed to say that if the cost were no object I would choose to stay there above all others.

Unfortunately cost usually is an object, and just to get this matter out of the way (so that those readers who habitually write to ask: 'Why do I go on so about the impossibly out-of-reach?' can skip the rest of this entry), the rooms here cost 500f to 1,000f, with breakfast a hefty 60f on top, six apartments are from 1,200f to 1,500f and the menu is 250f. So there. The rooms are not even particularly large or grand. Just very, very nice.

Neither is the building outstandingly de luxe – it was the old hunting lodge of the comte de Rostaing, enlarged into what we might call a manor; it is creeper-hung, white-shuttered, grey-slated, with a small tower on one corner; white chairs and tables are set out on the lawn by the huge lake pullulating with fish, and the 30 surrounding hectares ensure that whatever stress the guests had to cope with in order to afford to stay here will soon be dissipated.

The food in the pleasant beamed dining-room is like the rest of the set-up – restrained good taste. Chef Gérard Hummel learned his craft from Girardet, and learned at the same time not to gild the lily. Try his roulade of salmon with dill, red mullet simply grilled with herbs, lamb fillet with thyme.

If you can afford the best, you'll like the Domaine.

Pont d'Ouchet
(HR)S–M
50 Grande Rue
54.20.70.33
Closed Sun.
p.m.; Mon.; 1/
12–1/3

A simple but good little hotel in the village centre. The big plus is the welcome by patrons Louisette and Antonin Cochet, but the 10 rooms are fine and cheap – 85–120f, and the food way above hotel average. Go for the 68f menu. Half-board obligatory in season.

Auberge de
Beau Rivage
(HR)S
Escures
54.20.70.39
Closed Sun.
p.m.; Mon.; 15/
9–1/4

On the N 152.

I missed this one but, having read the following comment, will certainly check it out for the next edition:

'I would certainly recommend the Beau Rivage. It has a saucepan in the Logis guide and was the best presented meal we had, with an unusually wide selection of vegetables served separately.' – Pat Nappin.

Auberge de la
Croix Blanche
(R)S
54.70.25.28

At Veuves, some 4 kilometres away, on the north bank. Highly recommended by the Château des Tertres as being small, pretty, cheap and good.

Map 1J

ORLÉANS (Loiret) 130 km S of Paris; 112 km NE of Tours; 138 km E of Le Mans

---

45000

Ⓜ *Every day*

Joan of Arc's city. Reminders of the Maid of Orléans everywhere. There are statues, triumphant in the cathedral, contemplative by the steps of the Hôtel de Ville (as well she might be, blasted by bullets from the last war), mounted, in the place du Martroi (the Renaissance frieze is the best bit, illustrating events in her life) and determined on the quai du Fort des Tourelles on the south side of the Pont Georges V, where she was wounded by an arrow); there is the Maison Jeanne d'Arc, on the site where she lodged in 1429, there is the rue Jeanne d'Arc, lined with smart shops, there are ubiquitous restaurants, cafés, a bookshop, there is even a school, all dedicated to her name.

Joan has been good commercially to Orléans and Orléans is good to Joan, having continued to laud and honour her centuries after her death, where elsewhere she is forgotten. The Orléannais still celebrate every year, in great style, the feast of thanksgiving on 8 May, which Joan herself instituted in 1430, and nothing, not even the Revolution, has been allowed to interrupt that commemoration.

The city of Orléans, capital of the Loiret and of the administrative division of Centre Val de Loire, is far too big, too complex, too interesting a proposition for me to attempt to tackle here in detail. But, like its great rival, Tours, it is a city whose heart, once penetrated, can be covered on foot, however intimidating its *periphérique* and suburbs might strike the first-timer. So abandon the car, perhaps in the huge new underground car-park by the cathedral. My maxim in an unfamiliar city is always to follow signs to the cathedral, invariably in the oldest and most interesting sector, and start orientation from there. This works well in Orléans, where the approaches to Ste Croix are wide and open and location is easy. The vista towards the 'wedding cake' cathedral from the rue Jeanne d'Arc which fronts it is particularly inspiring and always provides a fresh shock of delight.

Ste Croix, approaching the size of Notre Dame, has had a long and hazardous career. Just consider that its foundation stone was laid in 1287 and that the nave and central spire were only completed in 1829 and it is not surprising that what we see today is a unique assembly of architectural and decorative fashion. Oddly enough the result is not inharmonious.

The apse is the oldest part – 13th and 14th centuries – the nave and transepts are four centuries younger, but still in the Gothic style, thanks to the enlightened instruction of Louis XIV, at a time when anything Gothic was generally despised.

During the Wars of Religion Orléans was a centre of concentrated violence and the original huge Romanesque tower and most of the nave was shattered by Huguenot explosives; the replacement towers and façade were added just before the Revolution.

Inside, look out for the rose windows in the transepts, sun-rays to honour the Sun King, Louis XIV, and the magnificent chandeliers which bizarrely owe their location to the Jacobins, who 'borrowed' them from Châteauneuf for the Feast of Nature and Reason. The 18th-century wood carving, particularly in the choir stalls, is among the most stunning it has ever been my good fortune to enjoy.

Around the corner, to the north of the cathedral, is the new arcaded **Musée des Beaux Arts**, housing a fine collection of paintings – Italian primitives, Tintoretto, Corregio, Van Goyen, a remarkable Velasquez St Thomas, and an evocative collection from Richelieu's château (see p. 125). Courbet, Boudin, Gauguin and Soutine represent the 19th and 20th centuries.

The **Hôtel Groslot**, a 16th-century red-brick mansion in the place de l'Étape, used to be the king's residence for Charles

IX, Henri III and Henri IV. François II died here, only three months after he had introduced his child-bride Mary, later Queen of Scots, to Orléans. It has been the town hall since 1790 and contains some fine Renaissance furniture and paintings and Joan memorabilia; her emotive statue is a bronze replica of a marble original by princesse Marie d'Orléans, daughter of King Louis-Philippe.

In the **Musée Historique** in the Hôtel Caby are statues from a pagan temple built in Gallo-Roman times near Orléans. Its most precious exhibit is a handsome stallion; its bronze was hand-beaten nearly 2,000 years ago.

There is a colourful little flower market in the place de la République, but for comestibles make for the **Nouvelles Halles**, off the rue Royale, a grand shopping avenue whose arcades were built in 1755 at the same time as the Pont Royal (George V now). The *halles* are a treasure trove of the freshest local produce from river and pasture, and a perfect antidote to a wet day. They are usefully open Sun. (but closed Mon.).

There are few hotels of any great character in Orléans, but the chains are well represented, with a Sofitel which overlooks the river at 44 quai Barentin (38.62.17.39) and which incorporates a good restaurant, La Vénerie.

Jackhôtel
(H)M–S
18 r. Cloître St-Aignan
38.54.48.48
Open every day
CB

This would be my choice for a small, central, unpretentious hotel, furnished with taste, and with the enormous bonus in a city, of a small garden. Just in front of the Church of St Aignan. 180–260f.

Terminus
(H)M
40 r. de la République
38.53.24.64
Closed 24/12–7/1
AE, CB, EC

Lacking the character of the Jackhôtel, but strong on mod cons, with a bath for every room, TV, video, double glazing against the city noise, recently refurbished and good value at 200–280f.

Les Cèdres
(H)M
17 r. du Mar. Foch
38.62.22.92
Open every day
AE, CB, DC

Practical modern hotel near the centre, in a quiet road. Nice interior garden. 34 rooms from 150f to 320f.

> **La Crémaillère**
> (R)L
> *34 r. N.D.-de-*
> *Recouvrance*
> *38.53.49.17*
> *Closed Sun.*
> *p.m.; Mon.;*
> *Aug.*
> *AE, CB, DC*

Indisputably No. 1 in Orléans, with two Michelin stars and 18/20 in Gault-Millau in confirmation. The 190f menu is a bargain not to be missed by anyone interested in real food, real cooking.

Paul Huyart comes from Brittany, which may account for a certain down-to-earthiness that distinguishes between fad and worthy innovation, and is not averse, in his fifties, to accept the latter and marry it to his own tradition of butter and cream and prime ingredients. The result is dishes such as his langoustines, barely cooked, wrapped in filo pastry, with a subtle bitter-sweet sauce – an almost Chinese presentation of Breton basic ingredient; Breton crabs he serves with a 'confit' of onions – a thick almost-chutney, and sharpens the rich crabmeat with lime; Breton turbot he is content to present very simply, with a wonderfully fresh sauce of herbs and spinach.

Desserts include unlikely masterpieces such as a compôte of rhubarb (brave man – the French have a blind spot about serving rhubarb as a dessert) flavoured with wood strawberries, and a definitive orange salad like no other orange salad ever tasted.

An arrow for excellence. Think what you'd get for £19 in England!

La Poutrière
(R)L
8-10 r. de la
Brêche
38.66.02.30
Closed Sun.
p.m.; Mon.; 1/
3–7/3
AE, CB, DC, EC

An attractively chic/rustic restaurant in an old market-gardener's house south of the river, not far from the quai des Augustins. The dining-room extends onto a terrace, leading to a garden where meals are served in summer, and a swimming pool. Chef Marcel Thomas makes good use of fruit and vegetables and cooks traditionally. Menus: 130f (lunchtime midweek), 180f.

> **Les Antiquaires**
> (R)M
> *2–4 r. Au Lin*
> *38.53.52.35*
> *Closed Sun.;*
> *Mon.; Easter; 3*
> *weeks in Aug.;*
> *25/12–1/1*
> *AE, CB, DC*

As the name implies, the furniture is antique, the décor rich and elegant, in this old restaurant near the Pont George V. Classic cooking, with imaginative flair from chef Michel Pipet: veal kidneys with horseradish, fillets of red mullet and brill cooked with saffron, and worth-leaving-room-for *pâtisserie* such as a pineapple gâteau or a confection of chocolate and bitter cherries appear on menus from 100f (weekdays only) and 160f. Good value to have this quality at these prices, and arrowed accordingly.

Le Lautrec
(R)M
Pl. du Châtelet
38.54.09.54
Closed Sun.
AE, CB, DC, EC

A little restaurant near the covered markets, specialising in dishes from the local region and the Tarn, whence hails Bruno Boulais, chef. You can eat on the terrace if you wish. Pink trout is cooked with prunes, hare with celery, and the local Tarte Tatin is given a new twist – it becomes Tarte Sologne, with pears included.

The good-value 110f menu should please most, otherwise it's 240f.

Chez Jean
(R)S–M
64 r. Ste-
Catherine
38.53.40.87
Closed Sun.
except fêtes
AE, DC, EC, V

Good budget-eating, on menus at 64f, with cheap carafe wine. Usefully near the cathedral.

Even cheaper ideas: **Le Bannier**, 13 faubourg Bannier (huge helpings); **L'Estouffade**, 5 rue de la Cerche (quick but good); **Le Khédive**, rue des Carmes (very French, lively café, *tabac, brasserie*); **Les Mouettes Blanches**, 2 quai de la Madeleine (brochettes, good value); **La Vieille Auberge**, 2 faubourg St Vincent (quick service, modest prices).

SHOPPING
Orléans has a particularly fine range of food shops:
Cheeses: **Lavarenne**, Halles Châtelet, wonderful choice from all over France, but particularly local cheeses.
Bread: **Plisson**, rue Bannier – not only the superb *baguette* but bread flavoured with onion, nuts, etc.
Pastries: **Morin**, 209 rue de Bourgogne – irresistible cakes, ices and home-made chocs.
Confectioners: **Chocolaterie Royale**, 53 rue Royale – the best in town, long established. Try cotignacs orléanais or quince paste. **Thouvény**, 8 rue des Carmes, has superb chocolates too.
Charcuterie: **André Lenormand**, 318 faubourg Bannier – a 'Meilleur Ouvrier de France' (an award given to the best worker in his category of food). Terrines and pâtés for picnics and bring-homes.

Map 3H　　　　**OUCHAMPS** (L.-et-Ch.) 16 km S of Blois

41120
Les Montils

Turn off the D 764 onto the D 7 to arrive at the village of Ouchamps. Le Relais is well indicated from there.

Le Relais des Landes
(HR)L–M
54.44.03.33
Rest. closed
Wed.; dinner
only except
Sun.
Hotel closed 2/
11–27/3
AE, CB, DC, EC

Relais de Silence, Logis de France, Château Indépendant – you name it – will appeal to some more than others. I describe it here because I know a great number of readers follow trustingly these chains, and they can then make up their own minds if the Relais is for them.

It is certainly all that those three organisations presume: certainly quiet, set down a lane in the flat Sologne countryside, certainly clean and well run, and certainly of interesting character. It's hard to describe – I would say an ugly pile of a building of uncertain age, but the brochure describes it as a *gentilhommière* of the 17th century. The rooms are spacious, comfortable and well equipped, with flowery wallpaper and fake beams, but it's expensive with the considerable asking price of 520f. I didn't care much for the modern leather furniture in the lounge either. However, it's obviously very popular and was fully booked in October. Menus start at 180f.

Map 3C	**LES PONTS-DE-CÉ** (M.-et-L.) 5 km S of Angers

49130
(M) *Fri.*

On the south bank of the Loire, which splits into three here, the southernmost stream becoming the Louet. The bridge in this little town, almost a suburb of Angers, crosses all three channels.

Le Bosquet
(H)S (R)M
41.57.72.42
2 r. Maurice
Berné
Closed Sun.
p.m.; Mon.; 20/
8–6/9

A simple modern building, agreeably situated on the water's edge, which would make a good inexpensive stop for those not wishing to get embroiled in the Angers traffic. Children are welcomed here by swings in the garden.

The rooms are unexceptional good-value at 105–150f, but the cooking would make a visit here a particularly attractive proposition, even for those staying elsewhere. Proprietor Michel Adams uses regional seasonal ingredients and presents them without undue fuss. His fish terrine with baby spring vegetables and his matelote of eel are worth homing in on. Menus from 78f, others are 115f and 190f.

More reports welcome for this potential arrow.

Map 3C	**PORT BOULET** (I.-et-L.) 5 km S of Bourgueil, 16 km N of Chinon

37140

The countryside around is dull but ideal for château-bashing, and remarkably quiet.

➤ **Château les**
Réaux
(C)L
47.95.14.40
Open all year

Cross the bridge over the untroubled water that surrounds the red-brick, white-stone, chequered château and you are light years away from the route nationale stress; the odd train does occasionally rumble somewhere near in the other world beyond the chestnut trees and the birds and the little family chapel.

The Renaissance château has been in the family of Florence Goupil de Bouille for well over a century. She has taken over from her grandmother and personally and physically renovated all the 10 bedrooms in different styles, so that now, in pleasant contrast to the imposing severity of the château, they are light and bright and cheerful, with pastel chintzes and stripes.

The dining-room has a wonderful, recently rediscovered, painted ceiling and glittering chandelier but it is not at all grand and conversation-impeding. Neither is the rest of the house – distinctly *familiale*, with all the warmth that that implies. The young staff smile. Florence has been hostessing for 10 years now and if not strictly a pro, she is far from amateur. She doesn't have to do the cooking herself, so unlike some private châteaux-bases you don't have to feel guilty that your hostess is working so hard and offer to carry out the dishes.

I would heartily recommend a stay under her hospitable roof for those who would like to sample life in the grand style, with a chance to dine among interesting fellow guests of all nationalities. You don't have to eat in (table d'hôte, 175f, includes four dishes and lots of home-grown veg. and salads) but you'll be missing a fascinating experience if you don't).

Rooms cost 400–800f, all with private bathrooms.
Arrowed for comfort and style.

Le Château des Réaux

Map 4E   **RICHELIEU** (I.-et-L.) 19 km SE of Chinon

37120
(M) 1st, 3rd
Mon. of each
month

An enchanting little town. La Fontaine called it the finest village in the universe and I can see why. Worth considering is the journey from Chinon by steam train, which puffs away every weekend from 25/5 to 15/9, stopping at Champigny-sur-Veude, Coutureau and Ligré Rivière. Further information from 47.58.36.29 on days of trips only.

Cardinal Richelieu's dream, the town was conceived in 1621 as an accessory to the extravagant palace and park he built there and filled with great works of art. The approach, via pedimented gatehouses, the Grande Rue, is still lined exclusively with dignified Louis-XIII-style houses, in white tufa stone. They lead through two wide squares to the gates of the park. The demolition of the palace is a great loss but the vast undertaking of one man has bequeathed us a unique fly-in-amber example of early town-planning, and at least no château means fewer tourists. The vast park remains, criss-crossed with canals and avenues of planes and chestnuts. Just inside the gate, past the dry moat, a statue of the cardinal welcomes his guests.

Back in the town, in the place du Marché is a fine 17-century market hall, with magnificent beamed roof, currently being restored. A new garden square was being planted out when I last visited, and very attractive it's all going to be.

Hôtel Le Puits Doré
(HR)S
Pl. du Marché
47.58.10.59

In 1987 a nice young couple took over the old run-down hotel and are gradually doing it up. Don't, therefore, be put off by the scruffy exterior. Proceed through vociferous bar to the lace-curtained dining-room, and, I guarantee, at lunchtime, you will find it full of sensible locals tucking into the 48f menu. Incredible value, especially when compared with the prices not many kilometres away in better-known towns.

It is sensible to stick to this bargain, because, when a young patron/chef, whose ambitions perhaps outweigh his experience, attempts something more demanding he tends to come unstuck. One of us was very happy with crudités, sweetbreads meunière (imagine – for 48f) and cheese; the other sampled the next price up at 70f, and was delighted with the tarte de légumes – perfect rich flaky pastry, satisfying savoury leek and bacon filling – but felt let-down with the more testing 'filet de bar, sauce dieppoise'. The lovely bass was overcooked to shreds and the sauce, which in its floury depths revealed but three tiny mussels, was hardly dieppois.

That said, at 110f the value seemed to return, with fresh duck foie gras for starters *and* half a lobster, followed by sole/scallops and duck crisped in honey. Sounds great. Perhaps the bass was a solitary error, and someone should tell me so.

The bedrooms have been refurbished in plush carpet-up-the wall style, but are really very comfortable indeed, and so cheap, at 120f for a double with bath.

Recommended for food and comfort at a remarkably low price in an under-appreciated and very attractive town.

Le Bourg
(C)M
Marie-Josèphe
Le Plâtre
1 r. Jarry
47.95.31.24 and
47.58.10.48
Closed 1/10–15/
4

Just off the main square, Mme Leplâtre's house, with brass sign outside for her doctor/vet husband, is white, elegant, very French, and approached through a quiet courtyard. She has two comfortable bedrooms with en suite bathrooms for 180f.

Château de la Vrillaye
(C)M
47.95.32.25

From all the recommendations I receive, there was one in the Loire Valley area that stood out as being particularly attractive, and not-to-be-missed on any account. Particularly frustrating it was therefore that problems arose on the day I had set aside for a visit to the Château de la Vrillaye, and so I have no personal experience to pass on. However, Mrs Hume's letter is so comprehensive that no doubt other readers will feel as encouraged as I was to try out her proposal.

'This château is owned by an Englishman, John Hadman, which for people like myself with little French is a great relief! He gives visitors a warm welcome and provides excellent meals (not English) – five courses for 130f, using produce from the home farm. Local wine is about 22f per bottle.

*'My husband and I spent three nights here and plan to return for a
longer period with time to enjoy the surrounding countryside and
relax in this beautiful, well-furnished and comfortable environment.*

*'The bedrooms are large-to-enormous, some en suite, from 350f to
650f per night B and B.'* – Angela Hume.

There are three other *chambres d'hôte* in the vicinity which were
personally recommended to me as being especially comfortable. I
did not, alas, have time to check them myself, so any first-hand
reports would be particularly welcome. They are:
Mme Picard, Le Bois Goulu. At Pouant, which is 5 km west of
Richelieu on the D 61; 49.22.52.05. Three rooms, sharing bathroom.
120f for two, 150f for three.
Château de la Roche du Maine. At Prinçay, which is 10 km south-west
of Richelieu on the D 46; 49.22.84.09. Four rooms with bathrooms,
swimming pool. 250f for two.
Château de la Grillère. At Faye-la-Vineuse, 6 km south of Richelieu on
the D 757; 47.95.66.06. 17th-century château; three rooms furnished
with antiques and four posters, private bathrooms. Price
undisclosed.

Map 3G	**RILLY-SUR-LOIRE** (L.-et-Ch.) 13 km NE of Amboise, 21 km SW of Blois, 17 km N of Montrichard

41150
Onzain

On the south bank of the Loire.

**Château de la
Haute Borde**
(HR)M
*54.20.98.09
Closed Sun.
p.m.; Mon.; 15/
11–1/4*

I found the rooms and welcome of this once-imposing manor house
disappointing, but just look at the location and distances from prime
Loire attractions and consider the price – 188–225f for a double room
– and shortcomings can be accepted. Another asset is the large
grassy garden, sloping down to the river.

I am told that the food, served in the rather grim dining-room, is
good too, at 65f upwards, so it's horses for courses, and the Château
de la Haute Borde gets a qualified recommendation.

Map 4E	**LA ROCHE-CLERMAULT** (I.-et-L.) 5 km S of Chinon

37500
Chinon

Signposted off the D 759 to Loudon and the D 751. Follow the single
track lane, bumping higher and higher above the valley of the
Vienne.

Le Haut Clos
(HR)S–M
*47.95.94.50
Closed Sun.
p.m.; Mon.
o.o.s.; 15/12–7/
1
EC, DC*

A lovely position, so close to the tourist belt and yet so high above it,
in quiet countryside.

The main hotel has a nice rustic dining-room and simple flowery-
papered bedrooms, with showers, for 99–150f. The annexe has the
more expensive rooms with baths, for 220f, but if you don't mind a
shower, go for the cheaper ones – much prettier. Menus from 65f to
170f.

Map 3F	**ROCHECORBON** (I.-et-L.) 3 km E of Tours

37210
Vouvray

Take the N 152 out of Tours.

Les Fontaines
(H)S–M
6 quai Loire
47.52.52.86
Open all year
AE, DC, EC, V

The description in the brochure of Les Fontaines as a *Manoir Napoléon III sur bord de la Loire* is a little misleading. The road east following the north bank of the Loire (the N 152) very soon escapes the suburbs of Tours and becomes surprisingly rural, but it does pass between the hotel and the river, which is hard to spot from the hotel grounds; first and very fleeting impressions of a turreted manor house soon give way to the recognition that this is a very agreeable but simple Logis de France, where a double room will cost not more than 280f with bath, or as little as 170f with shower.

None the worse for that; in fact all the better, since grand establishments are ten-a-penny in the Loire and good simple family hotels thin on the ground. These rooms are very comfortable and unplasticised, the outlook is on to a green *parc* and the management is very friendly and efficient. No restaurant but no hardship, with all the restaurants of Tours to try out in one direction and several others personally recommended by Mme Lafaye within walking distance.

L'Oubliette
(R)M
34 rue des
Clouets
47.52.50.49
Closed Sun.
p.m.; Mon.;
Jan.; 12/11–30/
11
CB, EC

Turn away from the Loire into the village of Rochecorbon to find this curiosity – an upmarket troglodyte restaurant. There is no indication from the cottagey exterior that, once past the reception area, you will be dining in a cave. A very elegant cave, well lit, with whitewashed stone walls and flowers on the tables, small, cosy, lots of atmosphere. A far cry from the origin of the name – an *oubliette* was a dark hole where prisoners were left and forgotten.

Patron Thierry Duhamel was apprenticed to the great Barrier in Tours, so he knows a thing or two about cooking. I commend his 95f weekday menu, and his short and to-the-point carte for dishes such as an escalope of foie gras, sharpened with honey vinegar, or pigeon with caramelised shallots.

The caves also provide ideal cellarage and a wonderful range of Vouvray wines.

Map 3B	**ROCHEFORT-SUR-LOIRE** (M.-et-L.) 20 km SW of Angers

49190
Ⓜ *Wed.*

Not really on the Loire at all but on a small side-stream, the Louet. From here westwards to Chalonnes the road is known as the Corniche Angevine, well worth an excursion along a stretch so totally different from most of the Loire Valley, all hairpin bends with spectacular views of the river far below, vineyards as far as the eye can see in all directions. The local Quart de Chaume is highly alcoholic, quite individual and very delicious, improving with age, up to about 20 years.

There are ruins here of a castle with turrets and watchtowers, a reminder of the vigilance necessary for previous inhabitants.

Le Grand Hôtel
(HR)S
Rue Gasmier
41.78.70.06
Closed Sun.
p.m.; Mon.
o.o.s.; 15/1–15/
2

A misnomer if ever there were one, since this little Logis on the main road is more faded and dusty than grand, but it's a very popular stop for those who like their hotels and patrons French-style. The house postcard says it all: *'huit chambres d'amis dans une demeure de tradition'*. The rooms cost 140–160f, the cooking is good, on menus from 68f.

'Visited three times. Young M. and Mme Allaire were very welcoming. Food excellent. Eight bedrooms, all lino-floored.' – Sue Biggart.

M. Allaire will arrange a very good wine tour of the region for 'next-to-nothing'.

Map 3C   **ROCHEMENIER** (M.-et-L.) 8 km N of Doué-la-Fontaine

On the D 69.

LE VILLAGE TROGLODYTIQUE

A visit to the most interesting of the troglodyte villages is an experience well worth seeking, particularly if you go, as I did, on a broiling summer's day, when the caves provided a welcome coolth and the sun filtering down through the periodic skylights was as dramatically strong as a spotlight.

The tour around the two farm dwellings and twenty rooms that make up the exhibition is unusually well set-out, with sensible explanations on each wall of the life and activities that went on there, sometimes not so very long ago.

It struck me how well-off the cave-dwellers were. Having scooped out their cave from the soft tufa stone, they sold the excavated material and moved into their new des. res., air-conditioned and well insulated. As every addition to the family necessitated more space, so another three-sided bedroom was added on to the living area.

All possible activities, holy and secular, were catered for. The beasts had their quarters, the winemaking and storage took place in ideal conditions, the chapel, in the shape of the cross, was large and lofty enough to accommodate all comers, but most of all I admired their community centre – a hall for meetings, eating, drinking, story-telling, dancing. Modern high-rise dwellers might well envy them their lifestyle.

Map 3I   **ROMORANTIN-LANTHENAY** (L.-et-Ch.) 68 km S of Orleans; 41 km SE of Blois

41200
(M) *Wed.,*
Fri., Sat.

Capital of the Sologne, that gentle, flat, wooded area dotted with lakes, south of Orléans in the bulge of the Loire, that used to be wasteland, Romorantin is an agreeable town from which to explore the river in either direction.

It sits astride the river Sauldre, with lots of flowers on its banks, around the old creeper-covered mill on the island, and in its particularly attractive public gardens flanking the river. No restaurant takes advantage of the view, alas – the Post Office has the prime site – but a picnic in the gardens would be a very pleasant substitute.

If you are lucky enough to be there on a Wednesday, an added attraction is the thriving market, both in the streets and in the covered market halls, where local stalls brim over with produce from field, lake and forest. Look for the more unusual offerings – the herbs that will appear later on the Lion d'Or's tables, the quails' eggs, the wild mushrooms, the game, the freshwater fish.

In the centre of the main street stands a very well-known hostelry:

➤ **Grand Hôtel Lion d'Or**
(HR)L
69 rue Clémenceau
54.76.00.28
Closed Jan.– mid Feb.
AE, DC, EC, V

Relais et Châteaux, but only rated three star for some unfathomable reason, so the taxes and prices are lower than most in this prestigious chain. 400f buys a highly luxurious room and a bathroom en suite, or an appartment will cost 550f.

The reception rooms and dining-room are gorgeous and there is a welcome green and calm interior courtyard, unsuspected in the middle of the town, where a drink or breakfast, or just a moment of repose on that expensive gardenware would surely induce a sense of well-being.

The food more than matches the quality of the hotel. Two Michelin stars, 18/20 in Gault-Millau, reflect a chef of rare talent. Didier Clément is the son-in-law of the owners, Colette and Alain Barrat, who over the past 10 years have restored this ancient Relais de Poste into the most comfortable, nay luxurious, hotel in the region. Their daughter, Marie-Christine, studied mediaeval cookery at university, and has inspired her husband to experiment with some of the herbs and spices used in those days, many of which have fallen out of modern culinary repertoires. The result of this marital harmony is nothing short of miraculous. Didier never allows the flavourings to dominate the other ingredients, only to enhance them. Give him some perfect langoustines and he will do the impossible – improve on nature. His 'Langoustines rôties aux épices douces' are pure sorcery. And he uses another of Marie-Christine's research discoveries in a dish called 'Noisettes d'agneau de pré-salé "au tabac de cuisine" ', the 17th-century name given to dried mushrooms reduced to a powder (and it tastes infinitely better than it sounds).

The meal continues as it starts – with superb ingredients cooked with imagination and flair. A soufflé of prunes, served with a cream flavoured with tea, baby waffles stuffed with fraises du bois, and a definitive cheeseboard, with some cheeses found but rarely elsewhere.

Genius doesn't come cheap. There is a mid-week menu at 240f, but otherwise the cheapest is 390f. And *demi-pension* is obligatory in high season, so this will not be a cheap stop. But what a memorable one!

Arrowed for a comfortable hotel and probably the best food in the book.

Le Lanthenay
(HR)M
Pl. Église,
Lanthenay
54.76.09.19
Closed Mon.;
Sun. p.m.; 22/
9–30/9; 15/2–
15/3
EC, V
Parking

Lanthenay got its name tagged on to Romorantin only recently; in fact it is a separate community, 2.5 kilometres north of Romorantin. Turn left off the D 922 towards the church to find this little Logis, built 10 years ago, with bright and cheerful rooms. Some of them are suitable for the disabled, being on the ground floor, with French windows.

It's a good place to stay for those who rank peace and quiet high on their list of requirements, and not expensive, at 110–190f. Add to this the bonus of a good restaurant, meriting a red R in Michelin, and it begins to look like a potential arrow, lacking only confirmation. Menus 79–146f.

Hôtel d'Orléans
(HR)M
2 pl. Gén. de
Gaulle
54.76.01.65
Closed 8/12–22/
12
EC, V

For those who cannot afford the Lion d'Or's prices, the Orléans, at 110–220f for a double room, offers alternative town accommodation. The rooms are adequate, but ask for one *au calme* away from the main road. The restaurant is way above hotel average, with good cooking on menus starting at 75f.

Le Colombier
(HR)M
10 pl. Vieux-
Marché
54.76.12.76
Closed Mon.
except fêtes;
15/9–23/9; 10/
1–11/2
AE, DC, EC, V
Parking

A pretty little restaurant (just 15 covers), with a terrace and a nice garden, and 10 rooms which I failed to see, since they were all occupied. They cost 196–210f and reports would be most welcome.

The food is interesting, substantial, and very well cooked by patron Maurice Dupuy, with traditional dishes featuring strongly – pigs' trotters, beef with its marrow – and a bouillabaisse that the Mediterranean would be proud of. The 72f (not weekends) menu is a bargain, but the next price up, at 145f, is also good value.

Les Vénitiens
(R)S
5 r. des Poulies
54.96.02.05
Closed Mon.;
Tues. lunch

I don't often include restaurants whose cuisine derives from any other country than France, because I feel that (a) Brits go to France to eat French, and (b) ethnic restaurants back home are usually better than in France, where they are handicapped by the prevailing chauvinism. However, because it was obviously the most popular place in town when I visited Romorantin, and because it was the only cheap eatery I feel I can suggest, here is an exception.

Family-run, like all the best Italian places, with M. Terrana as chef, this little back-street trattoria offers pasta and standard Italian dishes at the kind of prices that families can afford.

Map 3D

LES ROSIERS (M.-et-L.) 24 km SW of Angers; 14 km NW of Saumur

---

49350
(M) *Mon*

A busy little town on the north bank of the Loire, focussed on a square with some good food shops, especially the *poissonerie*, where, even if you have not occasion to buy, you can bone up on the different varieties of river fish to be found on local menus. Then you can take a drink at a table in the square, watching *le monde* go by.

Auberge
Jeanne de
Laval and
Résidence Ducs
d'Anjou
(H)M (R)L
54 r. Nationale
41.51.80.17
Closed Mon.
except fêtes;
10/1–15/2
AE, CB, DC

Named after Good King René's second wife, whose statue graces the square outside this classy *auberge*, set back in its leafy garden, where you can eat in summer. If you like to dine extremely well and fall into a comfortable bed at prices that are not astronomically high, you could hardly do better than here.

I met a couple who, having toured the whole Loire area for many years had no doubt that this was their favourite hotel, and I can see why.

It's been the family home of the Augereau family, who still run the place, for many years. All the rooms have been recently redecorated and whether yours opens out onto the flowery garden of the Auberge or onto the banks of the Loire from the Résidence, you will find every comfort included in the price of 260–450f; extra praise for the fine breakfasts.

The restaurant is a lovely room – all light wood and pastel colours, looking out onto the garden. Michel Augereau cooks divinely – using local ingredients wherever possible – without undue fuss. His is the definitive beurre blanc, served with zander, pike, and salmon, caught in the river down the road. Or you can have more modest fish in a perfect friture. Other classic dishes such as braised sweetbreads or 'col vert' (green-collared duck) roast *à l'ancienne* are equally commendable. As is the best tarte aux pommes in the Loire. Not cheap, alas; lunch weekdays have a menu for 170f, otherwise it's a hefty 300–350f.

Arrowed for comfort, welcome, superb food, in a good position.

Val de Loire
(HR)S–M
Pl. Église
41.51.80.30
Closed Mon.
o.o.s.; Sun.
p.m.; Feb.

Overlooking the square, an old-fashioned hotel and restaurant, whose food occasioned praise from every local I asked. So don't be put off by grim-ish entrance. Simple rooms are 135–170f. Menus from 50f to 140f.

La Toque
Blanche
(R)M
41.51.80.75
Closed Sun.
p.m.; Tues.
p.m.; Wed.; 23/
8–9/9

A useful restaurant 500 metres westwards on the main road (the D 952), whose good cooking on the 58f menu has earned the coveted red Michelin R. Nothing chi-chi – just good French value. Reports needed please.

Map 3C   **SACHÉ** (I.-et-L.) 8 km E of Azay

37190
Azay-le-Rideau

Follow the north bank of the Indre, the D 84, for a delightful green ride past orchards and watermills, to cross the bridge to the village of Saché.

The **Château de Saché** was the home of dear friends of Balzac, and became more truly home to him than his birthplace in Tours. He spent many happy hours here and worked on some of his most famous masterpieces; it is now a delightful museum, regrettably bypassed by most tourists, where the spirit of the author lives on, prompted by the sight of his simple belongings and manuscripts, proofs and first editions. One of the more interesting literary shrines in France and all the better for the tour being unguided, so that you can spend as little or as much time on any aspect as you please.

Auberge du XIIe Siècle
(R)M–L
47.26.86.58
Closed Tues.;
Feb.
AE, CB, DC

As the name suggests, an ancient beamed house, approached by steep steps from the village street. Inside a choice of ambiences – I would suggest one for winter, one for summer. In bleak weather the original small dining-room, all dark wood, copper log fire, flowers, is intimate and cheering; when the sun shines, what a clever alternative is the new addition – an adaptation of an old barn, attached via the kitchens, with plaster between beams replaced by glass to let in light and air and a view of the pretty rear garden. All is brightness and quite delightful, furnished with the same elegance as the original and famous restaurant.

Jean-L. Niqueux's cooking is among the best in the whole area, and the 150f menu is a bargain. From it you might eat dishes that appear simple on the menu – a soft boiled egg with wild mushrooms for example – but in fact require perfect judgement to present them attractively and deliciously. Fish is good – I ate some wonderful monkfish served with spinach, but on this particular evening after a week of gastro-excesses, Husband was longing for a plain steak. He got just that – but of such flavour and cooked so exactly à point that he was more than happy to forgo the more recherché dishes.

Leave room for superb desserts.

Arrowed for exceptionally good cooking in pleasant surroundings, at a good price.

▶ **La Sablonnière**
(C)M
47.26.86.96

Cross over the bridge and turn towards Azay to find this *chambre d'hôte*. I drove smartly past, paused for thought over what I had glimpsed, reversed and drove smartly back. How right I was. La Sablonnière is a modern house, carefully built in local style, so that its stone walls blend with those of its neighbours. What caught my eye was the sizeable conservatory, in which Mme Balitran and friend were sitting having coffee. This proved to be en suite with a *very* comfortable bedroom indeed, with its own highly luxurious bathroom. Beyond it is another, smaller bedroom, suitable for two children perhaps.

This makes a self-contained suite, with its own entrance. The spacious glassed-in terrace is a delightful place to sit for breakfast, or indeed at any other time, with comfortable lounge chairs and tables.

Mme Balitran is a renowned cook and although she does not wish to take on evening meals at this stage (no shortage of restaurants of all categories in nearby Azay or Saché), I am told her breakfasts, included in the price of 260f for two are exceptional. A good find this one, and arrowed accordingly.

Map 3H	**ST-AIGNAN-SUR-CHER** (L.-et-Ch.) 39 km S of Blois; 61 km E of Tours

41110

A delightful little town on the river Cher, with lots of character, tumbling down via cobbled streets to the river. Pleasant walks along the banks, good picnicking, and a little beach, which alone would merit the trip.

The church of St Aignan dates from the 11th and 12th centuries, with a Romanesque porch and crypt. Opposite is a wide flight of steps leading up to the 16th-century castle, which is inhabited and unvisitable. You can stroll round the courtyard though and take in the views down to the river.

Grand Hôtel St Aignan
(HR)M–S
7 quai Jean-Jacques Delorme
Closed Sun. p.m.; Mon. o.o.s.; 15/12–1/2

A nice old-fashioned French hotel overlooking the river. Full marks to the management, in the afternoon of a May *fête* day, when the last red-faced lunchers were threading their unsteady way to the car-park, for agreeing to let me see the rooms.

They vary enormously, as reflected in the price range – those at 75f obviously being simple; at the top end, for 255f, very nice indeed.

The service in the large dining-room can be overstretched at busy times, but generally it's all good news. With menus from 65f. A good choice in this price bracket, and priced accordingly.

'Right beside the Cher and of plenty of character. It is privately owned, family-run, with M. Ragot as the chef, while his wife deals with reception, rooms, etc. The Ragot family have lived in St Aignan for years – the present owner's grandfather was Mayor, while the rue Ragot runs from the hotel into the town centre.

'St Aignan is a good base for exploring Cheverny, Chenonceaux, Chambord, Beauregard, Le Gué-Péan, and M. Ragot obviously knows the area well and is very anxious to advise on trips around.

'Our party of six stayed at the hotel for four nights in April and thoroughly enjoyed the old-fashioned "Frenchness" of it. The food we found excellent and reasonably priced.' – David Compton.

Le Relais de la Chasse
(R)M
8 av. Gambetta
54.75.01.89
Closed Wed.; 20/12–5/1; 28/6–12/7
CB

Another aspect to the town, on the hill leading down into it, opposite the sloping car-park. An old inn, with exposed beams much in evidence. High quality cooking, with lots of fresh river fish on menus from 42f (weekdays only) and 90f. Carte 150–200f.

Map 1K	**ST-BENOÎT-SUR-LOIRE** (Loiret) 10 km SE of Châteauneuf

45730

On the D 60.

I wonder what proportion of tourists hell-bent on ticking off the châteaux bother to divert to the little village of St-Benoît. If they do, they will find first a sign pointing importantly to 'Le Port', winding on to a wide stretch of river bank, a campsite, a periodical fun-fair and a seedy *plage*. The river here might once have needed a port to handle its commercial traffic, but no longer. The town too is a disappointment. But follow the next sign to 'La Basilique', down a plane-lined avenue, park in the quiet square, and in this unassuming setting, the ample reward will be one of the finest Romanesque churches in France.

The present crypt, chancel and transept were built between 1067 and 1108, and the nave at the end of the 12th century. The belfry-porch, with its delicately carved golden Nivernais stone, glowing in the evening light, is a particularly graphic example of mediaeval art. Spend a moment here discovering the bizarre animals, luxuriant foliage, scenes from the Bible, and the story of St-Benoît.

He was the founder of the Benedict order, died in the 6th century, and was buried in the monastery of Monte Cassino. The abbot of what was then the Abbaye de Fleury decided that the saint's relics would be the very thing to enhance his abbey's prestige and income and sent off a raiding party of monks 700 dangerous miles to Italy to accomplish an almost unimaginable coup – to rifle the sepulchre under the Monte Cassino monks' noses, steal the saint's bones, and then bring them back on horseback to Fleury. The game monks must have got carried away, for they added the relics of St Scolastica, Benoît's sister, to their loot (and later gave them to the monks of Le Mans, who had abetted them in their journey.)

The saint's remains apparently did the trick because the gifts and endowments began to flow in from wealthy pilgrims and the Abbey of St-Benoît embarked on its most glorious reign, becoming one of the most esteemed centres of learning in Christendom. One of its monks, Oswald, went on to become Bishop of Worcester, and founded the see of York.

That abbey was burnt down in 1026 and its successor, as we see it today, developed into the finest abbey church in all the Loire Valley. It continued to prosper (Louis VII borrowed money from the monks to finance his Second Crusade), but with the Revolution its wealth was annexed, and the monks dispersed. They returned in 1944 and now their Gregorian chant, sung during services which the public are allowed to follow, is world-renowned.

Hôtel Labrador
(H)S
38.35.74.83
Closed Sun.
o.o.s.; 1/1–15/2
EC
Parking

A comfortable, if modest, hotel, right opposite the porch of the abbey, where a peaceful night's rest is guaranteed. It has a *salon de thé* in an adjoining building, above which there are bedrooms at 220f; in the main building they range from 100f to 200f with bath.

Map 2H   **ST-DYÉ-SUR-LOIRE** (L.-et-Ch.) 14 km NE of Blois

41500
Mer

A disappointing stretch of the Loire, and a dull village on its south bank, sliced by the main road, the D 951.

➤ **Manoir Bel Air**
(HR)M
54.81.60.10
Closed 10/1–20/2
V
Parking

Ideally situated on a route nationale but set well back, backing onto the river. Most of the rooms have river views, as does the very pleasant dining-room.

It's spacious, extremely well run, well equipped, light, moderately priced, with helpful friendly manager. The pleasant bedrooms cost 180–330f, the menus start at 65f. With Chambord a few minutes' drive through the park, and Blois nearby, it would make an ideal base for touring the châteaux, and is arrowed accordingly.

Map 4F   **ST-ÉPAIN** (I.-et-L.) 16 km S of Azay; 30 km SW of Tours

37800
Ⓜ *2nd Wed.*
of each month

Follow the D 57 south of Azay, or turn west off the route nationale, south of Tours, onto the D 101 and D 21, to arrive in this deeply verdant valley, where Joan of Arc pitched her camp on the way to Chinon. At Eastertime the pastures were technicolour green, sprinkled lavishly with cowslips and primroses. Climb the bosky hillside past some imposing but roofless ruins. Fear not – this ancient crumbling château of the dukes of Choiseul is not the hotel. The orangerie, further up the hill, built in the last century, makes an altogether more manageable setting for a luxurious and utterly peaceful stop, just a short drive from the more famous châteaux of the Loire.

Hostellerie du Château de Montgoger
(HR)L
47.65.54.22
Open all year
All credit cards

Mme Christel Débat Cauvin is both patronne and chef, and operates skilfully and agreeably at both levels. She has learned her craft alongside some very top chefs indeed and serves with aplomb dishes such as clams in their own juice, flavoured with truffles, and steamed duck liver in a millefeuille, layered with spinach. Not exactly simple country fare but very well done, and accompanied with baby veg. from her own *potager*. The 160f menu gives a good selection of her range.

There are 10 hedonistic bedrooms at the moment, some with canopied beds, all with luxury bathrooms, with more planned soon, at 400–750f. *Demi-pension*, at 700–1,000f for two people, is obligatory in high season. It includes especially good breakfasts, served on the terrace in summer, with a birdsong good-morning.

The Hostellerie stays open throughout the winter, when log fires contribute to the feeling of well-being.

Map 3A   **ST-FLORENT-LE-VIEIL** (M.-et-L.) 42 km SW of Angers; 15 km E of Ancenis

49410
Ⓜ *Fri.*

On the south bank of the Loire.

This stretch of the south bank is remarkably rural and peaceful, dotted with pretty villages, and infinitely the preferred route when time is not of prime importance. You have only to cross the swinging bridge from Varades to see how the mood changes instantly, from built-up hassle to country slow-down.

St-Florent is a charming little town that would make a good base for an unsophisticated holiday. Climb up its narrow cobbled streets to the spur high above the river, where a wide tree-lined square fronts the imposing church. From the viewing point you can look way, way down on the river, divided here by the Île Batailleuse, on to the toy-like boats carrying oil from Nantes. Lots of good picnic spots here, either in the gardens by the church or down in the town by the river bank.

The important church comes as a surprise in this modest erstwhile fishing village. Rebuilt in the early 18th century, it is a handsome classical building, with octagonal tower and galleried porch. David of Angers carved the huge statue of Bonchamps, a hero of a Royalist insurrection after the execution of Louis XVI in 1793, which stands in the north transept. It was a thank-you to Bonchamps for sparing the life of David's father, a Republican taken prisoner by Bonchamps' men. *Grâce aux prisonniers* he inscribed beneath it.

Hostellerie de la Gabelle (HR)S
41.72.50.19
Closed Fri. p.m.; Sun. p.m. o.o.s.; 23/12–3/ 1; 13/2–23/2

A perfect site for this little Logis, right down by the river, with only a grey cobbled quayside, frequented by hopeful fishermen, between it and the water.

The rooms are small but wholesome, and good value at 150f with shower or bath. Four people can share, at 220f. Cooking is way above average, as the number of French-registration cars in the car-park on Sunday lunchtimes shows, with menus from 55f. Altogether good news, and a welcome find in this price bracket.

'It sits on a slab of concrete bordering the Loire by a rather unromantic bridge across part of the river. A lovely view if you look to the right rather than at the bridge, and an interesting area. The food is varied and appetising, but I found that the cheapest meal is not good value and there was an English invasion the last time I was there. However, I would stay there again, but for the fact that the prices of rooms appear to have rocketed.' – Hilary Neiland.

Map 4E

ST-GERMAIN-SUR-VIENNE (I.-et-L.) 2 km S of Candes-St-Martin; 13 km NW of Chinon

37500

The short stretch of the D 751 from Chinon, driving north-west, is the prettiest imaginable. The Vienne is a deep green fast-flowing river, very different from Old Man Loire, into which it flows a few kilometres further on. St-Germain is a hamlet on its grassy banks – an ancient church, a café, a few beflowered houses and the best picnicking spot for miles around, where you can park your car under a wide-spreading tree and sit watching the river zip by. Not much else zips anywhere and I have yet to see a fellow GB on this road.

L'Anguille Vagabonde
(R)S
Pl. de l'Église
47.95.96.48
Closed Thurs.
and Sun. p.m.

A simple bistro, quite rightly specialising in river fish, as its name might indicate. The locals drive out of a summer weekend to feast on a friture or fried eels.

The service (not over-smiling at any time) can get harassed at busy times, but just ignore this and appreciate the pleasant situation for a simple meal or a drink under a parasol at a table facing the river.

There are five rooms at 80–130f, which I was not allowed to see but would expect to be modest. However, they were all taken at a not very busy time of year, so maybe they've very good news. Any reports most welcome.

Map 1l — **ST-HILAIRE-ST-MESMIN** (Loiret) 7 km SW of Orléans

---

45580
St-Hilaire-St-
Mesmin

A pleasant residential suburb of Orléans, on the D 951 on the banks of the Loiret.

➤ **L'Escale du Port Arthur**
(HR)M–S
205 r. de
l'Église
38.76.30.36
Open all year
AE, DC, EC, V
Parking

A hideous modern concrete building on a perfect site, right on the river's edge (at least take a picnic to this particularly attractive grassy bank, if a longer stay is not on the cards). A wide terrace, for summer sipping and scoffing, makes the best of the view.

The 19 rooms have recently been completely renovated, and now offer very good value, at 120–230f, all with private bath or shower. Obviously bag one overlooking the river, if possible.

The interior rusticated dining-room (one of three) has a good log fire in winter and menus are 80–220f.

With friendly management, these prices, this position, an arrow is indicated.

Map 3C — **ST-MATHURIN-SUR-LOIRE** (M.-et-L.) 25 km E of Angers; 25 km NW of Saumur

---

49250
Beaufort-en-
Vallée
Ⓜ *Tues.*

On the north bank of the Loire.

There is a pleasant stretch of road between Angers and Saumur, flat, not too *camion*-bedevilled, and with good river views. Along it are several restaurants to choose from, but try:

La Promenade
(R)M
41.57.01.50
Closed Sun.
p.m.; Mon.
AE, EC, V

The décor may be garish but the vibes are right. A handwritten short menu is always a good sign, and so is a friendly greeting from the chef/patron. Both in evidence here, where M. Minschina cooks simple food simply. He does have his posher specialities too – salmon soufflé, gratin of langoustines, sweetbreads feuilléte – for which the bill would come to about 180f, but I would go for something like Loire zander with beurre blanc and pay about half that amount.

Mme Minschina and their daughters make up the family team. A good recipe altogther.

Map 3E	**ST-PATRICE** (I.-et-L.) 9 km SW of Langeais; 34 km SW of Tours

37130
Langeais

Turn north off the busy N 152, which follows the north bank of the Loire, and follow the signs to the Château.

> • **Château de Rochecotte**
> (HR)M-L
> *47.96.90.62*
> *Closed 15/1–15/3*
>
> hotel
>
> food

How, I wonder, would one set about furnishing an historic house – sorry château – from scratch, with the intention of turning it into a luxury hotel, but without unlimited resources? The options would seem to be: gradually assembling furniture of the period (18th century in this case) – perfect eventually but what of the meantime?; buying a job lot of repros, like most other hoteliers would do – boring, boring; or boldly furnishing with the best of contemporary schemes.

The Pasquier family chose the last course, and very successful, to my mind, has been the result. Pale and flowery chintzes at the tall windows, lots of peaches and cream, painted cane, neutral plain carpets, and the glorious plasterwork on the ceilings inventively accented in delicate apricot and palest green.

My bedroom had the minimum of furniture – a huge comfy bed, a transparent plastic desk (better than it sounds) and pink-painted chairs, relying on its beautiful proportions, white panelled walls and cheerful light chintz bedcover and curtains to give the feeling of luxury. The bathroom was likewise unfussy, brand new, spacious, dazzlingly white; its towels were many and snowy but not the deep, deep pile with which the top hotels spoil their guests; minimal freebies too.

This may all sound negative criticism, but not so. I can do without smart soaps and the loan of a bath robe if their loss is duly reflected in the price. The leap from three- to four-star rating comes costly; the Château's three stars mean that a beautiful room in a beautiful château in one of the most popular tourist areas in France costs as little as 270f.

It truly is a beautiful château. Talleyrand thought so – he bought it in 1828 for his beloved niece and mistress, La Duchesse de Dino, who lived there until her death 10 years later. It must be especially lovely in summer, when tables and chairs are set out on the wide terraces, the fountains coolly trickle and the long lime-shaded avenues are welcome retreats. In late October the carpets of wild cyclamen were so abundant that I could not resist picking a bunch for the toothglass in my room.

The dining-room is mightily impressive and a lot of originality and daring has gone into its décor. Four terracotta classical pillars are fitted with spotlights focussing on a giant palm. The entrance is via a library, all black, and a salon, all peachy. What courage, and they get away with it!

Service and reception is via three highly attractive, well-dressed girls. When all three Pasquier daughters graduated from hotel school three years ago, their parents decided to buy the château and run it as a co-ordinating family. So this is not like many other Loire private châteaux receiving guests, which are sometimes flagrantly amateur in everything but price.

In order to get established, the Pasquiers are keeping their charges

Château de Rochecotte.

to the level of many a more modest establishment. The cheapest room, spacious, comfortable, well equipped, with bathroom, costs 270f for two. The most expensive – the duchesse's own chamber – is 420f. A bargain if ever I saw one.

The food is proportionately expensive. The 140f menu looked boring – salad, chicken, cheese, pud. – so I was driven to eat à la carte. Salad with warm scallops was not bad – lots of scallops but not amazingly tasty; then a fillet of beef with wild mushrooms, of which I cannot speak too highly, and a trendy fruit gratin. Allow 250f for three courses.

All the family are charming. I consider the combination of efficiency, friendliness, superb location and delightful rooms makes the Château de Rochecotte one of the most agreeable places to stay along the length of the Loire.

Map 2C | **ST-SYLVAIN D'ANJOU** (M.-et-L.) 5 km NE of Angers

49480
(M) *Sun. a.m.*

Take the N 23 out of Angers.

**Auberge
d'Éventard**
(HR)M
Rte de Paris
41.43.74.25
Closed Sun.
p.m.; Mon.; 2/
1–25/1
AE, CB, DC

The new autoroute is bound to relieve the congestion on the route nationale and although this ancient coaching house is unlikely to regain its erstwhile rural tranquillity, it will undoubtedly end up being an even more agreeable place to eat and stay.

Even now it's pretty good news. Family-run, with the nephew of chef-patron M. M. Maussion an attentive and knowledgeable *maitre d'hôtel*. It's an elegant, rather formal set-up, with food to match. M. Maussion commendably keeps his menus short and sweet. The 'Menu Touristique' at 150f includes upmarket items such as six oysters or marinated salmon, followed by 'poisson du marché or noisettes of hare, then cheese, then good desserts; preceded as it is by amuses-bouche and followed by complimentary sweetmeats, it represents excellent value; the next prices are 220f for the 'Menu Gastronomique' and 275f for the 'Dégustation'. In summer there is service in the floodlit garden.

M. Maussion is a dedicated and passionately involved chef, ambitious for the future. I hear there are plans afoot to extend or move his establishment, and I for one would not be at all surprised to hear that Michelin had recognised his considerable talents with a star.

One apartment at 430f and nine rooms from 110f to 270f, all overlooking the garden, are furnished in smart/rustic style.

This combination would well suit anyone not wishing to get involved with the Angers conglomeration, but wanting to eat well and stay in comfort near the city.

La Fauvelaie
(HR)S
Rte du Parc-
Expo
41.43.80.10
Open every day

Just behind the Auberge d'Éventard is a huge building-site, desolately barren (late '88), but destined to be the site of an exhibition centre. All the more impressive, therefore, to find, just one road back, an oasis of greenness, in which is set La Fauvelaie. Its 3 hectares of grounds will protect it from the busyness that goes on all round.

It was once a farm and has been sympathetically converted into a simple little Logis de France. The dining-room, made cheerful with yellow cloths and fresh flowers, faces away from the road onto the garden, with wide French windows letting in the sunlight. Proprietor M. Juhel serves straightforward food on a 100f menu. The bedrooms are comfortable and good value at 110–160f.

There is a nice family atmosphere about the place, and it would make a good cheap base from which to explore Anjou.

Le Clafoutis
(R)M
41.43.84.71
Closed Sun.
p.m.; Wed.
p.m.; Thurs.;
Aug.
AE, EC, V

For cheaper, less formal eating on the outskirts of Angers, Le Clafoutis should provide a happy answer. Serge Lébert and his wife Violette opened this little restaurant three years ago and have already won much local praise for their high standards and reasonable prices.

Their 70f (weekdays only) menu is a bargain – feuilleté of smoked salmon, duck, super desserts. Well-chosen wine list with sensible prices. Other good menus at 105f and 130f. Carte say 180f.

Map 3L

ST-THIBAULT-SUR-LOIRE (Cher) 4.5 km E of Sancerre

18300
Sancerre

A delightful way to arrive at St-Thibault is to take the tree-lined road along the canal from Ménétréol, the D 9. It's a lovely drive at any time but particularly on a sunny autumn day when the vivid leaves are reflected in the still waters. Eminent picnicking country.

St-Thibault is a lively little village, with a bridge over the Loire. There is a stretch of slow-running river here between the islands, where it is safe to bathe – a very agreeable spot on a sultry day – and many of the villagers occupy themselves with providing aquatic activities. This is one of the few places where, with some advice on the unique local conditions from the *école nautique*, you can hire a sailing boat and attempt to master the currents that rip and swirl between the islands.

Altogether St-Thibault makes good use of its river site. Two restaurants profit particularly:

L'Étoile
(H)S (R)M
36.54.12.15
Closed Wed.;
15/11–1/3
Parking

A wonderful position, actually on the water's edge, long-established, very popular. This could all spell trouble in the form of cashing-in and giving poor value, but not so at L'Étoile. The standard remains high in service, décor (this is no scruffy tourist caff) and quality of food.

M. Boursin specialises in terrines, fish, charcoal grills; his cheapest weekday menu, at 74f, is a snip. Otherwise it's 107f upwards. Don't think of going at the weekend without a reservation.

The hotel is something else: situated across the road, in a funny, rambling, old-fashioned building, shabby and paint-peeling, it's hard to credit that it has any connection with the polished restaurant. But it certainly is under the same management. Although it appears vast, in fact only 11 rooms are in service. They are far from luxurious, but spacious and very cheap at 82f, up to 140f with bath.

The road between the hotel and the river is a very minor one, so for those who like to stay somewhere quiet, paying the minimum for bed, and eating well, L'Étoile might well be worth considering.

L'Auberge
(HR)M
37 r. Jacques-
Combes
48.54.13.79
Closed Tues.
o.o.s.

In a side street just off the main road and not far from the river is this modest little building, whose exterior looks more like a suburban villa than a restaurant/hotel. Inside is an unexpectedly pleasant rustic décor, and in fact the house dates from the early 17th century.

M. Cormeille cooks the kind of simple country food, such as trout in Sancerre and boeuf bourguignon, that is hard to pin down in a sophisticated area like the Loire Valley.His 78f menu is a good one and so is the 110f Sunday lunch, but you can pay as little as 52f (or 70f). In summer it is possible to eat, very agreeably, in the little garden.

'*Recommended cheap stop over. Food excellent, good value, full of locals. Rooms very basic with loo and shower down corridor.*' – Mary Birks.

Le St-Roch
(R)S
48.54.01.79 and
48.54.10.75
Dinner by
reservation
only.
Closed Mon.;
Tues.

Le St-Roch is not beside the water but actually on it. Two old barges, jauntily painted shiny red and black, are tied up a bit further along the river path from L'Étoile, and you cross the gangway to find a jolly, nautical-flavoured restaurant, with the river slapping its sides. It would be good choice for lunch on a fine day or perhaps to take a glass of Sancerre on a summer evening (it's a bar too).

Menus are from 79f but you can eat just a petit friture of river fish if you wish. Book at weekends.

Le Jardin
(R)S
7 r. des Ponts
48.54.12.28
Closed Wed.

Pretty green-and-white bistro, with rear garden for simple grills and snacks. Menu from 55f.

Map 3L   **SANCERRE** (Cher) 46 km NE of Bourges

18300
Ⓜ *Tues.;*
Sat.

It has to be admitted that, for the most part, the Loire Valley is flat and same-ish; you go there for the châteaux, not the landscape. Many of the mediaeval buildings perished in the 1940 and 1944 bombardments of strategic bridges. All the more delight, therefore, to come across a complete contradiction.

Sancerre stands proud on a hill, with a panoramic view far below of the countryside all round, encompassing not only the misty loops of the Loire, the curves of the viaduct of St-Satur, the hills of Burgundy, but also its own particular *paysage* – the vineyards. Sancerre owes its allegiance first to the grape, second to the river.

Because the wine of the area is of high quality, it is feasible for even a very small vineyard to be commercially viable, and so the hillsides in all directions are picturesquely patchworked with holdings of a mere acre or so.

Charming position, charming town, devilish parking. Rather than get embroiled in the Indian-file, twisting, ancient streets that lead up to the market square, where one delivery van can block the way indefinitely, better abandon vehicle near the ramparts and climb the last bit on foot. No hardship, since there is much to admire on the way. It's all so quiet and sleepy, flowery and venerable, essentially photogenic, all the way up to the square, where the Maison de Tourisme has had the sense to bury its modern functionalism beneath ground level. Here there are cafés and bars with tables outside, and arrowed walks to lead you round the town's backwaters and, most important since the way is tortuous, back again for a rest from those cobbles.

The wine notes on pp. 179–89 will supply the technical details for the wines of the region, but may I add a personal recommendation here? Many readers will want to sample and perhaps purchase some Sancerre while they are on the spot – Britain is a top market for the fruity/dry subtleness; they will encounter at every turn invitations to taste and to buy from *vigneron* or *négociant*. The choice can be bewildering and sometimes advantage is taken of the unwary. May I heartily recommend, whether a purchase is envisaged or not, a visit to the *caves* of the Gitton family, at Ménétréol-sous-Sancerre.

Marcel Gitton *père* started with less than an acre just after the war and has built this holding up 75-fold. He told me how each small vineyard, within a few yards of the next with the same appellation, has such a distinctive character. The Gitton family has developed this deviation and they bottle under different labels six different Sancerres grown on flinty soil and four on chalky soil. You can taste them all at their *caves* on the hillside above the attractive village of Ménétréol, just below Sancerre, and decide which pleases you most. A case each of Les Belles Dames and La Vigne du Larry proved a splendid buy for us, but you can order a mixed bag if you are not sure.

Unlike most Sancerre producers, who hasten to pick, ferment and bottle, in order to get the wine rolling out and the cash rolling in, the Gittons prefer the old-fashioned way of allowing body to develop slowly for 11 months in oak casks, and they maintain that their wines can be kept and even improved over a period of time. They are the produce of old vines bearing an almost-forgotten low-yield Sauvignon grape. Their red wines too are made in traditional fashion – three weeks in vats, two winters in casks – and can be kept over an extended period. All the loving care and high standards might mean a few francs more on the bottle but the splendid wines will still cost far, far less than the same quality back home.

Sancerre's goats are becoming almost as well known as their wines. Their little round cheeses have become the darlings of modern chefs, who use them warm in salads as well as on their cheeseboards. Their name – 'crottins' – is perhaps too descriptive. It means goats' droppings. All around the countryside, particularly in villages like Chavignol, a few kilometres away from Sancerre, you will see advertised *dégustations*, offering crottins with a glass of wine. And a very good scheme too – no light lunch problems in this area.

M. Gitton warned me again that some were not to be recommended, but went on to tell me about his favourite, which I should certainly never have found undirected. It's a farm called Chèvrerie les Chamons at Ménétréol. You take the bridge over the canal, continue down a track and follow the signs to the right, bumping over the fields for about half a mile, until you come to a dreadful looking tin-roof affair. That's it. Go in the first door and you find yourself in a shop where you can choose a perfect crottin for your picnic. Their pungent pong mingles with that from the hundreds of brown goats herded in pens at the rear of the shop. Next door is the eatery, so highly recommended by M. Gitton as being honest and good. Here, if they are open, and that's never certain, you can eat splendid simple fare like omelettes, salads, soups and, of course, crottins.

Hôtel Panoramic and **Restaurant Tasse d'Argent** (H)M (R)M
Rempart des Augustins
48.54.22.44 *(hotel);*
48.54.01.44 *(rest.)*
Rest. closed Jan.; Wed. o.o.s.
AE, EC, V

It would not have been my choice. Assertively, incongruously modern, in this otherwise ancient town, with a 'Bar Américan'. Locals said 'Forget it – he never changes his menu.' But I was a guest, and who am I to look a nosebag in the face, so, albeit reluctantly, I lodged at the Panoramic and ate at its appendage, La Tasse d'Argent.

The former was functional and efficient, with the undoubted bonus of a wonderful view to justify its name and compensate for the lurid orange bedspreads and plastic *partout*; the latter, *garni* with hunting trophies and a poorly inhabited *vivier*, was not at all bad, especially if you ate in daylight to profit from the view, and do not suffer, as I do, from pop-musak allergy. (It seems to be the cross I have to bear – pleasant background as I arrive, mind-splitting blast as I sit down.)

So starting several notches in arrears, the meal was a pleasant surprise. Don't touch the carte – far too expensive – and the other menus looked dull, but for 110f I ate a salad with the local goats' cheese, grilled, and a house speciality, 'l'Entrecôte des Vignerons', which was the best piece of beef that has come my way for many a moon. Inauspiciously served with meat and veg. all plonked together on a plate swimming in too much sauce, garnished with a superfluous tomato and an even more superfluous pink umbrella, it proved to be the kind of flavour and texture I thought had been forgotten in the onslaught of poncey modern cooking.

And the wine – a red '86 Sancerre – was special. I had no idea a red Sancerre could have such interest. No half bottles but they charged for what I drank (a lot).

The cheeseboard was better than average, with some 15 varieties, in good nick. If you were unwise enough to order an ice-cream *spécialité* you qualified for more plastic umbrellas, stuck, I regret to say, in commercial vanilla or strawberry, layered with out-of-season fruit, embellished with cocktail cherries. Yuk.

Next day I sussed the town out thoroughly and reckoned that I'd probably picked the best of a disappointing bunch of hotels. Rooms are 190–250f.

Hôtel du Rempart
(HR)S
Rempart des Dames
48.54.10.18
Open all year
AE, DC, EC, V.
Parking

This one looks more interesting from the outside, a Logis de France, older and more characterful, with a cellar dining-room, but the rooms are not so good and it lacks the stupendous view. Cheaper though, at 130f with bath, and five menus to choose from.

I button-holed a family just leaving and they said, much as I expected: 'Fine, nothing special, food OK, rooms clean.'

Certainly the Merottos are friendly patrons and for a family hotel you can't go far wrong here.

Restaurant de la Tour
(R)M–L
Pl. Halles
48.54.00.81
Closed Mon.
AE, V

No doubt in the mind of anyone I asked that the Tour was the best restaurant in town. Pascal Gitton (see above), who thinks nothing of driving into Burgundy for a three-star meal and consequently has very high standards, praised it lavishly and I was cross that my itinerary left no time for me to put it to the test.

It's in a charming old building on the corner of the market-place, with a choice of two moods within. You can stick with the prevailing 14th-century on the ground floor, all dark and cosy and pampered, with a log fire in the bar bit, or settle for the 'Salle contemporaine' on the first floor, which has for its décor (via sloping glass windows) the panoramic view over the vineyards of Sancerre.

In either setting Daniel Fournier serves modern food, beautifully arranged, on menus from 88f to a well-spent 220f for the 'Menu Dégustation'. Dishes like a fish mousse, striped with chunky salmon, served with two sauces, tomato and beurre blanc, or strips of rare duck with caramelised peaches are his style.

An arrow, I suspect, as soon as first-hand reports are available.

L'Écurie
(R)S
Pl. Halles
48.54.00.81

Next door, around the corner, is a pizzeria/bar/*crêperie*/grill under the same management, useful for a more modest meal but with similar high standards (apart from the musak).

➤ **Joseph Mellot**
(R)S
16 pl. Halles
48.54.20.53
Closed Wed.;
18/12–15/1
EC

M. Mellot's family have been growers and producers of wine since 1513, and now he has the brilliant idea of combining a shop selling his produce with a bar/restaurant. In the square, the building is a handsome, elegant one, and the quality throughout is high. You can sit at wooden barrel tables by the window and sip a glass or two (£2) or take a light meal (until 9 p.m.) or excellent terrine, smoked ham, omelette, crottin. Allow 50f.

Arrowed for doing something simple so well.

Map 3D | **SAUMUR** (M.-et-L.) 66 km SW of Tours; 125 km E of Nantes

49400
Ⓜ *Sat., Tues.*
and Wed. a.m.

A delightful town, which in spite of extensive wartime damage manages to retain a good deal of character, helped considerably by clever restoration. It has at least four claims to distinction – its massive dominating château, its equine traditions, its wine and its mushrooms.

Pedestrianisation of the main shopping area has been a

good idea and it is most agreeable to sit here for a breather, or if the weather is not kind, to pop into the best *pâtisserie*/tea room in town, **La Duchesse Anne** in the rue Franklin Roosevelt, where you can sip a dainty cuppa and try one of the local chocolate specialities, bizarrely but vividly named 'Crottins de Cheval'. 'Could you please tell me the English word for Crottins', asked Mme la patronne. 'Droppings', I suggested. 'Ah bon', she said, 'the English customers always ask and I am afraid to offend.' Offend or not, they're the best horse droppings I've come across.

Saumur is very conscious of the horsey theme. It has long been famous for its Cavalry School and since 1974 has been the home of the National Riding School. When I was invited to visit the latter, I accepted, with poor grace, simply because it was raining so hard that I thought it would fill in a soggy hour or two under cover. In fact I was fascinated, and strongly recommend a visit. It's at St-Hilaire-St-Florent, just outside the town.

Its purpose is to instruct instructors; it has the most modern facilities in the world to pamper the 500 horses, from automatic feeding to automatic disposal of those crottins. The indoor dressage school is the largest in the world and shows are regularly put on for visitors (enquire at the tourist office) by the mightily prestigious Cadre Noir. This is a body of men (and now two women) recruited from both the army and the civilian world as the finest horsepersons in France. To wear their distinctive black uniform with gold epaulettes and Napoleon-style hat is the peak of a French equestrian's career.

Guided visits to the school take place from 1/4 to 31/10, at 3 p.m. and 6 p.m. on Sat., Sun., Mon. and *fêtes*, and other days at 10 a.m., 11.30 a.m., 2.30 p.m. and 4.30 p.m. Information and reservations from the École Nationale d'Equitation, 41.50.21.35, or from the tourist office, 41.51.03.06.

Back in the town, follow the signs for a steeply winding walk up to the castle on its pedestal high above the roof-tops, looking down on to the wide sweep of the rivers Loire and Thouet that it was built to defend. It's a bit of a puff and not for the infirm, but well worth it.

The present castle was started in the late 14th century by the brother of Charles V, Louis duc d'Anjou, finished by Louis XII and remodelled in the 15th century by René of Anjou. To my eyes it looks exactly as a proper castle should – like the ones we used to build on the sands, with lots of towers and turrets and pennants stuck on the top. Instead of offering the

visitor a few sparsely furnished public rooms, it wisely
concentrates on two unique collections. The first echoes the
prevailing horsey theme; attractively set in the two wings of
the timbered attics of the castle where the servants of the
dukes of Anjou used to lodge, it traces the history of riding
and saddlery from all over the world from BC to the present
day. Try guessing before looking at the labels where all the
magnificent saddles originated, from Tehran to Texas.

The other collection is equally fascinating and represents
the very different world of decorative arts. Particularly
impressive is the European porcelain and faience, a
collection of 1300 pieces, lovingly assembled by one man,
the comte de Lair, but there are tapestries, Limoges enamels,
sculptures and paintings too.

Drive along the left bank of the Thouet, just before it joins the
Loire, to the suburb of St-Hilaire-St-Florent and you will pass
an assembly of vinous household names, for Saumur
produces the best sparkling wine in France outside
Champagne. Many a bride's father has reason to be grateful
to the likes of M. Ackermann, who first applied the
champagne method to the local wines.

You can visit the 4½ miles of Ackerman-Laurance galleries
deep in the white tufa cliff every day from Easter to
September, 9–11.30 a.m. 3–5 p.m., and benefit from the free
dégustations. Gratien and Meyer, a very impressive
establishment, un-pass-by-able, is at the other end of the
town on the Chinon road, with similar facilities, but there are
dozens of smaller wine houses to choose from.

It is no coincidence that Saumur, the town of the horse, is
also the town of the mushrooms. Crottins again! Three
quarters of the national mushroom output comes from the
tufa caves in this area, whose dankness is ideal for growing
fungi. The very name of the town, Saumur – sous-le-mur,
comes from these caves excavated at the base of the tufa
walls. There are worse ways to spend an hour or so of a day
that is damp outside too than to visit the Mushroom
Museum, in the Caves Louis Bouchard at St-Hilaire,
41.50.25.01, from 15/3 to 15/11, 10 a.m.–12 noon and 2–4 p.m.

Anne d'Anjou
(H)M
32 quai Mayaud
41.67.30.30
Closed 23/12–4/
1
AE, DC, EC, V
Parking

Here's a bargain. The once derelict building overlooking the river has been gradually restored by its present owners into a comfortable hotel, which for some reason I don't understand, since it is clearly the top hotel in the area, is rated only two-star, and is consequently cheap.

Most of the rooms are furnished in a simple modern style, at 200f with bathroom, but there are four superior alternatives, in the grandest of which the British Ambassador recently lodged. They retain the original painted panelling and one, high, wide and handsome, overlooking the river, costs only 400f.

The choice of outlooks is between river at front and château at rear. Both are splendid. The English apparently choose the river, the French, nervous of the traffic noise, prefer the château. Wrongly, because the windows are all double-glazed and sound-proofed.

On one busy bank holiday, when everywhere else was full, I was put in the annexe at the back of the pleasant little garden, in another simple but pleasant room with bath, also for 200f. No complaints here either, but I would choose the main hotel if possible. Next door to this annexe is the restaurant Les Ménéstrals (see below).

'The bedrooms are large and very comfortable and good value for money. The proprietors were proud to tell us that Terry Wogan had slept there. They serve a most comprehensive self-service breakfast of juice, coffee, bread, cheese, eggs, pâté, preserves, cereals, etc. We

Hôtel Anne d'Anjou.

observed some customers consuming breakfast, lunch, dinner all at one go. It is an old building which they have renovated with great taste and they have built the most beautiful restaurant in keeping with the character of the castle, where we enjoyed a fabulous meal.' – Marion Smith.

Arrowed for good value, pleasant situation, in a popular town.

➤ **Central Hôtel**
(H)S
23 r. Daillé
41.51.05.78
Parking

A triumph to find in these parts an example of that rare breed – a good inexpensive little hotel. This one is situated in the town centre, in a quiet street, just one block back from the river. The rooms are sparklingly clean and very comfortable, with all mod cons, such as telephone, TV, private garage. You can have a bathroom and/or twin beds if you wish. From 118–189f, or 210f for a family room.

Arrowed on all counts, not least for the welcome and efficiency of the nice patronne.

La Gare
(H)S
16 av. David
d'Angers
41.67.34.24
Closed 1/10–1/4

Small, family-run hotel, impeccably clean, opposite the station. Twelve rooms, six with bath, from 115f to 240f.

Roi René
(HR)M
94 av. Gén. de
Gaulle
41.67.45.30
Rest. closed
Sun., p.m.;
Mon. o.o.s.
AE, EC, V

A big modern hotel on a busy crossroads in the Île d'Offard. Rooms are well equipped at 215–295f. Menus from 68f.

'Good modern impersonal hotel with unusual menu set-up – excellent help-yourself cold table plus main dish. Main dish determines price.' – Richard Cobley.

➤ **Les Ménéstrals**
(R)M
11 r. Raspail
41.67.71.10
Closed Mon.
lunch; Sun.; 15/
1–30/1
AE, EC, V

In the garden of the Hôtel Anne d'Anjou, a fascinating setting on the first floor of an old barn, with glass set between the rafters to allow maximum light. Elegant, super-efficient service and the kind of clever cooking that combines the new lightness and attractive presentation with substantial portions and lack of pretentiousness.

I chose, on the 103f menu, asparagus feuilleté. This can involve anything from a few tinned asparagus spears sandwiched between package pastry or, as in this case, a sublime presentation of this princely vegetable. I remembered just in time that it is only in England that it is acceptable to use fingers for asparagus, but then let the side down by mopping up, with quantities of home-made bread, the delectable mousseline sauce that accompanied. Then came Loire salmon on a bed of sorrel, and a 'soupe' of strawberries – like the asparagus, the first of the season. All perfect.

Arrowed for excellent food in an attractive setting.

Château de
Beaulieu
(C)L
Rte de
Montsoreau
41.51.26.41

Set back from the road behind a pleasant garden, within a short distance from the town centre, is this elegant manor, whose owners accept guests for the good reason that they enjoy doing so.

Their home is elegant and well-maintained, with none of the dusty and unacceptable shabbiness that obtains in many of the amateur not-quite-hoteliers. All six bedrooms are comfortable and have their own bathrooms. From 350f to 650f.

Saumur is oddly short of restaurants and I failed to find any recommendable bargains in the S category, but two recommended locally were the *brasserie* La Bourse, as being good value, and La Volume for prime grills. The Ascot piano bar too received praise as somewhere wholesome to retreat to for undemanding late entertainment. Any suggestions for alternative eateries particularly welcome.

Map 3F   **SAVONNIÈRES** (I.-et-L.) 7 km SW of Tours

37510
(M) *1st Fri.*
of each month

On the D 7.

Hôtel des
Cèdres
(HR)M
Rte du Château
de Villandry
47.53.00.28 and
47.53.07.15
Closed Feb.;
rest. closed
Sun. p.m.;
Mon. o.o.s

A Relais de Silence hotel, useful for those who do not wish to get involved in the Tours traffic tangle. It is strikingly pristine, sparkling with white paint, embellished with well-disciplined red geraniums in window-boxes and spelling out the hotel's name in the manicured lawns. A swimming pool alongside is equally immaculate.

Inside is not quite so admirable – a lot of busy brown and orange pattern on walls, curtains and carpets, but equally clean. The rooms cost 300–360f.

The adjoining restaurant is under separate management. Around 250f would be a wise assessment of the likely cost of a three-course meal, so an evening here is not going to be cheap, but there is no obligation to eat in.

Map 2H   **SEILLAC** (L.-et-Ch.) 7 km SW of Onzain; 15 km SW of Blois

41150
Onzain

From Blois a pleasant drive through the forest to the riverside village of Molineuf, then the D 131 from Chambon-sur-Cissé.

Domaine de
Seillac
(HR)M
54.20.72.11
Closed 19/12–5/
1
AE, DC, EC

In deepest countryside, an ideal, unusual, well-conceived base for a family holiday, where the kids could be left quite happily enjoying themselves by the swimming pool, lake, on the tennis courts, swings and in the 60-acre park, while the culture-bent went off to do their stint of nearby châteaux.

The complex centres round the Domaine, in which there are 10 comfortable rooms. Most families prefer to stay in one of the 60 triangular wooden chalets set in the grounds, enjoying the independence of their own balcony, double bedroom on ground floor, twin beds on mezzanine, bath or shower.

Meals are served either buffet-style at the poolside, on the terrace, or in one of the attractive stable-conversion restaurants. Prices range from 290f to 410f, including breakfast. Menu 125f. *Demi-pension* is 245–455f.

Map 3B | **SERRANT (LE CHÂTEAU)** (M.-et-L.) 2 km NE of St-Georges-sur-Loire; 18 km SW of Angers

49170
St-Georges-sur-Loire

Turn off the N 23 to find this little-known, little-visited château, which would be at the top of anyone's list in another area with fewer choices. Sumptuous Serrant, designed by Délorme, architect of the Tuileries, built between 16th and 18th centuries, floats in a moat extending to a lake. Its white, tufa-stone, massive, round, cupola-topped towers are reflected in the calm waters and all around in the great park, with its fine chestnuts and cedars, is peaceful and serene.

High spots of the excellent tour (in French but with English written translation) are: the room prepared for Napoléon, with gorgeous gilded bed still unused (he stayed at Serrant a mere two hours); the library with its 10,000 leather-bound volumes, many of them first editions, and its painting over the mantelpiece of Bonny Prince Charlie bidding farewell to his henchman, Antoine Walsh, comte de Serrant, on his way back to Scotland, and the many signed photos of the international royalty (our Queen Mother, Lord Mountbatten, Princess Marina among them) who have stayed here; the cunningly concealed bath and washbasin, in 1850 one of the first in France to have running water; in the Grand Salon, the indescribably intricate

Serrant

ebony cabinet, whose many-layered, delicatedly carved drawers, disguised as anything but drawers, the guide manipulates like a conjuror. But all the furniture is magnificent and many pieces are unique.

The family La Tremoïlle, of whom the present owner, the Prince de Ligne, is a descendant, is one of the oldest families in France, and its members have lived in Serrant since 1749, when Earl Walsh, of Irish origin, refugee from the 1688 revolution, bought the castle. With all this interest and these connections, I cannot understand why more Brits do not visit this beautiful and underestimated château.

Open from 1/4 to 1/11; closed Tues. except July and Aug. Open 9–11.30 a.m. and 2–6 p.m.

Map 1C **SOLESMES** (Sarthe) 3 km E of Sablé; 55 km NE of Angers; 44 km SW of Le Mans

---

72300
Sablé-sur-
Sarthe

The river Sarthe is a very different proposition from the Loire. Its waters are clearer, they tumble rather than flow, its river banks are denser, greener; at Solesmes it rushes through lovely countryside, bordered to the south by the deep Pincé forest.

From Sablé, a pretty, flowery little town, you can take a delightful boat trip, incorporating, if you wish, lunch on board, from Easter to November. Telephone 43.95.93.13 for information, or hire a fishing boat for the day (same number).

Attractive though it is in its own right, Solesmes' main claim to fame is its Benedictine abbey, founded in the 11th century (though most of the existing buildings only go back as far as the last century). The best view is from the opposite side of the river or from the bridge. Do try and contrive a visit in the morning to hear the Gregorian chant movingly sung by the monks. Mass at 10 a.m. on Sundays; 9.45 a.m. weekdays.

Allow time to admire the famous monumental carvings known as the Saints of Solesmes; the radiantly tranquil face of Mary Magdalene in the Entombment, dating from 1496, is particularly stirring.

Another possible reason for visiting Solesmes in this area of poor accommodation and so-so food might be:

Grand Hôtel
(HR)M
*16 pl. Dom-
Guéranger
43.95.45.10
Closed Sun.
p.m.; Feb.
All credit cards*

Right opposite the abbey, incongruously modern; one might almost say aggressively so in the dining-room, with its plastic and chrome chairs, picture windows and Japanese lanterns. It is run by Bertrand Jacquet, who cooks, and his sister, who runs the hotel side.

She is gradually renovating the bedrooms. They are all comfortable, bright and well equipped, but if you can afford the price – 350f – go for the best ones, which have balconies overlooking the peaceful gardens. Others start at 255f.

The food is smart and aimed at the local business community as well as the hungry pilgrim. Stick with the 90f cheapest menu to get best value.

Map 2J SOUVIGNY-EN-SOLOGNE (L.-et-Ch.) 44km SE of Orléans

41600
Lamotte-
Beuvron

14 km north-east of Lamotte-Beuvron by the D 101.

A delightful village, both *fleuri* and *gastronomique*, with two recommended restaurants and a popular *crêperie*, whose tables sit irreverently in the garden of the photogenic little church, with ancient carved wooden porch.

➤ **La Croix Blanche**
(HR)M
R. Eugène-Labiche
54.88.40.08
Closed Tues. p.m.; Wed.; 15/ 1–1/3
Parking

A valuable find, with nice Mme Molan presiding, and her husband cooking meals that exploit to the full regional ingredients and recipes. It's all very French, very countrified, very charming, and look at the midweek closing times – obviously very popular with the Parisiens at the weekends, when booking is essential. It was in fact a Sunday when I called in, at a time in the mid-afternoon when contented French families are sitting replete, flushed of face, amongst the crumbs and half-empty glasses, with their offspring at last released from the table, letting off steam in the garden. Mme Molan greeted me not with that pained expression that says all too clearly 'You're too late and we're full' but with genuine regret that she could not offer me a meal or a room. I had eaten anyway, but was glad that I'd risked a snub when I saw the two pretty dining-rooms, of which the rear one is particularly charming, and the bedrooms, which are well equipped and comfortable. Rooms 122f. Menus 60f, 90f, 127f.

I'm going to break a house rule and arrow this one for readers' attention, even though I have neither stayed nor eaten there. Someone please write soon and tell me my confidence is justified.

Le Perdrix Rouge
(R)M
54.88.41.05
Closed Wed.
Parking

This rustically chic little restaurant just opposite the church had recently changed hands when I visited, but already the Orléannais had discovered its merits and it was brimming with happy lunchers. Chef-patron Jean-Noel Beurienne's cooking is more sophisticated than the ambience of his little house might seem to justify, but it was early days when I visited and he told me that he would adapt to what the customers seemed to want. Dishes like a terrine of pigeon with wild mushrooms, perfectly fresh turbot cooked with leeks, and a vacherin of raspberries augur well for the future. Cheaper menus looked a trifle dull (65f, 90f). I would go for the 128f version.

Map 1K SULLY-SUR-LOIRE (Loiret) 42 km SW of Orléans

45600
Ⓜ *Mon.*

Think of Sully and you think of the château. Understandably nowadays, since the entire old town was wiped out in two devasting raids, in the original fighting in 1940 by German bombardment and four years later by the other side. The tall spire of St Germain still stands in the shattered ruins of its church.

The river frontage, with its tree-lined walks, is a pleasant refuge and parking here is usually no problem. Another bonus for the town is an unusual Monday market, when a visit to Sully can prove altogether more satisfying that in most shuttered towns.

But of course it is the château that dominates. First sighting of its vast solidity never fails to impress, especially approaching from across the bridge or, even better, from the D 119 from Ouzouer. It looks remarkably well-preserved for its five hundred years, satisfyingly like everyone's idea of a castle, with chubby round towers and pepperpot turrets, all reflected in the wide moat, fed by the river Sange. Look at the timber roof, the finest mediaeval example in existence they say, with its 14th-century chestnut timbers shaped like a keel, as good as, or better than, new.

Any interest in the Château de Sully requires the purchase of a specific guide book, since its history, rich with a pageantry of kings English and French, Ministers of State, writers, philosophers, and courtesans, merits a tome to itself. Just as an *amuse-gueule*, there are three salient historical associations:

It was here that Joan of Arc persuaded the vacillating Charles VII to go to Reims to be crowned, and here that she was imprisoned in 1430 by the castle's owner, Georges de la Tremouïlle, who was jealous at her influence over the king. She escaped a plot to drown her but never saw her king again.

The Chief Minister of Henri IV bought the crumbling château in 1602, restored it, and was subsequently created duc de Sully. He it was who planted out the magnificent park, added a wing to the castle and constructed the moat. You can see his office in the château.

The young Voltaire, in exile from the court in 1761 for his near-the-knuckle satires, spent several profitable and carefree seasons here with the incumbent duc de Sully, who built him a theatre in the grounds in which to perform his plays. It was in Sully in fact that he wrote his first play, *Oedipe*.

Guided tours of the castle (sparsely furnished) last ¾ hour: May–Sept.: 9–11.45 a.m., 2–6 p.m.; March and Nov.: 10–11.45 a.m., 2–4.30 p.m.; April and Oct.: 10–11.45 a.m., 2–5 p.m.

I settled for a picnic by the water but a happy alternative might be:

L'Esplanade
(HR)M
Pl. Pilier
38.36.20.83

Right opposite the château, with tables outside from which to take it all in, accompanied by a beer or cup of tea. 69f menu inside, in a smart, cheerful dining-room, or fast food outside or on the covered terrace. I discovered too late that there were five bedrooms, and failed to get a look at them.

Map 1K

SURY-AUX-BOIS (Loiret) 14 km NE of Châteauneuf-sur-Loire; 41 km NE of Orléans

---

45530
Vitry-aux-Loges

In very pleasant green countryside, in the heart of the Forêt d'Orléans. A good overnight stop on the route south.

Domaine de Chicamour
(HR)M
38.59.35.42
All credit cards

The Domaine, an elegant, cream-washed, white-shuttered country house, dating from 1830, was discovered by its present owners, M. and Mme Merckx, in 1983 and enthusiastically converted into a comfortable hotel, meriting its Relais de Silence membership. It is well situated for visiting the northern châteaux, but is also a good choice for those who like to mix more violent exercise with culture. Membership of its riding school and tennis club are bonuses that go with being a hotel guest.

The rooms are comfortable and well equipped, and good value at 350f, and local produce is the base of most of the food in the restaurant. Menus start at 90f.

Map 1I   **TAVERS** (Loiret) 3 km S of Beaugency; 28 km SW of Orléans

---

45190
Beaugency

La Tonnellerie
(HR)M
38.44.68.15
Closed 5/10–30/4
DC, EC, V
Parking
🪝 🔧

A welcome refuge from all the Loire busyness, particularly in summer, when the swimming pool and gardens are a delight. The hotel looks nothing special outside, set right on the road in the sleepy village of Tavers, but once inside the courtyard, with a first glimpse of terrace, pool and airy white-and-green dining-room, it becomes obvious that this is going to be good news.

My room looked out over the pool and it was a quick nip down the back staircase for an immersion that washed away all the stress of a long journey.

Minor grumbles – the bathroom, with a sit-up-and-beg bath, was dark and far from luxurious for the price – 320f for one person (doubles at 390–510f) plus 30f for breakfast, and the absence of fresh flowers anywhere, in restaurant, reception or bedroom, in an upmarket hotel in July, I found hard to forgive, but by the end of my second day I was looking forward very much indeed to returning to the cool comfort of such an agreeable base.

Menus in the very pleasant dining-room cost 150f, 179f and 225f. The food was good, fresh and generous, without being exceptional. *Demi-pension* is obligatory in high season. Staff and patronnne were all friendly and helpful and their welcome, combined with the hotel's position and comfort, make this an arrow.

Map 3H   **THESÉE** (L.-et-Ch.) 9.5 km E of Montrichard, 34 km S of Blois

---

41140
Thesée-la-
Romain

On the N 76, following the north bank of the Cher.

Map-reading can lead to disappointment. The roads following the Cher, which look as though they might offer romantic river views, in fact demand the driver's undivided attention, so busy are they. Thesée is a nothing-town on the route nationale, but has two modestly priced Logis, which might fill the bill for those not wishing to pay the generally inflated prices of the region.

Le Moulin de la Renne
(HR)S–M
54.71.41.56
Closed Tues. p.m.; Wed. o.o.s.; Jan.; Feb.
Parking

Well signposted from the main road to the east of the village. A mill nowadays it is not, nor even picturesque, but the river is certainly nearby and it is agreeably peaceful, set in its own grounds. A simple raftered room for two will cost 160f. Menus from 65f.

La Mansio
(HR)S
54.71.40.07
Closed Tues.
p.m.; Wed.
o.o.s.; 1/1–28/2
EC, V
Parking

An agreeable little restaurant offering good regional cooking on menus from 55f, with nine rooms. If you ask for one at the rear, overlooking the gardens, you will find it to be simple but attractive, and good value at 90f.

Map 3F

TOURS (I.-et-L.) 82 km SE of Le Mans; 140 km SW of Chartres; 102 km SW of Orléans

---

37000
(M) *Every day*

For the first-time visitor to Tours the sprawl of its suburbs and new industrial estates can be daunting, especially if you get lost in any of the outlying areas, where the boulevards do *not* run straight and true, as they do in the centre. A further confusion is the proliferation of water and bridges, so that it is easy, before familiarisation makes it all quite obvious, to confuse the banks of the Loire with those of the Cher. But do not be put off by the scale. The core of the city is the most interesting and that is confined in a manageable area, on which I shall concentrate, between the rivers, nearer the Loire.

A guide like *French Entrée* is no place to do full justice to a city of this size – one of the most important in France – and I shall not attempt more than a sketch of its attractions and a description of the impressions they have made on me during both recent visits and during the times when two of my children were at university here.

Stick to the main boulevards and you can't go wrong. Parking is not easy, but abandon the car at the first opportunity and explore on foot; the area covered here is all within half an hour's walk of the central place Jean-Jaurès. The shaded boulevard Heurteloup has hundreds of parking slots, and the square by the station is another good possibility, with the Information Bureau nearby, but it's a matter of cruising and not being too British-polite when you spot a space.

A university city (and Tours is particularly popular with language students, since the French here is held to be the purest in all France) invariably means lots of animation, lots of cafés and good cheap restaurants. The crossroads round the place Jean-Jaurès is the hub, with the avenue de Grammont lined with tables on the pavements, full of chatter and colour. Its extension on the other side of the square, the rue Nationale, is the main shopping street. Balzac was born here in 1799, when it was known as the rue Napoléon.

Since 1970 restoration work on the mediaeval *quartier*

around the place Plumereau, which was largely destroyed in the war, has brought new life to a most tranquil and attractive setting. The ancient streets, lined with fine 15th-century timber-framed houses, have been pedestrianised and it is now most agreeable to stroll past boutiques and bistros, with a chance to rest cobble-weary feet and watch the world go by at a table in the photogenic place Plumereau itself. Look out for the rues Briçonnet, Bretonneau, des Cerisiers, and the places du Carroi aux Herbes and de Châteauneuf.

The flower market in the centre of the boulevard Béranger (continuation of Heurteloup after place Jean-Jaurès) is famous, and rightly so. A riot of colour spills from the hundreds of stalls; promenade between them, learning the French names for the flowers and shrubs they offer for sale.

Other markets are the open-air flea market on Wednesdays in the place de la Victoire, for expensive amusing trash, and the covered Halles, daily, *not* to be missed for any lover of interesting foodstuffs, in the rue de la Victoire. This is undoubtedly the place to load up the car with all manner of take-home goodies, since there is a very useful car-park next door.

Tours

It never ceases to amaze and please me that in big French cities you have only to walk a few blocks to find a completely fresh environment and atmosphere. Just a short walk from the station and boulevard Heurteloup are quiet tree-lined squares and old streets full of bookshops, *antiquaires* and specialist food shops. Few tourists seem to bother to walk along the dignified rue Colbert, to my mind one of the most appealing streets in Tours, or the rue Scellerie, where Balzac went to school. They lead to the **Cathedral of St Gatien**, begun in the early 13th century and completed in the 16th, thus encompassing every stage of French Gothic architecture, with Renaissance embellishments.

The soaring west front, crumbling, alas, as tufa stone is wont to do, is the most impressive aspect, dominating the little square in which it is set. Inside is wonderful stained glass, 13th century in the chancel, 14th-century rose windows in the transepts and the 15th-century great rose window in the nave.

On the exterior north wall are the elegant Gothic-Renaissance cloisters, known as the 'Psalette', since psalms were sung here by the canons.

To get another fine view of the cathedral and its reckless flying buttresses, walk behind to the place Grégoire de Tours, on the left of which is the **Musée des Beaux Arts**. Open 9 a.m.–12.45 p.m. and 2–6 p.m. from April to Nov., and until 5 p.m. for the rest of the year. Closed Tues.

The building alone – the former Archbishop's palace built in the 17th and 18th centuries – is worth a visit in its own right. The panelled rooms are decorated with silk made in the city, and make a perfect background to the paintings and furniture.

Some particularly famous works of art, like Rembrandt's jewel of a *Flight into Egypt* and some wonderful Mantegnas, make a visit here a must, but I find the lay-out irritatingly confused, with gems often hidden away. Do a bit of homework before pentrating the maze, decide what you want to see, stick with it, and ignore the rest.

A highly recommendable preamble to the châteaux of the Loire, for which at least a little knowledge of the history of France, in which they so often played a rôle, is desirable, is a visit to a new museum in the Château Royal of Tours, the **Historial de Touraine**, produced by the Musée Grévin of Paris.

The château itself is steeped in history – Charles VII was married there in 1413 to Marie d'Anjou; Mary Queen of Scots wed the future Louis XI there in 1436; Joan of Arc stayed there on her triumphant return from Orléans; and the duc de

Guise escaped from the top of the tower which now bears his name.

All these characters and many others – 165 models altogether – act out the events which shaped the future of Touraine, France, Europe, the world. It's all a fascinating spoon-fed way to take on board some of the salient facts about such people as Clovis, Charlemagne, Richard the Lionheart, Agnès Sorel, Anne de Beaujeu, Anne de Bretagne, Leonardo da Vinci, Rabelais, Ronsard, Diane de Poitiers, Catherine de Médicis, Richelieu, De Vigny, Balzac, Gambetta, Anatole France, who are bound to keep cropping up and demonstrating your ignorance on future culture trips throughout the area. I wish I'd started off here.

Musée Grévin, Château Royal, quai d'Orléans. 47.61.02.93. Open: 16/3–15/6, 9 a.m.–12 noon and 2–7 p.m.; 16/6–15/9 from 9 a.m. to 9.30 p.m.; 16/9–15/11, 9 a.m.–12 noon and 2–7 p.m.; 16/11–15/3 from 2 to 6 p.m. The history of Touraine. The visit is not guided but you can buy a good programme for 3f.

Tours is exceptionally well served with both hotels and restaurants – it could almost fill a book. As in Angers or Orléans, the other large towns in the area, I would probably recommend staying outside in country-quiet, except in poor weather. On this basis I have selected a few town hotels which would seem to fulfil most requirements.

➤ **Hôtel Akilène**
(HR)M
22 r. du Grand Marché, 17 r. de la Rôtisserie
47.61.46.04
Always open
EC, V

The double address does not mean two hotels but one that spans the space between two old streets in the heart of old Tours. The Akilène is a nice old white-shuttered French hotel, with really attractive, comfortable rooms from 110f to 206f and friendly, multilingual management. It does have a restaurant, but I know nothing about the quality of the food. Menus are 68–130f and there is a reasonably priced house wine.

This would be high on my list if I needed a central base, but the snag is that too many other tourists agree with me and it is often full. Don't risk it therefore without a reservation.

An arrow for extremely well-priced accommodation, in a comfortable hotel in the most attractive part of Tours.

➤ **Hôtel Mirabeau**
(H)M
89 bis bvd Heurteloup
47.05.24.60
Closed Christmas hols.
AE, EC, V

An excellent choice of central town hotel. Built a hundred years or so ago, elegant but modernised, nice owners. The well-furnished, stylish bedrooms cost a very reasonable 250f a double, or 285f for one with four beds. Some of the rooms do overlook the main boulevard, but they have been sound-proofed. There is a lift, bar and little rear garden for sunny breakfasts.

Arrowed unhesitatingly for remarkable value in a central position.

Hôtel du Musée
(H)S
2 pl. François
Sicard
47.66.63.81

Definitely a hotel of character. Delightfully old-fashioned in one of the most attractive *quartiers* of Tours, near the cathedral, overlooking a quiet leafy square.

The patron is as colourful as his hotel – don't go if you like smooth impersonal service and a plastic cube. Here the bedrooms are spacious and comfortable and cheap – 70–180f with bath. Very popular, so often full.

Hôtel Balzac
(H)M–S
47 r. Scellerie
47.05.40.87
Open all year
All credit cards

Recommended on several counts – its central position in a quiet old street near the cathedral, its spic-and-span presentation with modern well-fitted rooms, friendly reception and good value; 74–242f.

▶ Jean Bardet 🏠
(HR)L
57 r. Groison
47.41.41.11
Open every day
AE, CB, DC

The opening times are a good clue (though how long they can last I cannot prophesy). They are just one indication of the enthusiasm and dedication of Jean and Sophie Bardet for their new restaurant, their new hotel, their new town, their new prestige.

Jean's rise to the dizzy heights of two stars in Michelin, 19/20 in Gault Millau, has been rapid. His background is not a typical one. He started cooking in a scruffy *steack-frites* in Maintenon, opened his own bistro in Châteauroux in 1972, aiming no higher than at the commercial-traveller market (not to be despised in France) and was 'discovered' by Gault-Millau in his next *plus présentable* restaurant in 1981. Four years later he had achieved the coveted fourth *toque* and joined only six other chefs in the whole of France in the 19/20 class.

The gods smiled on him when he discovered in the centre of Tours – well, just across the river – a faded 19th-century mansion with 3 hectares of land; an Englishman had owned it previously and created a *jardin anglais*, with mature trees, rare specimen plants, ponds, high walls – a perfect setting for the luxurious ensemble the Bardets were aiming to create. They and their architect have been unusually clever in achieving a building that looks as though nothing has changed for centuries, but which has in fact been custom-built to their specific requirements around the original shell. Two wings have stone balconies to every room – the new luxurious bedrooms – supported by impressive white classical columns; the dining-room is another bay looking out onto the garden. An old conservatory, with nice antique details such as the radiators curving round the bay, has been retained for the bar.

Inside all is light and bright and cheerful, with a predominately young staff and a feeling of cheerful enthusiasm rather than the kind of pomposity that dulls the tastebuds. Not sure about the silver lamé bow-ties though.

We certainly felt very cossetted, arriving just as dusk was falling, in time to enjoy a stroll round the garden and the swimming pool, sniffing the evening scents, then, as we sipped aperitifs in the conservatory, watching hundreds of fairy lights beginning to wink in the trees.

To eat à la carte would cost at least 500f – more if one explored some of Jean's rarer, classier wines. He has a wonderful list, particularly of local wines, and plans to produce his own from a newly planted vinery. Wine courses are also envisaged.

Menus are 195f, 280f and 360f. We saw no reason not to eat on the cheapest, the 'Cuisine du Marché', which gave me a memorable fricassée of baby eels from the Vendée and Husband a ragoût of oysters on a mound of watercress mousse 'reinforced' with Muscadet; then came a shoulder of roast lamb, with a ragoût of haricot beans and little fresh peas – and it is a measure of Jean Bardet's stature that he can cook an apparently simple, familiar, dish like roast lamb and make you feel you never tasted such before – and calves' sweetbreads with preserved lemon slices. All quite quite perfect. A souffléed crêpe, stuffed with caramelised almonds, was a satisfyingly spectacular dessert, but I stuck with an old favourite brought with Jean from Châteauroux – a China-tea sorbet perfumed with jasmine and mango.

Altogether a memorable experience; if you can afford it, don't miss it.

The rooms are from 420f to 700f, furnishings all different. All very luxurious but some more successfully styled than others.

Arrowed for outstanding cooking.

La Roche le Roy
(R)M–L
55 rte de St-Avertin
47.27.22.00
Closed 1/8–20/8
AE, CB

In the suberb of St-Avertin, near the southern exit onto the autoroute, Alain Couturier has found a gorgeous 16th-century house, and moved there in 1987 from his successful base at La Poivrière in central Tours. He used to cook at La Gavroche, and married an English girl, Marilyn, who now welcomes and copes with language problems.

So those who like the idea of eating Gavroche-style without making the major investment necessary in London will do well to make the journey here, where the cheapest menu is a mere 148f, and eating à la carte will only set you back another 100f or so. A salad of red mullet with saffron, salmon with a confit of leeks, flavoured with orange zest, and a flaky tart topped with red fruit coulis are the kind of dishes Alain likes to present.

The house, setting and garden are truly delightful, and a summer lunch or dinner here, eating outside perhaps, would be a treat. The Couturiers are still young, enthusiastic, and hardworking, and their food is good value. Go soon.

La Gourmandine
(R)M
49 r. Bernard Palissy
47.05.13.75
Closed Sun.;
24/12–3/1, 13/7–16/8
AE, CB

A subdued, rather serious little restaurant in a quiet street off the boulevard Heurteloup and not far from the station which is a favourite with local gourmets (so book).

Patron Patrick Terrien has just returned from a spell in Japan, where he has acquired the taste for delicacy and precision native to that country. He also likes to use spices such as ginger, with which he delicately flavours the odd uses in dishes such as a salad of langoustines. A bitter-sweet salmon dish is sprinkled with sesame seeds, turbot is cooked in Vouvray on a bed of Japanese seaweed. But he does not ignore his Gallic origins and serves a regional menu too, and, of course, excellent Loire wines.

The 95f weekday menu could be a gastro-experience for those who like to dare a little.

L'Odéon 🏠
(R)M
10 pl. de la Gare
47.20.12.65
Closed Sun.
p.m.; Mon
AE, CB, DC

Easy to find, just by the station, in a vaguely thirties-style *brasserie*. Run by the oddly named M. Lhopiteau, who cooks fairly straightfoward dishes in the modern style, such as red mullet in Chinon, duck in cider, followed by extra good pâtisserie. Go for the 85f menu.

Le Relais
(R)M–S
Pl. du Mar.
Leclerc
47.05.46.12
Closed Fri.
p.m.; Sat. o.o.s.

A station buffet would you believe, but unlike any other buffet I know. Who would have thought a décor of green trellis and roses to be appropriate here? Yet it works and offers a pleasant shock as you enter from the grey station approach.

An ex-chef from Barrier cooks un-station-buffet-!ike dishes – a mousseline of whiting in a crab sauce, skate with a chervil-flavoured sabayon and an excellent tête de cochon for those who remember what brawn used to taste like. Good menus from 60f including wine (weekdays only), 85f and 130f.

L'Ecuelle
(R)S
5 r. du Grand
Marché
47.66.49.10
Closed Mon.

They advertise a *cuisine d'autrefois* in this attractively beamed little bistro in the old quarter. That involves piled steaming platefuls of fricassée of veal, boeuf bourgignon, coq au vin and the like. Husband tucked happily into a substantial whack of home-cured ham cooked with lots of carrots, boiled potatoes and lentils – un petit salé aux lentilles – wonderful warming winter fodder. I, less hungry, was cheerfully served with just a bowl of home-made soup, which, with lots of that gorgeous bread, a Tarte Tatin, and a pichet of cheap wine, filled the lunchtime gap nicely.

We were just snacking, without too much time to spare, but there are very popular three-course menus at 50f, or a plat du jour – such as chicken chasseur with rice – at 38f.

Recommended for a good value tuck-in.

Tart' Annie
(R)S
15 r. du Grand
Marché

Ideal for light lunches. What the French call *coquette*, with an *ambiance féminine* (but it was pretty unisex when we were there).

The menu centres round quiches, savoury and sweet, with a choice of about five different fillings. My 'provençale', with leek, onions and ham, was great. So was the salad with hazelnut dressing. Husband had an onion omelette, which came plump, sizzling and enticingly golden. Then a chocolate mousse for him and a pear-and-almond tart for me. All top class. With a 75cl carafe of wine, coffee and mineral water, our bill came to under a tenner. Takeaways for picnics too.

Le Grandgousier
(R)S
88 r. du
Commerce
47.20.75.21
Closed Wed.
CB

A pioneer in the recently discovered (for France) genre of wine bars. Not open long but already popular for its excellent value: 68f buys a choice of several entrées – rillettes, crudités, soup – and the dish of the day – chicken, guinea fowl, steak – plus cheese or pud. – fruit tarts, all of commendable quality. What a sensible formula, combined with *dégustations* of splendid Touraine wines. This is a good place to buy take-homes too.

163

Eating: **La Grange**, 22 rue Lavoisier (good crêpes); **Le Grill du Roy**, 16 rue du Grand Marché (salads and grills); **Chez Plum'reau,** 6 rue du Grand Marché (famous *crêperie* in the centre of the place Plumereau); **Le Taste-Vin**, 33 rue du Grand Marché (open all hours, local wines, good snack dishes); **L'Univers**, 8 place Jean-Jaurès (central *brasserie*, the oldest in Tours, with superb 1900 glass). *Drinking:* **Le Corsaire**, 187 avenue de Grammont (cocktails); **Le Duke**, place Plumereau (jazz); **Le Palais de la Bière**, 29 place Gaston-Pailhou (200 beers and 60 whiskies); **Le Vieux Murier**, place Plumereau (usefully sited).

SHOPPING

The central markets in Tours are so magnificent that most food shopping will no doubt take place here, but some ideas in the town are:
Boulangeries: **Berruet**, 57 rue du Commerce; **Le Fournil**, 7 place des Petites Boucheries.
Pâtisseries: **La Marotte**, 3 rue du Change (best cakes in town); **Poirault et Sabat**, 31 rue Nationale (wonderful chocs and best *salon de thé*).
Charcuteries: **Chaude**, 6 rue Émile-Zola; **Au Cochon Fin**, rue Colbert; **Lebeau**, 34 rue des Halles.
Wines: **Caves de la Sellerie**, 43 rue de la Sellerie (good selection of local wines).

Map 3D   **TRÈVES-CUNAULT** (M.-et-L.) 3 km SE of Gennes; 12 km NW of Saumur

---

On the south bank of the Loire.
    The stretch of river road between Gennes and Saumur is a peaceful and pleasant drive, with little mediaeval villages, like Chênehutte-les-Tuffeaux, strung along the way. Nothing very dramatic happens until you come suddenly upon the magnificent abbey of Cunault, claimed to be 'the most majestic and the most beautiful of the churches of Anjou'. And I wouldn't be surprised.
    To step down from the bright sunshine into the dimness of the great nave is to leave the rest of the world behind – exactly what the building was intended for. It was built in the 11th and 13th centuries, with massive 11th-century bell-tower and 15th-century tower.
    Gradually, as the eyes become used to the light change, one realises that this is not at all a dark and gloomy church but, thanks to the gleaming tufa stone, great height, and wide side-aisles, one radiating brightness.
    The 223 carved mediaeval capitals are worth some craning of the neck. Traces of their original polychrome remain, to set you guessing how the ensemble first appeared.

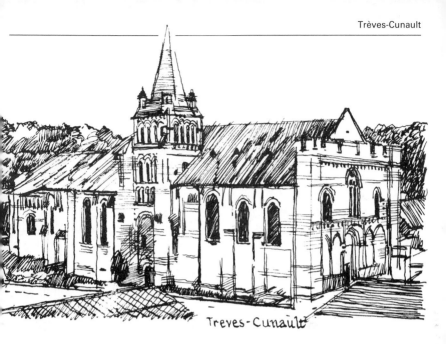

Treves-Cunault

A mile or so further east and another Romanesque gem awaits – the church at Trèves, beside a striking 15th-century tower. Another smaller example of a vast light nave, arcade bordered.

Both villages are well worth a detour, to see these rare examples of Angevin Romanesque church architecture.

Map 3E   **USSÉ (Le Château)** (I.-et-L.) 14 km NE of Chinon; 32 km SW of Tours

On the D 7, on the south bank of the Indre.

Try and approach the château from the north, having perhaps followed the pleasant and peaceful little D 16 along the Loire and taken a turn south just as the road peters out, to cross a bridge over the Indre. From here the white tufa stone of the castle's many towers and pinnacles, set halfway up the escarpment, with the dark forest of Chinon as backdrop, is truly enchanting.

Perrault is said to have used it as a model for his tale of the Sleeping Beauty, a fact well capitalised on inside the castle where waxwork figures present the story in a series of rooms. In order to peer into these set-pieces, you must scramble round the narrow passageways that wind around the towers, and in so doing must perforce encounter a body of fellow tourists hell-bent in the other direction, involving a mêlée of conflicting purposes. On the way out you might well curse them for being so obtuse. On the way back you will have realised that there is no choice; some crazy planner has arranged a two-way system in a single track. What the result must be in high season I cannot imagine. At Easter it necessitated much

Ussé

holding in of stomachs and pressing of backs to walls, which meant that everyone emerged looking distinctly ghostly from such proximity to the powdery tufa. All adding to the fairy-tale quality.

The rest of the castle can be visited on a guided tour but there's not really a lot more to see. Best spend the time appreciating the romantic assembly of stern fortress and elegant residence from the courtyard and terraced gardens overlooking the valley. The oldest part – the keep in the south-west corner – is 15th century.

In the grounds stands a lovely 16th-century chapel, still Gothic in style, enlivened with touches of exquisite early Renaissance decorations, like the sculpted shell over the doorway. Most striking is the dazzle of the tufa, which looks as though it was cleaned yesterday but in fact is no more nor less snowy than when it was built.

To bring the fairy tale into the 20th century and for a truly memorable view (and lots of special photos) you could take a helicopter ride from the meadow beside the castle. From 150f for each of four passengers. You can do the whole of the Loire Valley in this fashion if you have 80 minutes and 1,700f to spare.

There is a café just below the castle for urgent refreshment but for something more substantial make for one of my favourite stops at Bréhémont. See p. 51–2.

Map 4I	**VALENÇAY** (Indre) 55 km S of Blois

36600
(M) *Tues.*

A town on the D 956, undistinguished apart from its two major attractions, Talleyrand's castle and the hotel named after the Spanish princes once kept in luxurious exile there.

Valençay is at the southern extreme of the usual tour of the Loire châteaux and is often left off a hasty itinerary; more's the pity because here is a mini-Chambord of manageable proportions, with hordes of peacocks and deer rather than Japanese cameramen. 'Impressive' is the word most often used to describe Chambord. 'Beautiful' is more appropriate for Valençay.

Napoleon deemed it important that Talleyrand should be able to offer prestigious hospitality, in return for diplomatic favours, and so subsidised his purchase of this Renaissance gem in 1803. With sunny, wide terraces enclosed by its wings and elegant white classical façade, well-stocked parks and astonishing range of original furniture, so well preserved that they look like Maples, made-yesterday, it's an agreeable place to while away an hour or two.

The feeling of being in a home (the heirs retain a few rooms there still) rather than an institution is a pleasant one and the personality of Talleyrand, his family and mistresses, is potent. The dreadful surgical boot he was forced to wear is one of the souvenirs that present him as a man not a plaster image.

The park is open all year, except 25/12 and 1/1. In the lovely formal garden, black swans, peacocks and other fowl wander freely. To the west of the château is an enclosure for llamas, kangaroos, dromedaries and deer.

The château is open 9 a.m.–12 noon and 2–7 p.m. between 15/3 and 15/11; weekends o.o.s. 10 a.m.–12 noon and 1.30–4.30 p.m. *Son et lumière.*

Château de Valençey

➤ **Espagne**
(HR)L
*Av. Château
54.00.00.02
Closed Sun.
p.m.; Mon.
o.o.s.; 1/1–1/3
AE, EC, V*

The Relais et Châteaux chain can be proud of this member. It costs a lot to stay there but, since this book is all about value for money, it qualifies for an arrow since the value is patently obvious, in the attention to detail, the quiet courtyard full of flowers and shrubs and white tables and chairs, and in the delightful balconied bedrooms. I think my bed in 'l'Hermitage' was the most comfortable I have ever slept in, and only a heavy programme the next day persuaded me to leave it. Breakfast is always a strong Relais et Châteaux point and here it was well up to standard, served in pretty pink-and-white Limoges china with very un-plastic jam and butter. The rooms cost 300–500f.

The restaurant, with a Michelin star, is worthy of the hotel and the castle. A no-choice 150f menu suited my fancy very well, with a salad of duck breast, colourfully enlivened with strips of red and green pepper, then calves' sweetbreads and the house flight of fancy – bombe Talleyrand. Chef Maurice Fourrée has a track record that includes Lucas Carton, so here is a chance to try top Parisien cuisine at provincial prices.

Reception and service are particularly friendly and helpful. A truly delightful place to stay.

Hotel d'Espagne

Map 3A	**VARADES** (Loire-Atlantique) 39 km SW of Angers; 48 km NE of Nantes

44370

On the north bank of the Loire. A somewhat ugly town on the N 23, improving considerably as it approaches the river and the bridge, at La Meilleraie.

Le Petit Pêcheur (HR)S
40.98.33.64
Open all year

This little restaurant has a fine terrace, facing south over the river, which I imagine must be a very popular spot in fine weather. It was a miserable wet day when I was there, late for lunch, and disappointed in Varades. I parked across the road and prepared for nothing more than a necessity stop. In fact it was one of the most delightful meals of the trip, not least because of the friendliness of the owners and the other customers.

There was a 95th-birthday party in progress, and in came a complimentary cake, glittering with sparklers, amid much general

169

mirth and goodwill. When the time for toddling off arrived, the patron buttoned up the coat of the birthday-boy's equally aged wife, implanted a firm kiss on her wrinkled rosy cheeks and saw the couple off to their car.

The food was another pleasant surprise. On the 78f menu (another, at 48f, called itself a 'Menu Rapide' and included duck pâté, entrecôte, cheese and wine), I ate a mouclade (mussel stew) flavoured lightly with curry, 'le poisson Petit Pêcheur à l'estragon', some OK cheese and a home-made crème caramel. A 50cl pichet of wine set me back another 19f. The rain cleared and I could appreciate the fine view of the Romanesque church of St-Florent across the river; somehow matters had improved dramatically during the hour I had spent there.

The rooms are modest but clean with good river views, at 90f. Arrowed for good value, welcome and site.

Map 1G   **VENDÔME** (L.-et-Ch.) 32 km NW of Blois; 56 km NE of Tours

41100
(M) *Fri.,*
Sat.

An enchanting little town, built over several streams of the river Loir, so that bridges and banks appear unexpectedly in the middle of the pedestrianised area and through the public gardens (good picnicking), and the main river curves protectively round the back gardens of nice old white-and-grey slate houses.

At the other end of the town is the massive 14th-century Porte St-George and, high above another arm of the Loir on 'la Montagne', is the ruined château, dating from the 13th and 14th centuries. From the terraces up here there are good photo opportunities of the old town and Loir Valley.

The Abbey of La Trinité presents an astonishing façade of flamboyant Gothic stonework, wonderfully intricate, built in the early 16th century. Contrasting with its lacy delicacy is the solid belfry, standing independently and constructed four centuries earlier. It is said to have been the model for one of the two towers – the 'Clocher Vieux' – of Chartres Cathedral.

Altogether a pleasant little town in which to stroll and pause for refreshment at one of the cafés in the place St-Martin. Also a good overnight stop on the route to and from the ferries, so my mission was obviously to find a hotel.

Le Jardin du Loir
(HR)M
Pl. de la Madeleine
54.77.20.79
Closed Sun. p.m.; rest. closed Mon.

Walking along the river bank I spotted the garden of this newly opened little hotel and restaurant, and struck lucky. It's light and bright and cheerful, excellently situated in the town centre but facing onto the garden and another terrace on the river. Here in summer you can eat a simple grill menu, sensibly served from an outside bar. Three courses – crudités, grilled meat or chicken, dessert, for 55f. More sophisticated fare in the delightful little pink-clothed restaurant, on menus from 90f.

The eight rooms are simple but agreeable and relatively unplasticised. A bargain at 125–270f, with choice of twins/doubles/shower/bath.

Reports welcome to justify what I anticipate will be an arrow for cheerfulness and good value.

Le Vendôme
(HR)M
15 fbg Chartrain
54.77.02.88
Closed 20/12–3/
1
CB, EC

The obvious choice – and none the worse for that. Prominent in the main road, recently given a facelift, now an Interhôtel. The rooms are all being modernised and are now impersonally efficient and comfortable, at 205–315f. 3 people can share for 275–350f.

The Chapeau Rouge restaurant has been agreeably contrived on one side of the hotel, maximising light and brightness. The menu to go for is the cheapest at 90f, including wine, with an hors d'oeuvre trolly, dish of the day (such as braised beef with carrots) and pud. (such as chocolate gâteau). But this is weekday lunchtimes only; at weekends prices shoot up to 220f.

Le Daumier
(R)M
17 pl. de la
République
54.77.70.15
Closed Sun.
p.m.; Mon.;
Jan.

Just in front of the abbey, a little restaurant with bags of character, based, as one might expect from its name, on the *fin-de-siècle* décor. The result is a warm *brasserie*-like ambience. The food is interesting and good, leaning towards sea-products, like a millefeuille of mussels, fillet of rascasse, grey mullet with green lentils, or shin of veal with garlic purée. Menus at 85f, 130f, 200f, all good.

Chez Annette
(R)S
194 bis fbg
Chartrain
54.77.23.03
Closed Thurs.;
no annual
holiday
AE, CB
Parking

A good cheap stop, with a wide range of menus, served in a rustic-style dining-room. Good hors d'oeuvre trolly, pike with beurre blanc, escalope of veal normand; 60–110f.

Le Petit
Bilboquet
(R)M
Rte de Tours
54.77.16.60
Closed Sun.
p.m.; Mon.; 2
weeks in Aug.

One restaurant I feel no need to test for myself – although I greatly look forward to an eventual meal there – since it was recommended by Jane Grigson, who knows better than most what constitutes good cooking.

The specialities are veal kidneys *à la Ronsard* and fish, cooked by patron M. Bissa. Allow 180f à la carte.

Map 3G   **VERNOU-SUR-BRENNE** (I.-et-L.) 15 km E of Tours

37210
Vouvray
Ⓜ *Thurs.*

One of the nicest aspects of this region is that you have only to head a few miles away from the busy Loire and its bordering routes nationales to find sleepy villages and deep countryside. Take the D 46 from Vouvray for just such in Vernou.

➤ **Hostellerie**
Perce-Neige
(HR)M
13 r. Anatole
France
47.52.10.04
Closed Sun.
p.m.; Mon.
o.o.s.; 2/1–2/2
AE, CB, EC

Hotels like this are hard to find in the Loire Valley. All one asks for is that they should be comfortable, countrified, peaceful, attractively furnished, with a passable restaurant, and not expensive. The Hostellerie fits the bill on all counts. It's a pleasant, creeper-covered house set in substantial grounds, lawns scattered with white chairs.

M. Metais cooks better than passably. You will eat very well on his 103f menu (others are 147f and 195f) – fish with a basil sauce, kidneys en croûte in port wine.

Mme. Metais welcomes and shows you to the pretty, well-equipped rooms, which at 116–250f are excellent value. Arrowed accordingly.

Map 3F   **VILLANDRY** (I.-et-L.) 20 km W of Tours, 10 km NE of Azay-le-Rideau

---

37300
Joué-lès-Tours

A blessed relief after the busyness of the N 152, the south river-bank road west of Tours, the D 88, is narrow and relatively free from heavy traffic, with good views over the river.

One is spoiled for choice château-wise in this area and, in order to avoid cultural indigestion, it is advisable to work out a personal programme before the trip of the châteaux most likely to appeal, for reasons many and varied. I think the one that would appear on everyone's list is Villandry, simply because it is so very different from all the rest.

Villandry is the last of the Renaissance châteaux built along the Loire Valley, its soberly grey elegance presenting a very different picture from the exuberance of some of the early Renaissance buildings. All that remains of its 14th-century origins is the incongruous keep in the south-west corner of the gardens. Inside are Spanish furniture and paintings collected by the Carvallo family, whose descendants still live in the château.

But the main reason for visiting Villandry, of course, is its unique gardens; the finest in France they say, and they could well be right. At the beginning of this century, Dr Carvallo, father of the present owner, began reconstructing the original formal French garden, which had previously been landscaped in the casual English park style. He designed the gardens on three levels, the water garden, the ornamental garden, and the vegetable garden, all neatly encompassed by trimmed box-hedges and yew trees. The best view of the resulting delightful and amazing spectacle is from the terrace of the château, bordered with lime trees. From here you can see across the valley to the meeting of the Loire and Cher and, on a clear day, pick out other neighbouring châteaux: Langeais, Cinq Mars and Luynes.

The present M. Carvallo has made an inspiring video film of the gardens, under the theme of the 'Four Seasons'. While Vivaldi provides the background, this not-to-be-missed pictorial treat

Villandry

explores the spring planting, the summer exuberance, the autumn colours, and finally the winter resting time, when armies of gardeners can get on with their intimidating job of pruning the hundreds of lime trees.

The vegetable garden is particularly fascinating, with its stunningly vivid displays of purple cabbages, emerald leeks, lime-green lettuces, all disciplined into intricate geometric patterns.

Whatever time of year you happen to be in the district, I can promise a special treat in store here. Allow plenty of time to roam round at will and enjoy it all.

Cheval Rouge
(HR)M
47.40.02.07
Closed Mon.
o.o.s.; 1/11–15/
3
EC, V
Parking

On the D 7 a few hundred yards from the château towards Tours.

A modern hotel with a splendid reputation for fine cooking by chef Christian Rody, who specialises in the traditional cooking of the area: Loire fish, charcoal grills and pastry are good choices on the menus, which at 135f and 220f are good value for this quality.

The 20 rooms, all with bathrooms, are conventional but very comfortable. Ask for one at the back. They are oddly priced at 263f and 268f.

Map 4H	**VILLELOIN-COULANGÉ** (I.-et.L.) 2.5 km SE of Montrésor; 36 km S of Montrichard

37460
Montrésor

Between Montrésor and Nouans on the D 760.
A lovely spot of green country, following the valley of the Indrois.

Château les Genêts 🛏️
(C)M–S
47.92.61.01

Bowling along from Montrésor, feeling pretty good after the discovery of that delightful village and ready for more delights, I came across the newly painted sign for Les Genêts, *chambre d'hôte*. No hesitation about turning up the drive but a certain self-consciousness to see two figures on the terrace of the château watching my progress with curiosity. *'Bonjour Madame'* I said by way of introduction. *'Hello. How nice to see you'*, said Rosemary Farley.

She and her farmer husband Peter, together with their son and his girlfriend, moved from Wiltshire to start a new life in France; here they have 800 acres of land and a dairy herd of 150 cows, based around a 19th-century 'château' which Peter, an ex-architect, describes as 'pretty horrible'. I wouldn't go that far. Faded yes, hardly classical, but, given a coat or two of paint on the peeling brown shutters and ironwork on the conservatory, I could think of worse habitations.

The Farleys now have launched out into taking PGs. 160f buys a double room and breakfast, English if required, or 650f for five nights. The 75f table d'hôte dinner including wine is based on home produce – meat, fowl, fish, veg., fruit, cheese. If the weather's right it'll be a barbecue.

On Sundays Rosemary has come up with a 'Dimanche en Campagne' formula for non-residents. 100f for the day offers a tour of the farm and dairy, walking along forest tracks, fishing in the lake, and a buffet lunch. What a treat for kids of all ages.

The rooms are basic but comfortable – remember this may be a château but first it's a working farm.

I predict that Les Genêts will be addictive.

Châteaux

It is highly advisable to be selective about châteaux-visiting, in order to make the experience an enjoyable and profitable one. Here is a list of the châteaux described in this book, with a rating system based on what I found in 1988:

Three star, not-to-be-missed

Angers: impressive fortress, unique tapestry.
Chambord: elephantine extravagance.
Chenonçeau: incomparable, everyone's favourite.
Le Lude: superb harmony of styles, particularly interesting *son et lumière*.
Villandry: unique gardens.

Two star, meriting a detour

Amboise: superb site, interesting historically.
Azay-le-Rideau: picture-book pretty.
Cheverny: classical elegance.
Chinon: ruins, superb site, interesting historically.
Loches: fortress, interesting historically.
Saumur: superb site, interesting collections.
Serrant: privately owned, elegant, original furniture, British connections.
Valençay: mini-Chambord without the crowds.

One star, go if you can

Beauregard: privately owned, unique picture gallery.
Blois: interesting historically.
Brissac: privately owned, spectacular furnishings.
Langeais: fortress, interesting historically.
Meung: fortress, interesting historically.
Montreuil-Bellay: superb site.
Le Plessis-Bourré: privately owned, unique ceiling.
Ussé: superb site, fairy-tale castle.

The others, still mostly interesting

Beaugency: ruins.
Chaumont: don't bother with interior.
Châteauneuf: mostly ruins.
Gien: hunting museum.
Montpoupon: privately owned, hunting museum.
Montgeoffroy: privately owned, elegant furniture.
Montrésor: privately owned, superb site.
Montrichard: ruins.
Montsoreau: not a lot to see.
Sully: substantial fortress.

Chambres d'hôte

This is a category of accommodation that has won more plaudits from previous *French Entrée* readers than any other. In Normandy and Brittany particularly it has been found that a stay in a well-equipped farmhouse, manor or modern house, with well-briefed hospitable hosts, has brought more in the way of interest and comfort than many a more expensive hotel. But because these hosts are not professionals, the standard of vetting must be strict. Just following any old *chambre d'hôte* sign at the roadside can sometimes lead to disaster; personal experiences are vital.

In *FE6* and *FE7* I was unable to explore this possibility further because the regions they cover do not seem to encourage the *chambre d'hôte* system, so I was delighted to see that the contrary was the case in the Loire, which has probably the best network anywhere in France. I could easily write a whole book on just these.

However, their number has meant that I could not personally visit every one that has been recommended to me, let alone those I just stumbled on. Those I did stay in were, without exception, stars, and so I have little doubt that others which have been equally highly praised are too. The answer seemed to be to compile a list and leave readers to do the hard work. Please do write and tell me of any triumphs (and horrors if necessary).

I apologise for the sketchiness of the addresses. Now you can see how I earn my keep!

Indre et Loire

Artannes-sur-Indre. Thierry Keufer, La Mothe. 47.26.80.18.
Azay-le-Rideau. Thierry Poireau, 'La Petite Loge'. 47.45.26.05.
Bréhémont. Maurice Chevalier (!), Le Bourg. 47.95.65.79.
Loches. Françoise Gaillard, Les Ées, Ferrière-sur-Beaulieu. 47.59.33.62.
Genillé. Alain Couturie, Domaine de Marolles. 47.59.50.01.
Langeais. Claude Venon, Château de Chemilly. 47.96.33.06
　　　Mme. Halopé, L'Épeigne. 47.96.54.23.
Larçay. André Lesage, Le Château de Larçay. 47.50.39.39.
Vernou-sur-Brenne. Geneviève Bellanger, Les Landes, 47.52.10.93.

Loir et Cher

Cellettes. Renée de Chevigné. 45.70.48.14.
Fay-aux-Loges. Nicole Sicot, Les Charmettes, Donnery.
   38.59.22.50.

Sarthe

La Bruère-sur-Loir. M. Thibault, Château du Grand-Perray.
   43.44.72.65.
Poncé-sur-le-Loir. M. et Mme Sevault, La Tendrière.
   43.44.45.27.

Maine et Loire

Les Cerqueux-sous-Passavant. Jacqueline Tilkin, 'Montsicard'.
   41.59.90.93.

Wines and spirits by John Doxat

AN INTRODUCTION TO FRENCH WINES

Bonne cuisine et bons vins, c'est le paradis sur terre. (Good
cooking and good wines, that is earthly paradise.)

King Henri IV

French food positively invites accompaniment by wine, albeit
only a couple of glasses because one is driving on after
lunch. At dinner one can usually be self-indulgent. Then wine
becomes more than a sensory pleasure: with some rich
regional meals it is almost imperative digestively. Civilised
drinking of wine inhibits the speedy eating that is the cause of
much Anglo-Saxon dyspepsia.

The most basic French wine generically is *vin ordinaire*,
and very ordinary indeed it can be. The term is seldom used
nowadays: *vin de table* is a fancier description – simple
blended wine of no particular provenance. *Vins de table* often
come under brand-names, such as those of the of the
ubiquitous Nicolas stores (Vieux Ceps, etc.) – and highly
reliable they are. Only personal experience can lead you to
your preference: in a take-away situation I would never buy
the absolute cheapest just to save a franc or so.

Nearly every restaurant has its house wines. Many an
owner, even of a chain of establishments, takes pride in those
he has chosen to signify as *vins de la maison, vin du patron*
or similar listing. In a wine-rich area, house wines (in carafe
or bottle) are likely to be *vins de pays*, one step up from *vins
de table*, since this label indicates that they come from a
distinct certificated area and only that area, though they may
be a blend (thus sometimes an improvement) of several
wines.

Ever since they invented the useful, if frequently confusing,
Appellation d'Origine Contrôlée (AC) the French have created
qualitative sub-divisions. An AC wine, whose label will give
you a good deal of information, will usually be costlier – but
not necessarily better – than one that is a VDQS. To avoid
excessive use of French, I translate that as 'designated
(regional) wine of superior quality'. A newer, marginally
lesser category is VQPRD: 'quality wine from a specified
district'.

Hundreds of wines bear AC descriptions: you require
knowledge and/or a wine guide to find your way around. The
intention of the AC laws was to protect consumers and
ensure wine was not falsely labelled – and also to prevent
over-production, without noticeable reduction of the 'EEC

wine lake'. Only wines of reasonable standards should achieve AC status: new ones are being regularly admitted to the list, and the hand of politics as much as the expertise of the taster can be suspected in some instances. Thus AC covers some unimportant wines as well as the rarest, vastly expensive vintages.

Advice? In wine regions, drink local wines. Do not hestitate to ask the opinion of patron or wine-waiter: they are not all venal, and most folk are flattered by being consulted. By all means refer to a vintage chart, when considering top class wines, but it cannot be an infallible guide: it has no bearing on blended wines.

OUTLINE OF FRENCH WINE REGIONS

Bordeaux

Divided into a score of districts, and sub-divided into very many *communes* (parishes). The big district names are Médoc, St Emilion, Pomerol, Graves and Sauternes. Prices for the great reds (châteaux Pétrus, Mouton-Rothschild, etc.) or the finest sweet whites (especially the miraculous Yquem) have become stratospheric. Yet château in itself means little and the classification of various rankings of châteaux is not easily understood. Some tiny vineyards are entitled to be called château, which has led to disputes about what have been dubbed 'phantom châteaux'. Visitors are advised, unless wine-wise, to stick to the simpler designations.

Bourgogne (Burgundy)

Topographically a large region, stretching from Chablis (on the east end of the Loire), noted for its steely dry whites, to Lyons. It is particularly associated with fairly powerful red wines and very dry whites, which tend to acidity except for the costlier styles. Almost to Bordeaux excesses, the prices for really top Burgundies have gone through the roof. For value, stick to simpler local wines.

Technically Burgundies, but often separately listed, are the Beaujolais wines. The young red Beaujolais (not necessarily the over-publicised *nouveau*) are delicious, mildly chilled. There are several rather neglected Beaujolais wines (Moulin-à-Vent, Morgon, St Amour, for instance) that improve for several years: they represent good value as a rule. The Maconnais and Chalonnais also produce sound Burgundies (red and white) that are usually priced within reason.

Rhône

Continuation south of Burgundy. The Rhône is particularly associated with very robust reds, notably Chateauneuf-du-Pape; also Tavel, to my mind the finest of all still *rosé* wines. Lirac *rosé* is nearly as good. Hermitage and Gigondas are names to respect for reds, whites and *rosés*. Rhône has well earned its modern reputation – no longer Burgundy's poorer brother. From the extreme south comes the newly 'smart' dessert *vin doux naturel*, ultra-sweet Muscat des Beaumes-de-Venise, once despised by British wine-drinkers. There are fashions in wine just like anything else.

Alsace

Producer of attractive, light white wines, mostly medium-dry, widely used as carafe wines in middle-range French restaurants. Alsace wines are not greatly appreciated overseas and thus remain comparatively inexpensive for their quality; they are well placed to compete with popular German varieties. Alsace wines are designated by grape – principally Sylvaner for lightest styles, the widespread and reliable Riesling for a large part of the total, and Gerwürtztraminer for slightly fruitier wines.

Loire

Prolific producer of very reliable, if rarely great, white wines, notably Muscadet, Sancerre, Anjou (its *rosé* is famous), Vouvray (sparkling and semi-sparkling), and Saumur (particularly its 'champagne styles'). Touraine makes excellent whites and also reds of some distinction – Bourgueil and Chinon. It used to be widely believed – a rumour put out by rivals? – that Loire wines 'did not travel': nonsense. They are a successful export.

Champagne

So important is Champagne that, alone of French wines, it carries no AC: its name is sufficient guarantee. (It shares this distinction with the brandies Cognac and Armagnac.) Vintage Champagnes from the *grandes marques* – a limited number of 'great brands' – tend to be as expensive in France as in Britain. You can find unknown brands of high quality (often off-shoots of *grandes marques*) at attractive prices, especially in the Champagne country itself. However, you need information to discover these, and there are true Champagnes for the home market that are *doux* (sweet) or *demi-sec* (medium sweet) that are pleasing to few non-French tastes. Champagne is very closely controlled as non-French tastes. Champagne is very closely controlled as to region, quantities, grape types, and is made only by secondary fermentation in the bottle. From 1993, it is prohibited to state that other wines are (under EEC law) made by the 'champagne method' – even if they are.

Minor regions, very briefly

Jura – Virtually unknown outside France. Try local speciality wines such as *vin jaune* if in the region.

Jurancon – Remote area; sound, unimportant white wines, sweet styles being the better.

Cahors – Noted for its powerful *vin de pays* 'black wine', darkest red made.

Gaillac – Little known; once celebrated for dessert wines.

Savoy – Good enough table wines for local consumption. Best product of the region is delicious Chambéry vermouth: as an aperitif, do try the well distributed Chambéryzette, a unique vermouth with a hint of wild strawberries.

Bergerac – Attractive basic reds; also sweet Monbazillac, relished in France but not easily obtained outside: aged examples can be superb.

Provence – Large wine region of immense antiquity. Many and varied *vins de pays* of little distinction, usually on the sweet side, inexpensive and totally drinkable.

Midi – Stretches from Marseilles to the Spanish border. Outstandingly prolific contributor to the 'EEC wine lake' and producer of some 80 per cent of French *vins de table*, white and red. Sweet whites dominate, and there is major production of *vins doux naturels* (fortified sugary wines).

Corsica – Roughish wines of more antiquity than breeding, but by all means drink local reds – and try the wine-based aperitif Cap Corse – if visiting this remarkable island.

Paris – Yes, there is a vineyard – in Montmartre! Don't ask for a bottle: the tiny production is sold by auction, for charity, to rich collectors of curiosities.

HINTS ON SPIRITS

The great French spirit is brandy. Cognac, commercially the leader, must come from the closely controlled region of that name. Of various quality designations, the commonest is VSOP (very special old pale): it will be a cognac worth drinking neat. Remember, *champagne* in a cognac connotation has absolutely no connection with the wine. It is a topographical term, *grande champagne* being the most prestigious cognac area: *fine champagne* is a blend of brandy from the two top cognac sub-divisions.

Armagnac has become better known lately outside France, and rightly so. As a brandy it has a much longer history than cognac: some connoisseurs rate old armagnac (the quality designations are roughly similar) above cognac.

Be cautious of French brandy without a cognac or armagnac title, regardless of how many meaningless 'stars' the label carries or even the magic word 'Napoléon' (which has no legal significance).

Little appreciated in Britain is the splendid 'apple brandy', Calvados, mainly associated with Normandy but also made in Brittany and the Marne. The best is *Calvados du Pays d'Auge*. Do taste well-aged Calvados, but avoid any suspiciously cheap.

Contrary to popular belief, true Calvados is not distilled from cider – but an inferior imitation is: French cider *(cidre)* is excellent.

Though most French proprietary aperitifs, like Dubonnet, are fairly low in alcohol, the extremely popular Pernod/Ricard *pastis*-style brands are highly spirituous. *Eau-de-vie* is the generic term for all spirits, but colloquially tends to refer to local, often rough, distillates. Exceptions are the better *alcools blancs* (white spirits), which are not inexpensive, made from fresh fruits and not sweetened as *crèmes* are.

Liqueurs

Numerous travellers deem it worth allocating their allowance to bring back some of the famous French liqueurs (Bénédictine, Chartreuse, Cointreau, and so on) which are so costly in Britain. Compare 'duty free' prices with those in stores, which can vary markedly. There is a plethora of regional liqueurs, and numerous sickly *crèmes*, interesting to taste locally. The only *crème* generally meriting serious consideration as a liqueur is *crème de menthe* (preferably Cusenier), though the newish *crème de Grand Marnier* has been successful. *Crème de cassis* has a special function: see *Kir* in alphabetical list.

THE LOIRE THROUGH A WINEGLASS

The most peaceful holidays I have enjoyed in France have been spent ambling (if one can amble by car) through the tranquil Loire valley, just before or after the summer holidays. We always avoided the large towns and showed minimal interest in tourist attractions, staying at random in secluded and very comfortable country hotels, lingering over delicious meals, and quaffing much pleasing wine.

Ignoring the glamour of the fabulous châteaux – one can easily understand why they were built there – I find the great virtue of the Loire to be its understated beauty. This gentle, civilised unpretentiousness is reflected in the variety of its copious reservoir of wines. The Loire does not boast of vintage rarities about which connoisseurs rave, for which huge prices are paid, nor does it attract writers to pen those fancifully adjectival descriptions of numbing inconsequence to the generality of drinkers. It is for the wine-lover of modest experience, intelligent but not over-demanding, that the Loire offers many delights and, unlike some wine regions, it produces no utterly bad wines.

Let us briefly examine the most important.

Muscadet

This is not the most splendid Loire wine but it is the most widely known. It comes from the westerly Pays Nantais: the great city of Nantes is the regional capital. Yet until comparatively recently, Muscadet – a grape, not a place – was little drunk outside its own principal locality, Sèvre-et-Maine, which is now almost synonymous with Muscadet.

The Muscadet grape originated long ago as the 'Burgundy melon'. It made a wine renowned as a sauce base: it is still in minor cultivation in Burgundy for a handful of gourmets. Around two and a half centuries ago, the vine was planted in the Loire region and did well. It is only in the last thirty years, or less, that production has rocketed to meet demand.

Muscadet is unique amongst French wines in that, for reasons I do not know, it is the only one to have a legal maximum strength – a perfectly adequate 12.3°. Muscadet is best drunk young: if more than one vintage appears on a list, choose the most recent. All but the simplest Muscadet AC is now described – or most is – as *sur lie* (on the lees). This is not racked but is bottled from the cask after short fermentation. It is easy to appreciate the popularity of Muscadet. It is reasonably fruity, makes no demands on purse or palate. It is a perfect accompaniment to the fish in which the adjacent Atlantic remains rich.

An important town of the Muscadet area is St Fiacre-sur-Maine. I mention this only as as an odd sacramental connection between drinking and driving: St Fiacre is patron saint of cab-drivers.

Anjou

The wines of this historic region are of great antiquity.

Charlemagne, first Holy Roman Emperor, owned vineyards here. Later, Anjou came under English rule. The prestige of Anjou wines was such that in 1194 they could bear a tax four times that applied to other wines imported into England. Notable French monarchs recorded a liking for Anjou's products: Louis XVI showed his appreciation by allowing the Layon river to be canalised to give Dutch vessels easier access to wine cargoes. Britain's Edward VII, a great wine-drinker, made a personal friend of his Loire vintner.

Simple Anjou Blanc, without further attribution, is an inexpensive all-purpose medium-dry wine. Anjou is particularly associated with *rosé:* Anjou *rosé* was famous before nearly every white wine producer started making this style. That said, there is nothing very exciting about Anjou *rosè*: reliable light beverage wine, highly suitable for summer.

It is with sweeter and dessert wines that Anjou really scores, and it is almost certainly these which attracted the high and mighty in times past. Our forebears did not share the modern vogue for 'dryness', or 'lightness'. They liked wines rich and strong. The best Anjou sweet wines rival all but the top Sauternes and are much less costly. They come from grapes affected by *pourriture noble* (noble rot), the curious fungus that appears to destroy over-ripe grapes: yet in practice it absorbs moisture, thus concentrating the sugar in the fruit. The *Chenin Blanc*, much grown in the Loire, is particularly susceptible to 'noble rot' which readily occurs by nature in Anjou, whereas elsewhere it may be necessary to introduce it. The affected Chenin makes into fine sweet wine. Look out for Coteaux du Layon for good value, or Coteaux de L'Aubance. Costlier, but worth every franc, are more specifically named Quarts de Chaume and Bonnezeaux.

Saumur

This region is part of Anjou but has claims for separate treatment. It produces the best, though not widely distributed, Anjou reds, led by Saumur-Champigny, and amongst *premiers crus* (first growths) is Parnay: it was the Parnay proprietor who was the king's friend mentioned above. There is also an outstanding white Parnay. Abroad, Saumur is best known for its sparklers, made, for the time being, by the 'champagne method', and also semi-sparkling *pétillant* varieties. Inevitably, there are also *rosé* and *créme* sparklers. I reckon you will do best with a Saumur AC *Brut*.

Touraine

The vinous virtues of Touraine were hymned by Rabelais,

Balzac and Dumas, amongst other writers. It lies in the heart of the long Loire valley and its centre is gracious Tours. This used to – still does? – enjoy the reputation of being the home of the purest spoken French: once it was almost obligatory for aspirant entrants to the Foreign Office to study there for a spell! Touraine produces sound, reliable whites from the Sauvignon grape, so a Touraine Sauvignon in itself guarantees a superior *vin de table*. It is Vouvray and Montlouis that are associated with the better whites. Touraine makes the most widely distributed reds of the Loire, notably Bourgeuil and Chinon. These can stand considerable bottle-age. Touraine *rosé* wines are comparable to the more celebrated Anjou *rosés*. Sparkling Vouvray, very lively, has a considerable reputation.

Sancerre

Commercially, this district has some affinity to Muscadet. From an ancient, not much regarded – even declining – wine area, Sancerre has, in about a quarter-century, become not only popular but distinctly fashionable. Prices have risen accordingly. The dominant Sauvignon grape produces excellent, crisp whites. Look for 'Sancerre' with a *domaine* designation for the better types, though you will find straight Sancerre AC more than adequate; sometimes over-priced because of the vogue the name enjoys. Reuilly and Quincy are place-names to remember, plus the slightly lighter Menetou-Salon. Reuilly reds and *rosés* deserve serious attention.

Pouilly

Likes to consider itself separate from Sancerre. Do not confuse its basic Pouilly-sur-Loire with the much more special Pouilly-Fumé, a delicious, dry, yellowish white. It must be stressed that Pouilly-Fumé has absolutely no connection with Burgundy's Pouilly-Fuissé, a more acidic wine. Pouilly-Fumé is usually drunk young, though it does gain with some ageing.

A general merit of most Loire white wines is that they are as suitable before a meal as during it.

> *If the alchemists of old had known your wines, they would have had no need to seek further for gold one can drink.*
> King Edward VII, to M. Crystal,
> Owner of Clos-des-Murs, Parnay (Saumur)

Condensed glossary
of French wine and ancillary terminology

Abricotine – Generic apricot liqueur. Look for known brand-
names.

Alcool blanc – Spirit distilled from fruit (not wine); not to be
confused with fruit-flavoured cordials.

Aligoté – Burgundy wine (from grape of same name); light
and dry.

Anis – Aniseed; much used in aperitifs of Pernod type.

Aperitif – Any drink taken as an appetiser (literally 'opener').
France has a huge range of proprietary aperitifs.

Appellation (d'Origine) Contrôlée – AC; see An Introduction
to French Wines.

Armagnac – Superb brandy of the Gascon country, now
achieving something of a rediscovery. See Hints on Spirits.

Barsac – Sweet Bordeaux wine (officially part of Sauternes);
wide range from excellent to sickly boring.

Basserau – Sparkling red Burgundy; unusual if nothing else.

Beaune – Prestigious Burgundy name (red), the best very
costly.

Blanc de Blancs – White wine from white grapes only. White
wine is often made from black grapes, skins being removed
before fermentation – as this is.

Blanc de Noirs – See immediately above: these are
essentially type descriptions; some prestige accrues to
Blanc de Blancs.

Bordeaux – See An Introduction to French Wines.

Bourgogne – Burgundy; see An Introduction to French
Wines.

Brut – Very dry; particularly with good Champagne.

Cabernet – Noble grape, especially Cabernet-Sauvignon. Just
its name on a label denotes a sound red wine.

Cacao – Cocoa; usually as *crème de cacao.*

Calvados – Apple brandy; see Hints on Spirits.

Cassis – Blackcurrant; *crème de cassis* widely favoured,
notably in Kir (q.v.).

Cave – Cellar.

Cépage – Indication of grape variety; e.g. *cépage Sauvignon.*

Chai – Ground-level wine store, exclusively used in Cognac,
frequently also in Bordeaux.

Champagne – See An Introduction to French Wines.

Clairet – Unimportant little-known Bordeaux wine, but
probably origin of English word Claret (red Bordeaux).

Clos – Principally Burgundian word for vineyard enclosed, or
formerly protected, by a wall.

Cognac – see Hints on Spirits.

Côte – Vineyard on a slope; no particular quality significance.

Coteau(x) – Hillside(s); much the same as *côte*.

Crème – Sweet, mildly alcoholic cordials of many flavours. Not rated as true liqueurs, but one exception is *crème de menthe* (mint). See also *cassis*.

Crémant – Sparkling wine, without lasting champagne-style effervescence.

Cru – Literally 'growth'. Somewhat complicated term. *Grand cru* only meaningful if allied to good name. *Grand cru classé* (officially classified great wine) covers greatest wines, but not all *cru classé* is *grand*.

Cuve close – Sealed vat; describes production of sparkling wine by bulk secondary fermentation as opposed to bottle fermentation of 'champagne method'.

Cuvée – Wine from one vat, unblended. Another confusing word; *cuvée spéciale* can have more than its literal meaning.

Demi-sec – Translates as 'medium dry'; in practice means sweet.

Domaine – Mainly Burgundian word; broadly equivalent to château.

Doux – Very sweet.

Eau-de-vie – Generic term for all distilled spirits.

Frappé – Drink served on finely crushed ice.

Glacé – Iced by immersion of bottle, or other refrigeration.

Goût – Taste. In some regions also describes rough local spirit.

Haut – 'High'; denotes upper part of wine district. Not necessarily a mark of quality, though Haut-Medoc produces notably better wines than its lower areas.

Izarra – Ancient, Armagnac-based Basque liqueur.

Kir – Excellent, now very popular aperitif: very dry chilled white wine (properly *Bourgogne Aligoté*) with a teaspoon of *crème de cassis* (q.v.) added, Kir Royale employs champagne.

Liqueur – originally *liqueur de dessert*, denoting post-prandial digestive use. Always sweet, so to speak of a 'liqueur Cognac' is absurd.

Litre – 1.7 pints; 5 litres equals 1.1 gallons.

Méthode Champenoise – Wine made by the champagne method.

Marc – Usually roughish brandy distilled from wine residue, though a few *Marcs* (pronounced 'mar') – notably *Marc de Bourgogne* – have some status.

Marque – Brand or company name.

Mise – As in *mise en bouteilles au château* (bottled at the château) or . . . *dans nos caves* (in our own cellars), etc.

Index

Notes

Notes

Notes

Notes

Notes

Notes